Rocky Mountain Mining Camps

The Urban Frontier

Rocky Mountain Mining Camps

The Urban Frontier

Duane A. Smith

UNIVERSITY OF NEBRASKA PRESS   LINCOLN

Library of Congress Catalog Card Number 67-24522

International Standard Book Number 0-8032-5792-9

First Bison Book printing: February 1974

Most recent printing shown by first digit below:

2   3   4   5   6   7   8   9   10

Bison Book edition published by arrangement with Indiana University Press.

Manufactured in the United States of America

For my mother and father

CONTENTS

Preface *xi*

ONE *The Urban Frontier* 3

TWO *Young America* 16

THREE *Not All Were Welcome* 29

FOUR *When Young America Finds a Good Gold Gulch* 42

FIVE *Boom Days* 59

SIX *Growing Pains* 78

SEVEN *Maturing in Spite of Itself* 99

EIGHT *Magnet in the Mountains* 124

NINE *Problems of Urbanization* 142

TEN *The Mature Camp* 159

ELEVEN *Community Leadership* 177

TWELVE *Life Was Never Easy* 193

THIRTEEN *A Time for Relaxation* 206

FOURTEEN *The Tiger Is Found* 221

FIFTEEN *The Promised Land* 242

Bibliographical Essay 255

Works Cited 260

Notes 273

Index 297

ILLUSTRATIONS

Map of Mining Camps Frequently Cited   2

Deadwood, South Dakota   5

Early mining camp, Central City, Colorado   43

Early mining camp, Gayville, South Dakota   43

Main street, Helena, Montana, 1865   50

Main street, Helena, Montana, 1874   50

Boarding house, Silver Reef, Utah   63

Star Hook and Ladder Company, Georgetown, Colorado   94

Business district, Virginia City, Montana   102

Business district, Alta, Utah   102

Brass band, Black Hawk, Colorado   117

Stagecoaching   120

Tabor Opera House, Leadville, Colorado   163

Baseball team, Silver Plume, Colorado   214

Skiing, Irwin, Colorado   218

Saloon, Leadville, Colorado   222

Hurdy-gurdy girls   236

PREFACE

The West of the mining camp is gone. In a few reconstructed or refurbished camps, in order to attract the tourist and his dollar, an attempt has been made to recreate life as it once existed. Here, far too often, the tinsel and glitter pass for the prosaic, everyday existence. That which was neither dangerous, exciting, nor glamorous is relegated to the background or conveniently forgotten. Consequently, if some of the original inhabitants suddenly reappeared, they would probably have trouble recognizing what was once their town. It is my hope that this book will help correct this misconception of the Western mining camp, present new insights, and encourage others to examine and study the mining camp seriously.

The year 1859, with the opening of the first gold rush into the Rocky Mountains, is a convenient starting point. Within three decades the area was explored, picked over, and mined, leaving only a few more discoveries after 1890, the termination date of the study. The old mining West was almost gone by then, and the area where the prospector could wander had been narrowed. Roughly a generation had passed since the 1859 gold rush, and the mining West had matured. The Rocky Mountain states and the Black Hills and eastern Arizona mark the limits of this examination. They make a geographical and chronological unit separate from the Nevada and California camps. Certainly the role of the camps in these last-mentioned states is not less significant, but it is beyond the scope of this book.

The camps chosen were selected at random with an eye toward available source material and achieving a cross-section of large and small, temporary and permanent, mountain and desert. A few were placer camps, but most were hard rock mining communities, reflecting the predominance of the latter over the entire region. No differentiation has been made between the two. In each state several camps were studied in detail and others used when material was found. Just as in mining, a great deal of dead work had to be done to reach the valuable ore, but the search was rewarding and most fascinating.

In this search I have received the generous cooperation and guidance of many institutions, but special thanks must be extended to the staffs of the Montana Historical Society, the State Historical Society of Colorado, the Western History Department of the Denver Public Library, the Homestake Library (Lead, South Dakota), the Bancroft Library, the Arizona Pioneer Historical Society, the Museum of New Mexico, and the Wyoming State Archives and Historical Department. In these and other places I spent many weeks examining various records, and I owe to the librarians and archivists a great debt of gratitude.

To the University of Colorado I wish to express my thanks for the research grant which allowed me to spend one summer traveling in search of material. Many others who in some way contributed to the completion of this manuscript include Howard Scamehorn, who read it and offered helpful suggestions, Kay Eberl, and the staff of Indiana University Press.

Two people, above all others, assisted, prodded, and encouraged me to finish the project. Robert G. Athearn of the University of Colorado, who did so much to help a graduate student complete his work, offered numerous insights and stimulation, furnishing an example toward which to strive. My wife, Gay, deserves nearly equal credit with me, for she spent many tedious hours typing, proofreading, and correcting her husband's attempts to put his thoughts into logical and readable form. Words are but a weak expression of my gratitude.

D. A. S.

Rocky Mountain Mining Camps

The Urban Frontier

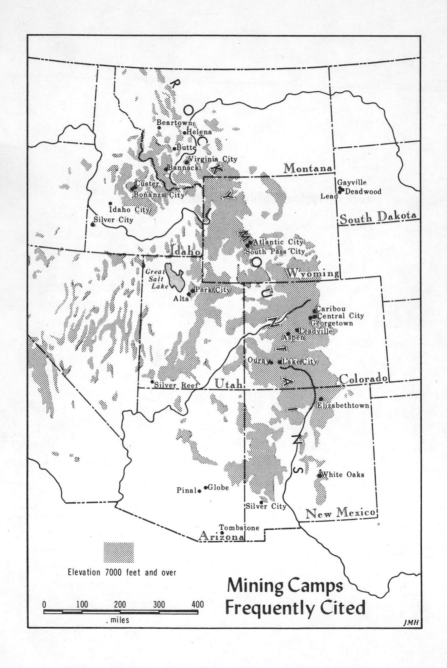

Mining Camps
Frequently Cited

Elevation 7000 feet and over

0   100   200   300   400
. miles

JMH

One

The Urban Frontier

Pᴿᴏʙᴀʙʟʏ few Americans in 1848, at the conclusion of the Mexican War, realized or even dreamed of the vast mineral potential of the country they had so recently wrested from their southern neighbor. Fewer still would have ventured to speculate that within a generation this land, and that previously acquired in the same area, would be crisscrossed by the miner and the prospector in an endless search for gold and silver, that valuable mineral deposits would be uncovered, and that permanent settlement would be so rapid. Yet these things happened in the western portion of the United States, from the Rocky Mountains to the Pacific Coast and from the Mexican border to Canada. The gold rush to California heralded the opening of the era; then, after a decade, 1859 witnessed the discovery of gold in Colorado and silver in Nevada's Comstock. Afterward came many other discoveries which sent the hopeful scurrying after elusive wealth until after the turn of the century. Few obstacles checked the advance of the mining frontier during these years.

Once having realized the potential of the region, Americans became extremely interested in it. Thousands left their homes to try their skill and luck; others followed the mining successes and failures vicariously through current magazines and newspapers. Almost anywhere, from page one to the financial news, the reader was likely to find an article or news item dealing with some aspect of the mining West. When transportation became easier and inconveniences and dangers fewer, Easterners and Europeans—reporters, investors, and the curious—came to examine, explore, and, for a brief period, experience the excitement of the wild West.

Mining itself, the core of the movement, was often too prosaic, too humdrum to arouse much interest in the mind of the average American of that day or this. The mining camp, however, was the heart of the excitement, the glamor of the frontier. Sensational, extraordinary, exciting episodes caught the fancy of the reading public. The names of such camps as Leadville, Colorado, or Deadwood, South Dakota, became bywords to most Americans for a few years, only to be replaced in the public's fancy by some other rip-roaring camp. Too frequently, as a result of this type of publicity, the mining community became stereotyped as the image of wickedness and extravagance. The bizarre became the norm, the unusual the accepted. Behind this false front was the real mining camp, less glamorous but more significant in American history.

The mining camp represented something different and, for the most part, new in the American frontier experience: urbanization. Earlier isolated examples of the same kind were Pittsburgh and St. Louis, which had been urban headquarters for the fur trapping frontier and for a time had been far in advance of general settlement. Sometimes urbanization appeared in the vanguard of the agrarian movement, with town promoters and would-be villages, although without the timing, numbers, or immediate significance of the mining camp. For centuries the frontier had been the home of the individualist, where men and women lived their lives in a basically rural environment. By choice or adaptation these people had become the cutting edge of civilization; behind their line of advance grew the refinements of rural life and the first signs of urban existence. In contrast, on the mining frontier the camp—the germ of a city—appeared almost simultaneously with the opening of the region. Individual prospectors or prospecting parties conducted the initial exploration, but their success quickly attracted others who formed the basis for the nascent community.

The urban nature of the movement increased the speed and di-

rection of development. Within weeks or months, the refinements
of civilization appeared to the frontiersman. By visiting the camp,
anyone with enough money could secure favors and pleasures which
had been denied to earlier frontiers for as long as a generation. Also

Deadwood in 1876, shortly after the rush to the Black Hills. It
became one of the most notorious of the mining camps. *Harper's
Weekly, October 28, 1876.*

available were newspapers, recent periodicals, the latest fashions,
and new equipment of all types which, together with other similar
items, gave the frontier an up-to-date and progressive character.
To be sure, this facade could disappear as quickly as it had come,
but in the participant and the observer it produced a different reaction to the frontier than would have occurred otherwise. These
reactions and their significance will be discussed in detail in later
chapters.

Urbanization meant that the problems which faced the more

settled regions were transported to the frontier and placed in an entirely new environment. Such problems as municipal government, revenue, and sanitation had to be faced and some attempts made to solve them before they got out of hand. Others such as law enforcement were magnified by the number and proximity of the people involved in the settlement and the exploitation of the area. The need for better transportation, for example, was not new or exclusive to this frontier, but its urgency meant the relative success or failure of the region. While a farmer could afford to wait to develop his farm and the fur trapper could get along with his personal means of transportation, the miner had to open and then develop the vital transport arteries before he could hope to make his venture profitable.

The camps were frequently isolated, a condition based not solely on distance but on terrain and climate as well. Isolation did not, however, produce the self-sufficiency often described as a typical characteristic of the American frontier. The miner could not hope to be self-sufficient, nor did he want to be. His time was spent in searching and mining. He could not stop to raise crops or make needed equipment, even if he had had the skill. Money was available and time could be saved by having someone else do the work so that he could purchase the end product. The miner could be, and often was, ingenious in improvising to overcome varied problems, but he was not self-sufficient in the sense of the pioneer farmer or family. He relied on his own luck and store-purchased grub and equipment.

As a result, the camps became attractive markets. Encouraged by this situation, farmers moved into regions which previously had been called deserts. Cheaper and faster means of transportation appeared. The ubiquitous traveling salesman and other merchants arrived on the heels of the first stampeders. Trading and even embryonic industrial towns developed to serve the surrounding camps. Except perhaps for the salesman, these were all signs of permanent settlement which came within a decade after the initial discovery.

The speed and often the magnitude of such developments placed the urban mining frontier in a category by itself.

The principal characteristic of this movement was the quick appearance of ready cash. The farmer might work for a season and have less than $100 in hard money. The miner, on the other hand, often enough found himself with a far greater sum after only a short working time. "Easy come, easy go" too readily became the motto. Why worry about tomorrow when your mine held more riches only waiting to be uncovered? This speculative, gambling instinct characterized many of the people. Money flowed freely in the camp, producing a way of life common to all boom situations. Not all were caught up in this sudden prosperity, yet all were influenced by it. The possibility of a financial windfall was one of the main factors in the rapid urbanization which accompanied the opening of the mines. Without it the camps could not have been founded or maintained.

Intellectually and culturally, the urban mining center acted as an assimilator and a transmitter for European and American ideas and traditions. The same might be said of other aspects of the American frontier, but the camps stood alone in their tempo and variety. Theaters, schools, debating societies, literary clubs, churches, and lending libraries often appeared during the first years of a camp's existence. The principal reason for their appearance was the urban nature of the camp, where people of similar views could associate. How deeply these traits were embedded in the life of the community is another question, but this does not measurably detract from the fact that great effort was made toward these intellectual attainments by some of the people for the possible benefit of all.

The urbanization of a mining region was the sign of prosperity to the miners and to many outsiders, who viewed the coming of the school, church, railroad, and other prominent features as indications of permanence and stability. The camp was caught in this cycle, promoting such developments to prove to the outside world that it was, in fact, here to stay. The townspeople were encouraged to support local endeavors as their civic duty. Thus this image became the goal of all budding mining communities. Certain features were symbolic of the best mining communities: a large and varied business district, a fancy hotel, a modern and attractive school or church, and stone or brick construction throughout the community.

Despite such developments, with few exceptions the camps declined. They aged rapidly and soon took on the signs of a depressed community. Now their urban nature reacted against them, as old camps were contrasted with new camps that were expanding. Such a comparison normally acted to the disadvantage of the older settlement. Thus the community's urban amenities became a yardstick of its prosperity and development.

In other parts of the country, after passing through the frontier period, a typical region moved into a more stable era characterized by the growth of towns and villages. Urbanization then, in essence, became a sign of that stability. This, however, was only partially true on the mining frontier. Permanence was indeed the goal, but such was the transitory, exploitative nature of this frontier that it frequently was not attained. The mines declined and stopped producing. The camps, which existed primarily to serve and be served by the mines, similarly declined. All that once had seemed so permanent was now abandoned, as the population drifted on to other, more promising regions. The camp became a mere ghost of its former glory, awaiting the ravages of nature and man. Such wastefulness and instability have too often been viewed as the sole result of mining. By the very nature of urbanization a much more important result had occurred, which was frequently overlooked.

Urbanization of the mining frontier developed without the preceding stages which normally served as a basis for growth. The urban mining centers had to encourage and promote the development of their surrounding areas during and after they were established. Such was the case, for example, with the early growth of agriculture, industry, and transportation. These suffered with the decline of mining, yet, after a period of recession, they became the backbone of permanent settlement which was no longer based upon mining. In this sense the urban mining frontier made a significant contribution to permanent settlement.

The mining camp is more than just a symbol of a gaudy, reckless era, more than a spot where tourists can gawk at restored or refurbished tinsel remains and then pass on, believing they have seen it all. The camp reflects the frontier struggle of man to build something lasting in a strange and frequently hostile environment. It becomes the story of the men and women who lived and died there, who called it home.

The mining frontier also represents another break with traditional patterns. The miners jumped hundreds of miles of wilderness to reach Colorado and Montana, over a thousand to arrive in California. Only in the case of the Oregon movement was a similar example of noncontiguous settlement found in such magnitude, following the initial landings at Jamestown and Plymouth. Miners broke away from the western edge of the Mississippi Valley to move into virgin regions in search of gold and silver. Mining districts and camps became isolated islands of settlement surrounded by wilderness, connected with the outside world only by long roads or thin telegraph lines. This was particularly true in the decades of the 1850s and 1860s. The miner, buried in the mountain valleys of Idaho and Montana, was further removed in travel time from his Midwestern neighbors than they were from England.

This isolation made urbanization of the mining frontier harder to achieve, while at the same time accentuating its varied aspects. The early mining camp could expect little or no outside help in such areas as government and law enforcement. Effective measures could come only from within. Further, the urban nature of the frontier clearly sharpened the disadvantages of isolation for its people. The pioneer individual or family could do without, or rely on its own resources, but in the mining camp or the surrounding district this could not be done for a very long period without serious repercussions. To overcome isolation was one of the first necessities of all mining communities.

The growth of the mining frontier cannot be described as a steady movement; in fact, almost the opposite was true. Of the mining camps of 1859, 1863, 1877, or any given year, some would prosper, decay, and die within a decade, while others languished for years before reviving or finally succumbing. The frontier, meanwhile, advanced to other areas. Nothing was less conducive to a steady progression or even repetition of events than the Western mining camp. Districts which at one time had been beehives of activity were abandoned, some to be resurrected later for further exploitation, most to remain monuments to the transitory nature of human accomplishment.

Instability was characteristic of mining. The miners dug out the ore, which they could not restore. No discovery had unlimited potential, and eventually the resources were exhausted. The fate of the district hinged on its adaptation to this inevitable change in economic fortune. As settlement developed in the Rocky Mountain region, this unstable condition became less significant. Still, until after the turn of the century, mining continually advanced and receded, but within a steadily diminishing area.

The mining camp in American history is not unique to the trans-Mississippi frontier. Here it developed to spectacular heights and became part of folklore and legend, but the mining camp had become part of the frontier long before the first adventurer moved across the Missouri in 1849 for California. In the Spanish Central and South American colonies, camps had existed for several centuries. Some followed the typical pattern of a short life, but others became important Spanish towns. The early explorers and even the English settlers in North America were motivated by the desire to find wealth. Their efforts were generally futile, but they made a few discoveries which stimulated the growth of camps.

Mining flourished particularly in the first half of the nineteenth century in the South. Virginia, North Carolina, Georgia, and Alabama went through mining booms, although nothing which compared to California or Colorado. Around the mines embryo camps developed. They displayed to a moderate degree the basic ingredients of their later counterparts—speculation, rapid growth, often shoddy construction, and subsequent decline. Concerning the antiquated appearance of a twelve-year-old camp, one visitor wrote: "Owing to the fact that the houses are chiefly built of logs and, having never been painted, [they] are particularly dark and dingy, but uncommonly picturesque in form and location." [1] Considering the age, this was peculiarly amazing to the Easterner, used to slower but more permanent development.

Even the settings would have been recognized by a later fortyniner used to Western camps. "The mining land, is nothing more than little vallies, which lie between hills, such as you see every where in a mountainous, broken country." [2] Farther north, around the lead mines of Missouri, Illinois, and Wisconsin, other camps grew up reflecting similar traits.

These, however, were like preliminaries to the main event. Gold was found in California in 1848, and the rush of the next year dwarfed anything previously known in American mining history. Almost overnight, camps sprang up throughout the new mining districts. In shape and substance they were similar to those which had preceded and those which would follow them. Speed was essential and construction costs high. Men were impatient to get on with the more important business of mining. As a result, little effort was made to achieve esthetics, comfort, or convenience. With typical carelessness, buildings went up in haphazard fashion, built along what approximated a main street. Evidence of the great rush and of the miners' impatience was littered everywhere. Despite this the community had a vigorous, lively, flourishing air.

The cost of living was high, but the denizens of the frontier crowded into the camps. It was a heterogeneous population composed of people from all parts of the world. They blended and mixed, producing a society which had characteristics of all their backgrounds, yet which would become typically American. Not only did they start from nothing to build their community, but these pioneers had to reconstruct from their previous experience a means to govern it and provide law and order. Out of their efforts grew the mining codes, local government, and rudimentary court system which became the foundation of much of the future growth of California. During the next few years most of the camps boomed, creating a carnival atmosphere which permeated the surroundings. Optimism and easy money set the tone of the day. Under such conditions vice in all its forms flourished. The good life became the easy life. The individual who came into contact with such conditions changed, too; restraints previously acknowledged were now honored more in their bending or breaking than in their acceptance. The legend of the mining camp had been born.[3]

Conditions which the Californians had come to accept as normal for a camp were carried by them throughout the West as they wandered away after the boom had passed. These forty-niners went north to British Columbia in 1858, and eastward into Nevada the next year. Ignoring the North-South sectional crisis and eventual Civil War, others went into Idaho, Montana, and Colorado in the early 1860s.

The land into which they wandered was vast and unknown. Through it ran the backbone of the continent, the Rocky Mountains—which, together with other shorter ranges, made much of it mountainous terrain. It was a land of vivid and sharp contrasts —scenic, climatic, and geological. Although richly wooded and watered valleys to the north lured the miner, stark deserts stretched to the south. In the high plateaus and mountain valleys winters were harsh, but in other areas they were mild. It was a region of rugged mountains and canyons, yet in South Pass or the Rio Grande Valley a traveler hardly realized he was crossing the Continental Divide. In some areas water was abundant to the point of being a handicap; in many other places, however, the arid environment was the greatest obstacle to settlement. Gold, the old-timers were fond of saying, is "where you find it," and it was found throughout much of this land. Eventually, silver, too, was discovered and then other valuable minerals such as copper, tungsten, and uranium, which together produced wealth far beyond the expectations of the hundreds of thousands of men and women who searched for it in 1859 and the years thereafter.

Rumors of a golden wealth in the Rocky Mountains had reached the Eastern states on occasion before the 1850s, but this remote and unknown land did not attract much attention. The forty-niners, on their anxious way to California, had swept over and through it without giving the region much more than a second thought. In the fall of 1858, however, with depression stalking the land, the Midwesterner was in a much more receptive mood when rumors and then evidence arrived of the new-found wealth in the region of Pike's Peak.

Once again, as in the winter of 1848-49, eager Americans made plans to depart the following spring for the new gold fields. Even the increasingly bitter sectional dispute was pushed aside in many areas as attention was focused on the great American dream of sudden wealth. In the late winter and early spring of 1859 the tide swept westward. While not so many as in the decade before, the fifty-niners, as they came to be called, numbered some 100,000. "Pike's Peak or Bust" was the slogan, but many turned back before reaching that promised land. Others persevered, overcame the discouragement of the initial disappointment in finding no great amount of wealth around Cherry Creek and the modern Denver, and turned their attention to the mountains, where gold was found.

Among the sightseers who braved the discomforts of stage travel to see the diggings during the summer of 1859 was the well-known reformer and New York newspaper editor, Horace Greeley. Writing his column as he journeyed, Greeley gave the Eastern reader one of the earliest word-portraits of a Rocky Mountain mining camp. Commenting on what would be Central City, Colorado, he wrote:

> As yet, the entire population of the valley—which cannot number less than four thousand, including five white women and seven squaws living with white men—sleep in tents, or under booths of pine boughs, cooking and eating in open air. I doubt that there is as yet a table or chair in these diggings, eating being done around a cloth spread on the ground, while each one sits or reclines on mother earth.[4]

From these humble beginnings came much of the impetus for the mineral exploration and settlement of the Rocky Mountain empire during the next thirty years.

Into Idaho and Montana, meanwhile, during the early 1860s came miners and settlers from California, Colorado, and the Mississippi Valley. They found riches, built their camps, and stayed. The same story was repeated to a lesser degree during the following years in Utah, Wyoming, Arizona, and New Mexico. Isolated to the east, the Black Hills were found to contain gold, and despite all that the Army and the Sioux nation could do to prevent them, the miners came during the 1870s. By the end of the year 1890, untold millions of dollars had been poured into the nation's economy from this Rocky Mountain treasurehouse; a frontier had passed, and the land had been settled.

In 1859, however, the whole saga of the frontier loomed before the fifty-niners. Probably few took the time to speculate where their wandering might take them or what might result. They were too engrossed in their personal, optimistic dream of great fortune to speculate on the future. Anything seemed possible and one had only to wait his turn to tap the bountiful golden blessings which nature had bestowed on this land.

> The gold is there, 'most anywhere.
>   You can take it out rich, with an iron crowbar,
> And where it is thick, with a shovel and pick,
>   You can pick it out in lumps as big as a brick.

Then ho boys ho, to Cherry Creek we'll go.
  There's plenty of gold,
  In the West we are told,
  In the new Eldorado.

Oh dear girls now don't you cry,
  We are coming back by and by;
Don't you fret nor shed a tear,
  But patiently, wait about one year.[5]

Two

Young America

THE mining camp is but a meaningless shell without the people whose lives gave it substance and meaning, thousands of now forgotten pioneers who lived out their years without personal recognition or fame. It was they who gave the intangible qualities of life and spirit to the camp. Individually, their achievements were small, although making a living or raising a family under the conditions they faced were monumental efforts; collectively, their achievements are an epochal story.

They came from the nearby Mississippi Valley, from all parts of the United States and the world. The merchant, the housewife, the saloonkeeper, the minister, the blacksmith, the lawyer, all in their various capacities serving the needs of their fellow residents, friends, and families—the daily activities of such ordinary people set the tone of their communities. Theirs was not a glamorous life. What frequently remained hidden from the casual observer was the heartbreaking, backbreaking toil which went into opening the wilderness and establishing civilization.

Nature exacted a ruthless price from the pioneers who dared to gamble on the fortunes of mining. Life in the camps, with its pathos, misery, and sordid conditions, too often remained the sole reward for years spent on the frontier. Men and women grew old rapidly under such conditions, their lives twisted by their environment. Upon reaching the end of their allotted life span, they could look back on the rotting cabins, deserted streets, and ugly mine dumps, all filled with memories, and perhaps wonder if their efforts had been worthwhile. Their accomplishments were illustrious, even if some were temporary. In a generation they had settled in a land larger than the one their forefathers had required more than two hundred years to settle. They left another heritage, a West which remained theirs forever. It cannot be buried by the plow or compost pile of humanity nor eroded by nature.

The fifty-niners and those who followed in their footsteps liked to refer to themselves as "Young America," and in truth they were young. "Young America," a fairly common term of the day, also referred to a group within the Democratic Party, but as used throughout this study, it has no political connotations. Exuberance, hope, optimism, and vision were their trademarks; these traits became closely related to the mining frontier which they helped to build. While not unique to this frontier or period, these qualities became symbols for the entire age. Indeed, it was a time when a person was almost free to fulfill his personal dream, to mold his own destiny; yet this hope could not be the ultimate reality for all. In Europe this possibility was gone for many, and in the eastern United States the situation was rapidly changing as the country emerged from the Civil War to be confronted by increasing business and industrial domination. In the West alone, for a time, there still remained a new, unspoiled land which belonged to the opportunist and the optimist.

It is not the notorious or the wealthy, who are remembered for their unique exploits, who shall be chronicled here. Rather, the vast legion who failed to strike it rich or gain fame shall hold the stage. They were the ones who primarily built the camps and created the institutions which will be discussed in the following chapters.

Descriptions of these people are found in many accounts, letters, and diaries. To give a balanced picture, their own observations as well as those of outsiders have been included.

An article which appeared in the Virginia City *Montana Post,* January 28, 1865, analyzed succinctly, from a local view, the personal characteristics of the residents. The editor felt that the "great features of our people" are enterprise, restless activity, and contempt for danger or privation. Hospitality was, he concluded, general and unaffected. Men "who can rough it" and ladies "of spirit and energy" were most welcome. Weighing this description against a certain amount of local pride and prejudice, one still finds a fairly accurate picture.

The editor might have gone on to point out the optimistic nature of many of these people. George Parsons, resident of Tombstone, Arizona, during the 1880s, summed it up clearly in his diary: "Keep a stiff upper lip and some day in the near future you may be rewarded for existence here. . . . Perhaps my day is some time off so I shall strive just the same for my purpose. I shall obtain what I want some day in this or a similar country."[1] The people, on the whole, were willing to work, yet sometimes their patience and endurance would wear thin and they would move on to a more promising district. This restlessness was frequently mentioned by visitors and recognized by the people themselves. It created problems for the community as a whole and was, on occasion, the point of some critical comments in the local paper about its effect on the camp.[2]

There were, to be sure, extremes in all camps—men of the highest ambitions and intentions mixed with those of the lowest. Openhanded generosity was matched on occasion by extreme selfishness. "Putting on style," as it was often referred to, was one thing, however, that was not tolerated. Labor might be the guide for many, yet there were always a few who would not tolerate it and looked to an easier living. The greater portion of the inhabitants were quiet, law-abiding citizens, yet in the larger camps, and in some of the smaller ones as well, there existed a criminal element which often dominated the scene during the early existence of the camp.[3] Citizens of a typical community represented a cross section of humanity. They viewed themselves neither as curiosities nor as a particularly new breed of Americans; they left classification to visitors and later generations.

Humor was typical of these people, perhaps reflecting one way to temper the reality of a situation. From subtle jest to the bawdiest humor and rough practical joke, humor in all forms appeared. The newspaperman, searching for a story, was apt to fall victim to some prankster, unless he was particularly careful. For instance, the local reporter of the *Montana Post*, June 22, 1867, wrote that he had been "taken" in a series of practical jokes which had just culminated in his traveling a mile to see the "cherry colored" cat. Upon arriving he was shown a "lank distempered specimen," black as a crow, and told, "black cherries." He vowed not to be taken again but no doubt had to break his vow. Not only did these diversions provide fun and relaxation, but they also served as an outlet, an escape from the humdrum and tedious workaday world.

One member of the mining community, the minister, had an excellent opportunity to observe his fellow men. He was a part of the community, yet somewhat isolated by his position from varied aspects of its activity. Reminiscing in later years, John Dyer commented that in his twenty-seven years of experience, mainly in Colorado, he did not remember an instance where a miner or prospector did not behave himself in church.[4] He and others reflected that the majority of people were generous, personally kind, and in the habit of doing their own thinking. Just as in the Eastern churches, clergymen found it hard to enlist volunteers to serve as teachers or hold church offices. To be sure, ministers often observed a good deal of drinking, gambling, and swearing, which aroused moralizing statements but did not detract from their general impressions.[5]

Visitors to the camps increased after the 1860s, and many wrote of their experiences in books or magazine articles. Their impressions were as varied as their backgrounds. Their attitudes were influenced by the stage of urbanization of the camp and any experience they might have had in the frontier environment. Generally, writers noted that indifference to failure seemed to be characteristic of mining camp dwellers. Some European visitors felt that these

Americans displayed a great adaptability to any employment but seemed content with a far lower standard of craftsmanship than that of Europe. American observers on the whole apparently took this situation for granted and glossed over it in their reports. Clothes, to the amazement of some, were not necessarily the mark of the man in the camps. Rich and poor dressed alike. The gambling nature of the inhabitants often created an unfavorable impression on the more puritanical tourists, who were not amused by the wasteful extravagance which was practiced as a rule.

Those visitors who took time to make more than just a cursory examination were often impressed with the scholarly knowledge possessed by some of "the boys." Yet a deeper penetration found the crudeness and roughness which were also a definite part of each person's life. While some were impressed by the peaceable, order-loving nature of the people, other observers completely disagreed. The reception given the wayfarer could have a great deal to do with his reaction, and the reception varied from warmth to indifference. The visitor, in fact, often was as much of a curiosity to the residents as they were to him. Like their descendants of the twentieth century, camp inhabitants were apt to litter cans, bottles, and all manner of waste material around the countryside, which marred the beauty of the site and left the visitor with an unfavorable first impression.

Generally, these observers seemed to have been favorably impressed with the majority of the residents of the camps. Terms such as, "kind," "civil," and "ordinarily obliging," were used to describe them. Certainly there were those who were not impressed or felt they observed more bad qualities than good. One such was a newspaper reporter who wrote of Leadville, Colorado:

> The average Leadvillite is a remarkably dry animal, and is wont to recklessly fling away his coin and ruin his constitution in the multitude of 'gin-mill,' concert-saloons, dance-halls, and other disreputable places with which the city swarms. He stands around in clustering glory blocking up the sidewalks making it necessary to

force one's passage through the highly odoriferous mass whose aggressive characteristics appear to be about an equal proportion of insensibility, stupidity and concentrated 'cussedness.' [6]

This criticism must, however, be tempered with the realization that this is an older mining region describing a new rival.

The miner, whether in the camp or outside it, was the object of much interest. The miners themselves and most visitors agreed that mining was monotonous, hard work, a job only for the strong. It was a profession which took skill and experience, although, particularly in the early days, a great many inexperienced men tried their hand at it. Beyond this, the opinions vary. Some tourists were of the opinion that, generally, miners appeared friendly and neighborly, although at least one thought he had never in his life seen so many hardened, brutal men. There was also a general divergence as to whether these men were peaceable. While some felt that miners had a low standard of living, others pointed out that, as a class, they lived better than the Eastern working man.[7]

A composite picture of the people, then, cannot be drawn. Too many variables enter into any series of accounts. Here existed a cross section of America, and quite often Europe, mingled together. Certain general characteristics stand out, but with the urban frontier the individual remained predominant. Extremes were tolerated if they did not endanger the community as a whole, and, within limits, the individual was allowed to pursue his own course without interference. In numerous cases the inhabitant of the mining community was but a transplanted Easterner or European who was following his old trade on the frontier. Some came to the frontier because of the relative freedom offered by this environment, but many tried to transplant what was familiar, what was accepted in the older communities.

This was a society dominated by men. Women appeared very early, though, in most mining districts, as Greeley's comment illustrated for Central City in 1859. The census returns for the years 1860-80 further support this contention. Throughout most of the period, however, especially in the decade of the 1860s, the arrival of women in a camp was an important event. Often the scarcity of women was a handicap, at least to the social side of the camp's life.[8] As settlement spread, this condition was gradually alleviated, but men still maintained their predominance. The influence on the community exerted by these women far exceeded what might have been expected by their limited numbers. To the raw frontier they brought gentleness and a degree of culture and refinement, as their ancestors had done similarly in earlier frontiers. They struggled to establish the social and cultural values they had known in their former homes. To whatever degree they succeeded or failed, the influence was felt; it could not be overlooked or ignored. In the end they succeeded in molding much of the frontier into a more refined and acceptable image.

The speculative air of the camp affected all who came under its spell. While men and women were trying to change the raw camp into a more civilized pattern, they were themselves being changed by the new environment. Matthew Dale wrote to his brother in 1861 after two years in the Colorado gold fields: "You cannot gain that self reliance and independence under all circumstances a few years here would impart, by remaining anywhere in the east." [9] In a predominantly male society, men were more tempted to turn to gambling, drinking, and similar activities for relaxation. Women, too, enjoyed more freedom than they might have had otherwise. They found higher paying jobs, especially with the scarcity of servant girls. The number of divorce proceedings reported in the newspapers indicated that the uninhibited ways of society affected both sexes. No longer did a woman have to tolerate poor marital relationships when so many eligible men were available. Urbanization also produced situations totally new to frontier experience. For instance, at the very outset the typical individualism of the opening of a frontier was modified, as the miners cooperated to set up mining laws and a mining district to govern their working relations with each other and to provide the framework of legal government.

If the adults were affected by the conditions, the children who lived in the camp were even more a product of their environment. Their impressionable years were spent in a situation which condoned and consented to much that was not considered part of the usual education of American youth. Boys and girls grew up quickly in a society where emphasis was placed on adult vocation and avocation. Girls, especially, in the masculine society short of women, matured rapidly. In early teens they began to be escorted to dances by older men, and soon they were married.

Boys must have found the life of the mining camp much to their liking, with what they considered to be its adventure and excitement. At an early age, unfortunately, many of them started to partake of its more seamy aspects. Newspaper editors commented, on occasion, about such matters as profanity, gambling, and drinking habits of some of the younger members of the community; in age the participants ranged from five to fifteen. The following quip from Virginia City, Montana, illustrates how readily the younger generation emulated the older:

> A party of five chips off the old block whose ages varied from ten downward and whose height ranged from 3 feet 6 to 4 feet nothing in their stockings was pointed out to us last Sunday sitting on some boards engaged in playing poker. A young gentleman of some eight summers appeared to be losing as he brought down his knuckles violently on the board, exclaiming, 'oh, h—l on it: I can't hold a pair, to which responded his companion of seven winter's growth: 'Steady, old hoss, it's no use getting riled.' [10]

To open this or any other frontier required cooperation. In the urban mining settlement cooperation was particularly noticeable in many ways which benefited the entire community and/or some individual. The whole settlement, for example, would benefit from a community roadbuilding project with everyone assuming a share of the work. In Elizabethtown, New Mexico, the district was handicapped by lack of water, so the residents and miners donated time and money to construct a ditch from the nearest available source to the mines.[11] On numerous occasions, camps sent money and supplies to a sister community which had suffered a disaster, usually a fire.

On a more individual basis the cooperative spirit of the people was reflected by their willingness to help some of their less fortunate neighbors. They aided those who were needy and sick, often responding willingly to the frequent subscription papers which were passed around. They helped in building churches or schools, if the sponsoring organization did not have the manpower and money. But these people were not in any sense socialistic—quite the contrary. Except in times of distress the other fellow was allowed to go his own way with little or no help or hindrance from his neighbor.

The mining camps presented a cosmopolitan appearance, reflecting the world-wide birthplaces of their inhabitants. A newspaper reporter observed of a Sunday crowd:

> Here were congregated the most varied elements of humanity and the most various types of human character: persons belonging to almost every nationality and every status of life—the Irishman, the Englishman, the German, the Italian, the Frenchman, the Russian, the fair-haired Scandinavian, men from every State in the Union. . . . all blended into one homogeneous equality.[12]

All these nationalities and probably more could be found in any camp. Men with mining skills were welcome whether they were German, Cornish, or American, but such skills alone did not always guarantee acceptance, as will be shown. The camp accepted those who had services or talents which were needed. For most foreign people it was a school of Americanization unmatched in speed and assimilation by the rural frontier.

The majority of these people were native-born Americans, coming from all the states and territories. Statistics from the original census returns reveal that New York, Ohio, Pennsylvania, Illinois, and Missouri contributed the greatest number of settlers. A regional distribution pattern was apparent if one divided the country into four sections. The Midwest or those states west of Pennsylvania, north of the Ohio River, and east of Kansas provided by far the most settlers. The East, or Pennsylvania and the Northeastern states, was second, while the South was a distant third. The remainder of the country made a negligible contribution in 1860 and 1870 but by 1880 became a considerable factor with the first generation of Western children.[13]

It must be kept in mind that these statistics reflect the *birthplaces* of the people and that many of them probably migrated at least once before appearing in the Rocky Mountain region. A breakdown of statistics reveals other interesting trends which shed more light on these Americans. When the census of 1860 was taken, the Pike's Peak gold rush had just been completed. The states which made the heaviest contributions were New York, Ohio, and Pennsylvania, but the number from the South was larger proportionately than it would be at a later date. The border states of Kentucky, Maryland, Tennessee, and Virginia, in that order, sent the only really appreciable numbers, while the deep South made a negligible contribution. Percentages from the Midwestern states greatly increased during the decades of the 1860s and 1870s, especially Illinois and Missouri. Although never contributing a large number, the far Eastern states of Maine, Massachusetts, and New Jersey always seemed to have a few natives in each camp. No doubt some of these people were on their second or third move before they reached the mining West.

The transitory character of this generation is well illustrated by the history of William Donald, who was born on Prince Edward Island in 1830. At the age of twenty-one he moved to Maine and later went to Michigan. In 1860 Donald followed the fifty-niners to Denver, soon turning to prospecting. To quote him, he "did not succeed well," and following a stint as a miner, he became the superintendent of a Gilpin County, Colorado, mine. When news of rich silver discoveries in neighboring Boulder County reached Donald, he migrated again. Although placed in charge of a group of mines, he now broadened his interests and opened a hotel. At last he found the opportunity for which he had been searching for twenty years and settled down. William Donald is not typical of all miners or even one group, but his career reflects a mobile tendency common to all. Mobility was an important feature of the mining frontier and a definite influence on the camps.[14]

The census returns tend to confirm the fact that the frontier was most attractive to those geographically near it, and even the wealth of the mining camps could not tempt distantly settled Americans. While California may have lured the Easterner, some of the glamor had subsequently worn off, and travel and living costs remained high in 1859. To reach the mining regions took more money than many people could hope to save in a decade of hard work. For the pioneering people of the Midwest, however, it was just another move in what had become a way of life. The attractions were perhaps more glamorous, the possible rewards greater, but the move itself was similar to what their parents had faced a generation before.

Of the foreign countries, the British Isles and the Empire were the best represented in the mining camps. The Irish, of course, were numerous. Following the English-speaking countries came the German states. There was always a scattering from other countries but none had any consistent percentage. The Chinese, in the decade of the 1870s, became an increasingly larger fraction of the population, particularly concentrated in the older mining regions of Idaho and Montana. The census returns of 1860 indicate a much smaller percentage of foreign born than in later years. The rush, however, had just started and it had not created the interest in foreign lands that California had in 1848-49. The immigration pattern as it developed was typical for the United States during these decades. The majority of emigrants came from England and northern Europe. There was one notable exception—the Scandinavians were never attracted in appreciable numbers to the camps.

To illustrate some of the general statements of previous pages, the 1880 census of two communities, Custer, Idaho, and Pinal, Arizona, will be discussed in detail. The following figures are based upon the total population of each community rounded off to the nearest tenth. Americans represented 59 percent of the population in Custer and 74 percent in Pinal. Of those of American birth, 39 percent in the former and 8 percent in the latter were first generation, one or both parents being born outside the United States. The largest foreign group in Custer was the Irish, who totaled 16 percent of the entire population, and in Pinal the Chinese, with 8 percent. The British Isles and Empire contributed one-third in Custer and 5 percent of the population of Pinal. In the former camp the percentage breakdown of those born in the Midwest, East, and South was 18, 25, and 8 and in the latter 20, 16, and 7. It was a male-dominated society, with only 4 percent women in Custer and 14 percent in Pinal.

Both camps had the normal number of Southerners but the border Southern states produced over half of the total. Since this census was taken in 1880, the West was well represented, mostly by children or youths in their teens. Nine percent of Custer's population and 31 percent of Pinal's had been born in the area west of Missouri. Custer had a slightly higher percentage of Easterners and a lower number of Midwesterners than was usual.

The mining frontier was primarily a youthful movement. One participant wrote some years later: "I was there a good many years before we saw a man with grey hair." [15] The reasons for this are fairly obvious, as George Parsons stated about his father's coming to Tombstone: "It's all very well for a young man like myself to take risks as I am doing or have done, as if all is lost I can recover myself soon, but [it] is quite another thing for my father with a dependent family." [16] The young were not tied down to family, business, and tradition. It was easier for them to follow the ever-changing fortunes and location of the camps. They could better withstand and adjust to the rigors of the life for it took youthful optimism to overcome the disappointments and failures. The land was young and they could grow with it.

The census figures provide support for this conclusion about the youthful nature of the participants, and indicate further some interesting trends. Considering only those people between the ages of 16 and 49,[17] the median age of the residents of Central City and Mountain City, Colorado, in 1860 was slightly over 27 and 28 years. In 1870 the average had reached 30 years or better in over half the camps tested. By the census of 1880, 14 out of the 18 camps averaged at least 30 years, with one camp reaching 39. Besides the gradual aging of the participants, another conclusion can be drawn: the newer the camp the younger its residents. For example, the two communities of 1860 were about a year old and in the next two censuses the camps less than five years old produced the lower averages. There are, of course, exceptions to these statements but strong indications of these trends are apparent.

This gradual rise in age of the population was at least partially responsible for the change which came over the mining frontier during the years of this study. Maturity came to replace the youthful exuberance of the earlier years. This had an effect on the way of life and the character of the camps which will be discussed in subsequent chapters. Regardless of the gradual aging, the camps of the frontier still remained young when compared to settled communities of the East.

Three

Not All Were Welcome

O_N the surface it might seem logical that everyone would be accepted into the social hodgepodge of the mining camp; that all would be welcome to try his or her luck, and depending upon skill and ingenuity, might succeed. This seems a fine theory, but it was not practiced. The camps were from the beginning predominantly inhabited by white, northern Europeans. This was not unusual for nineteenth-century Americans. They carried with them to the frontier their prejudices and traditions, and even the new conditions failed to modify these attitudes to any great degree.

For varied reasons certain minority groups found themselves facing discrimination. The Chinese, and frequently the Spanish-Americans and Negroes, quickly realized they were not welcome. The Mormons, too, on occasion, fell into this category, but for different reasons. The Indian, who had roamed the land before the coming of the whites, was excluded from almost all activities. His land seized, his way of life gone, he was left to fend for himself, preferably somewhere other than the immediate region of the mining frontier. In differing degrees all of these groups had an influence on the camp and its inhabitants, whether or not they were accepted members of the community.

Of the minority groups which actively participated in the life of the mining camp, the Chinese received by far the harshest treatment. They had immigrated to the California gold fields, spreading from there throughout the West. In most aspects of the life of the camp and district, Chinese were to be found, but almost as soon as they appeared resentment against them mounted. The Chinese problem as it developed had a cultural, social, and economic basis. Culturally, they were a race apart, hard to assimilate and hard to comprehend, even if their neighbors made the effort, which they rarely did. Their language, customs, and clannish nature created barriers which only time could erase. Socially, their racial characteristics isolated them and helped form a tacit, if not open, discrimination against them.

These differences alone could not have created the intense dislike of them, for other ethnic groups displayed similar traits. The spark which ignited much of the trouble was economic. Living on less, the Chinese were able to work for less. They represented a threat to the miner, Caucasian laundryman, or anyone else who had to compete with them in the labor market. Inherent also in the resentment was the fear or threat that property values would decline if the Chinese moved into the neighborhood. In addition, the thrifty and persistent Chinese could find gold in areas where the Americans and Europeans had given up claims which seemed to be worked out. For these reasons the Chinese arrival was looked upon with dismay by many, for it then appeared that the district was declining and profitable for none but Orientals. This created a state of mind which classified them as "harbingers of decline." [1] As a result of all these factors, a preconceived opinion developed against the race, which created a hostile atmosphere almost anywhere they chose to live and work.

The treatment of the Chinese was disgraceful for a country which prided itself on a democratic and equalitarian tradition. Urged on by racial and economic hatred, inflammatory editorials, and mob secrecy, the whites harassed the Chinese in innumerable ways. Even the Irish, who had received similar treatment in many Eastern port cities, reacted as had their persecutors to a new threat. Justification for excluding Chinese from the camps was both blunt and subtle. One newspaper editor wrote that no one could deny that the Chinese, viewed merely as members of the community, merited praise for their qualities of industry, promptness in paying debts, and obedience to the law. However, he went on to attack the Chinese slave trade in women and coolie labor, stating he would not allude to the fact that they were superstitious, took no interest in the prosperity of the land, and intended to return home with all the treasure which they could amass.[2] It made no difference that Americans often held similar views about future prosperity and returned home after making their Western fortunes; these were Chinese, and for them to do it was un-American.

Another editor became even more emotional, blaming Chinese cheap labor for the crime, vice, and destitution of the country. He described how this labor system drove many white children onto the streets to beg and made thieves of men who never carried "a dishonest hair on their heads when they could obtain work at reasonable wages."[3] Disagreement concerning Chinese obedience to American law was not unusual. There seemed to be two interpretations. Let any crime be committed in the Chinese section, and it brought forth editorial comments about the undesirability of the Chinese. Yet reliable evidence supports the other contention as well. The worst aspect of the hatred, emotionalism, and vileness of this type of attack was shown in one diatribe:

> The Chinese are the least desired immigrants who have ever sought the United States. . . . the almond-eyed Mongolian with his pigtail, his heathenism, his filthy habits, his thrift and careful accumulation of savings to be sent back to the flowery kingdom.
>
> The most we can do is to insist that he is a heathen, a devourer of soup made from the fragrant juice of the rat, filthy, disagreeable, and undesirable generally, an incumbrance that we do not know how to get rid of, but whose tribe we have determined shall not increase in this part of the world.[4]

The writer of this impassioned plea was disingenuous when he stated that he did not know how to get rid of the Chinese on the local level, for he and the entire frontier knew perfectly how they *had* been doing it. Violence or the threat of violence was relied upon as the solution. More often than not, the threat was sufficient to intimidate the Chinese. This was done by agreeing not to sell any property to them, by hanging out the banner "The Chinese must not come," and then enforcing the slogan if any appeared, or finally, by forcibly removing some as an example to others. If these methods failed, then the final alternative was total coercion, which could take the form of a mob or a more orderly group which would drive the "Celestials" away.[5]

If the Chinese once acquired a foothold, discriminatory taxes not only secured an amount of revenue for the district, but often discouraged further immigration. In the words of the Silver City, Idaho, *Owyhee Avalanche,* June 23, 1866: "They are in many respects a disgusting element of the population but not wholly unprofitable." Virginia City, Montana, by ordinance restricted the Chinese to a certain section of town, "owing to the immoral and filthy habits and also the extreme carelessness as to fires." [6] Other camps, by accepted practice, achieved the same result. This isolation only furthered the problem, for "Chinatown" became synonymous with vice and corruption.

Not all joined in this anti-Chinese sentiment; a minority spoke for justice and even acceptance. It was pointed out that the Chinese trade was profitable to the businessman and their taxes important to the local government, but this materialistic feeling in no way accepted the premise of racial equality. Quite to the contrary, it was reasoned that the Mongolian race was inferior, but the question was then asked, why should the superior race on every occasion "abuse and maltreat those unfortunates"? The Chinese after all had passports to come to the country, "they pay dearly for the protection they do not receive: but we hope, for the sake of common humanity to be able to record a change for the better before long." [7] Like a voice crying in the wilderness these ideas were pushed aside in the rush to stop the Oriental hordes.

This anti-Chinese sentiment failed to halt completely the influx of these people. They spread throughout the frontier, but especially into Idaho and Montana, where the placer or free gold regions quickly declined and the miners moved on to more profitable diggings. Where they were numerous enough, the Chinese built settlements within the larger mining community. They were miniature mining camps with Chinese gambling houses, merchants, prostitutes, restaurants, and—for an added touch—some had joss houses. These temples aroused a great deal of curiosity among outsiders. Here, too, were found opium dens, which did so much to give the Chinese bad publicity. These Chinatowns were much less numerous, however, in the Rocky Mountain region than in neighboring California.

Within their community or section of town the Chinese tried to carry on their way of life much as they would have in China. Their clannish and often secretive nature caused some problems with the jurisdiction of American law and authority. Trying to solve a crime committed among the Chinese could be a most frustrating and difficult experience for an American peace officer. For young and old alike their strange funerals provided wonderment, and the Chinese were often joined by their neighbors in celebrating the advent of the Chinese New Year. They were one of the social curiosities of the frontier, interesting to both locals and visitors.[8]

In those areas where the Chinese were not so numerous they were still rigidly limited to certain occupations. The laundry field was almost exclusively theirs, yet not without some competition. This need the Chinese were able to meet with better and cheaper service. So infuriated became the women of Helena, Montana, who were engaged in the same business, that they published a warning in the paper notifying the Orientals to leave or be visited by a committee of the ladies who presumably would enforce their edict. Chinese merchants operated all types of business in the camps, and Chinese restaurants and particularly cooks were in popular demand. Some raised small gardens, supplying the camps with vegetables. Many, however, held only the most menial jobs such as hauling water or wood.[9]

The Chinese did not remain in the Rocky Mountain West; they either returned to China or settled permanently on the West Coast. Few brought families and this, no doubt, with the alien environment, helped to explain their departure. While on the mining frontier, they represented an important economic force. By reworking the abandoned placer site with patient labor they redeemed the wastefulness of the previous owners. Many had come in gangs controlled by Chinese contractors, although not all were coolies of this sort. This was another factor which made them suspect to the Americans who thought more in terms of individual initiative. However, even though they were socially apart from the rest of the community, on an individual basis feelings of cordiality existed between them and some of their neighbors. Chinese cooks and servants endeared themselves to the families who employed them. On occasion schools were started by sympathetic persons to teach the Chinese to read and write English. On the whole, however, no matter where or. at what period of the mining frontier one looks, the Chinese were regarded as outsiders by the majority of their neighbors and co-workers.

The place of Negroes in the mining camps is harder to define. Bishop Daniel Tuttle wrote in 1867 that he encountered a considerable "squad of negroes mostly from Missouri" in Helena, Montana, yet other sources testified that the Negro was only infrequently found on the mining frontier. Census records confirm that they were there, but in varying numbers. Some camp newspapers mention them and their activities; others are silent on the subject. Whatever their aggregate, they were not so commonly encountered as the Chinese nor did they find restrictions against them so harsh.[10]

The Negro did not have to live in any specified section of the camp nor was he limited to certain jobs; but that discrimination existed cannot be doubted. The Englishman, Maurice Morris, who visited in Colorado in 1863, wrote that the ban against Negroes was strong. He stated that only a few white inhabitants were afflicted with what was popularly known as "nigger-on-the-brainism." In Central City, Colorado, as late as 1869, Negro parents retained lawyers to force the opening of the public school to their children. A letter written by a Negro mother of Park City, Utah, concerning the withdrawal of white children because her children entered the school has a poignant, almost timeless quality:

> My children's skin may be a shade darker than his but in all other respects they are equal to his. . . . I had supposed the terrible lesson this class [Southerners?] had been taught during the war would enable them to recognize the equality before the law, of the colored people, and not object to my little girls occupying seats in the same room with them.[11]

It is interesting to note that, in spite of the foregoing type of treatment, on at least one occasion a Negro participated in an anti-Chinese meeting, joining with his white neighbors in demanding that the Orientals had to go.[12]

Another form of discrimination was practiced, if not openly, at least tacitly. The papers reported stories of Negro balls, social associations, and clubs, indicating that the colored person was not accepted in similar activities sponsored by the white residents of the camp. Reflecting perhaps more than intended, a comment in the *Montana Post*, January 12, 1867, discussed the inaugural party of the colored Pioneer Social Club. After describing the ceremonies and addresses, the reporter mentioned that this "shows that they are competent at least in this Territory to attain a certain social standard to which entitled by the Creator." Such treatment was not unusual in post-Civil-War America.

Unlike the Chinese, the Negro was not an economic challenge to his mining white neighbors, for he did not readily have the opportunity to become a miner or prospector. Nor did contemporary sources consider the Negro a danger to the property values of the community. Politically, the colored people represented no menace because of their small numbers, nor did religion enter into the picture. The lack of a threat and the scarcity of Negroes produced primarily a climate of tolerance, if not outright acceptance, by the white community. Racial strife could not generate a full head of intolerance under such conditions.

Another minority group, the Spanish American, was present in southern Colorado, New Mexico, and Arizona, and in lesser numbers farther to the north. There was always a certain amount of ill feeling between the races, but the camps remained predominantly northern European-American stock. The Americans looked upon their communities as being distinctive because of this factor. Advertisements by Mexican merchants appeared in many papers of the more southern towns, indicating little business discrimination. On the whole, racial friction in the camps must have been at a minimum, for little note was taken of it.

The racial characteristics of the minority groups mentioned thus far easily separated them from the European stock. This was not the case with the Mormons, who, for their religious beliefs, especially the abhorred practice of polygamy, sometimes found themselves confronted with discrimination. Utah, their religious commonwealth, had an advantageous central location in the region under discussion. It had been settled for a decade before the great rush of 1859, but the church officials had taken a cautious attitude toward mining; this in itself was unusual in Western history. Nevertheless, the Mormons had profited greatly by their nearness to all mining centers and from those in their own territory. They found ready markets for their farm produce and other products, found good wages for skilled workers, and even the church dispatched exploring parties.

A certain amount of friction developed between the Mormons and the Gentiles, especially in Utah. An interesting contrast is presented by two Utah camps, Silver Reef and Park City. The former, located in the far southern corner of the territory, had little favorable to say about its neighbors. The editor of the camp's newspaper carried on a "war" against the "Latter-day slave owners," crying out against a supposed church practice of furnishing labor to Mormon merchants at low rates and to the exclusion of Gentiles. On the passage of the Edmunds bill (1882) outlawing polygamy, he happily entitled his lead article "Polygamy to the Rear and America to the Front." Park City, however, was located close to Salt Lake City and was much more moderate in its approach, stressing that Mormon and Gentile should work together. Anti-Mormon editorials and articles might appear in other camps, but the problem there was hypothetical and not a real one. Toleration was displayed, perhaps to a greater degree than was true for the Easterner of that day. According to the Leadville *Democrat* "so long as they obey the laws and make industrious self-sustaining citizens they should be welcome." [13]

There was conflict in individual camps among various minority groups, especially between the Irish and their rivals when competing for the same jobs. The threat of lower wages being accepted by members of some ethnic group played a major part in starting trouble. Such clashes depended on local conditions, the threat involved, and the strength of different groups. Some communities had their Cornish, Irish, or Welsh sections where people of similar background and cultures tended to group together. Here they often preserved their old world customs, but this was generally by choice rather than social mandate.

While the Indian had at one time claimed as his hunting ground all of the land over which the miners swarmed, his race was not directly involved in the exploitation of the mineral wealth. The mining frontier, however, had a direct bearing on the final disposition of the Indian question. Its influence was marked; for example, the opening of the Bozeman Trail to the Montana gold fields brought about the so-called Red Cloud's War of 1866-68, and the gold rush to the Black Hills resulted in the Sioux War of 1876. The mining frontier and the Indian were not mutually compatible, and the Indian had to give way or be overrun. Some of the more spectacular episodes and clashes between the Americans and the Indians resulted from this incompatibility.

Like other frontiersmen, the residents of the mining camps who lived anywhere near the Indian land seemed to have an uncontrollable desire to remove the red man from the country and open the reservation to settlement. That he resided there was reason enough, but many were convinced that he uselessly resided on the best land or mineral wealth available. The industrious whites could use the area in a much more advantageous manner. It was not, the argument ran, that they wanted to treat the Indians unfairly; they just felt that the Indians should be moved elsewhere to land more suitable for their needs.[14] Where this might be was left up to the government, for there was little space that some American settler did not want or feel he needed.

Reaction to the Indian problem in the camp newspapers remained fairly uniform throughout the entire period. The *Montana Post,* February 4, 1865, commented: "Christianize him sir, is whispered by the ignorant philanthropist of the day. A wolf knows no better and is shot and not tamed." A decade later the *Black Hills Pioneer,* August 26, 1876, recommended, "Kill all the Indians that can be killed. Complete extermination is our motto." These represented the more radical views of camps which were immediately threatened by an Indian danger. The farther one was removed from the danger, the less radical the position. As the years went by and the danger became less acute, the editors and others started to take a more reasonable approach to the question. While the Indian never became the noble savage so dear to many Easterners, at least he was examined in a more objective and more humane manner.

The local newspaper, as a result, turned its attention more and more to the government Indian policy, or lack of one. The mining camp editors had a field day advancing ideas as to what should be done—everything from making the Indian a citizen and compelling him to earn a living, to allowing him to roam and hunt freely as long as he remained peaceful, but dealing "death and destruction" to any who remained warlike.[15] A solution which would be economical, involve little or no supervision, and meet the problem seemed to be the desire of the hour. Such editorial speculation was harmless and had no effect on the Indian policy beyond being part of the mounting criticism of previous plans. Still, it did reflect the nature of the changing attitude toward the Indian, although an undercurrent of feeling remained that if the Indian was in the way, he had to go.

These were the people (with the exception of the Indians) who collectively made up the body of what may be termed the greater mining community. All of them were in some way affected by it and in turn influenced its development and life. That they are today individually unknown does not lessen their impact. On the urban mining frontier the individual gave way to the community, although the sum of the parts was still greater than the whole.

The society which was produced was democratic, at least as much as any other frontier settlement, yet it could also be intolerant. Minority groups, particularly the Chinese and to a lesser degree the Negro, faced discrimination almost everywhere they appeared in large numbers during these years. Society, though initially fluid, tended to become stratified as time passed. In the early days of a camp little attempt was made at distinction, because of the leveling influence of what might be termed "democratic poverty." Any social distinction was generally put aside, as the past was forgotten and life started anew in the camp. Society, however, in the sense of class consciousness, came early to this urban frontier. The riches of the mines produced a wealthy class, which included the leading merchants and professional people. This upper crust might not be exactly pretentious, yet pride and often extravagance marked their coming into wealth. Before long the respectable people would not appear at questionable places or affairs. The wealthy men, for example, might partake of the pleasures of the exclusive houses of prostitution, but look down on the "girls of the line." After the first few years, as mining became more costly and complicated, the cleavage between the laboring and capitalist classes emerged. No longer was the owner a worker in the mine, nor could the miner under normal circumstances hope to become an owner. Although they were not based upon money, there were often clannish feelings among the old-timers who opposed the newcomers. Riches or poverty were no barrier here. Social stratification was also reinforced with the coming of women, who brought with them or quickly copied the prevailing attitudes of the East.[16]

Thus the democratic social order, promoted by common dreams and poverty, changed with the success of a few and the failure of many. Social breaches along several lines appeared and infused themselves into the community. "Society," in turn, became a mark of distinction for the camp, a sign of its permanence.[17] Its coming further marked one phase in the passing of the frontier. The urban nature of the frontier strengthened society and was in turn strengthened by it. They were mutually compatible and to a degree mutually dependent. These effects were most notable in the larger settlements, but none escaped them in some form.

The question of whether the mining frontier acted as a melting pot cannot be conclusively answered. Some groups were never assimilated, others only partially so. To answer this question conclusively would require a study of many individual mining camps, an endeavor which, unfortunately, has been sadly neglected. A general examination would seem to indicate that the communities did act in this capacity, if for no other reason than that many camps failed to have a large enough foreign population from one country to produce a special section or clique, once again an exception being noted for the Chinese. The foreigners blended into the community or faced isolation. To most, this latter choice was undesirable and an unnecessary privation on the frontier.

"Young America" was molded and changed by the frontier environment of the mining West and also by the urban aspects of the mining camps. Each worked to produce an American who was different from his brother who had remained behind in the older states. It was not a radical difference but it was noticeable, as observers testified when commenting about the Westerner. Other frontiers produced similar results, modified by different economic and geographical conditions. The normal product of the frontier crystallized and out of it emerged regional America, of which the mining West was only one section.

Four

When Young America Finds a Good Gold Gulch

THE rush to a new mining bonanza could start with the merest rumor or a chance discovery by some prospector. It could begin with the influx of many people or just a few, depending on the location and the purported wealth. Regardless of the original circumstances, the scene soon changed. What was once nature's domain now became the workshop of man. Expectation, excitement, and optimism underlay the hustle of the hopeful, as they made their way to the bonanza to stake their claim, open their store, or in some other way try to make their fortune.

Almost overnight nature gave way to man. The first to arrive faced primitive conditions. This meant camping out on the ground and braving the elements until the first crude shelters could be constructed. Often the sites were in mountainous regions where the nights were cool, even in midsummer. The following description of Custer City, South Dakota, during the spring of 1876 illustrates a typical setting:

> There were but few houses completed, but many under construction. The people were camped all around, . . . , in wagons, tents and temporary brush houses or wickiups. The principal business houses were saloons, gambling houses and dance halls, two or three so-called stores with very small stocks of general merchandise and little provisions.[1]

Log construction and a haphazard, crowded appearance typify
the early development of a mining camp in Central City, Colorado, in the early 1860s. *Denver Public Library Western
Collection.*

Tents and log cabins provide shelter in this 1876 view of Gayville,
South Dakota. Note the garden in the lower right corner. *U.S. Signal
Corps, National Archives.*

Horace Greeley had drawn a similar picture of Colorado seventeen years before.

Men brought with them pack mules, horses, and in some cases wagons, and usually carried a supply of provisions to last for a few weeks. Everyone was on his own or, at best, a member of a small party. As a result, the site of the discovery took on the appearance of an irregular and awkward patchwork settlement with people camping almost where they pleased near their claim or on some other desirable location.[2]

On occasion a company would attempt to promote a site for a camp, hoping to make money by selling the lots to incoming settlers. Perhaps among the early arrivals would be a surveyor, who tried in a rude manner to lay out streets to serve as a guideline for buildings. These early attempts might or might not work, depending on the temper of the people who appeared. Usually, it was far from the miner's mind whether he was constructing his cabin, tent, or board shanty according to anyone else's idea of location.

Such humble beginnings did not long prove satisfactory. Very quickly more substantial buildings appeared among the temporary ones. Speed was essential; no time could be spared for painting or building anything beyond a simple, functional structure. The streets along which the settlement gradually organized itself were little better than beaten paths with uncleared stumps and rocks hindering passage. There was no neat grid arrangement; the roadways often wandered down the sides of mountains or up narrow canyons. Some of the buildings, almost from the moment they were completed, had a weatherbeaten appearance which gave the visitor the impression of a run-down Midwestern village. The camp, nevertheless, from the very start had a lively and booming air with people flocking in every day and a steadily expanding business life. An Eastern visitor described the scene as one of "vim, recklessness, extravagance and jolly progress."[3]

In a short time, a few weeks or months, the wilderness was transformed into a prospective urban community. As yet, it was

not a village in the New England or European sense, and indeed
it might never be, but it was a young mining camp. It happened
so suddenly that many were amazed. James Morley, a miner in
Montana during the 1860s, wrote in his diary that he was surprised
at how the country had improved in the past year. George Ingham,
who visited several mining regions in 1880, commented with wonder on the fact that the camp of Pitkin, Colorado, had grown
within six weeks to have some forty to fifty business houses and
saloons.[4] Many old timers took it all in stride, however, for they
had seen the same thing happen before in other places.

An examination of Rocky Mountain camps reveals a general
growth pattern. The discovery of ore deposits came first, followed
by a rush to the area. Along with hopeful and would-be miners
came merchants, gamblers, and others who immediately opened
places of business. On the heels of the original rush came freighters who kept the supply lines open and gave impetus to the development of the budding settlement. At first, no organization was
thought necessary to regulate the camp, but the desirability of order
soon became apparent. By common consent or through city government, regulations appeared first concerning the laying out of streets,
then regarding such matters as taxation. At this juncture, the future
evolution of the camp depended on the mines. If they proved pro-
ductive, then the community grew, attracting new business and
more people. If the mines failed, decline followed with the failure
to develop a more permanent economic base.

The history of any given camp was not characterized by steady
growth, but by fluctuations characteristic of the frontier. Even for
the more prosperous communities, the future was never wholly
bright, for the mines eventually declined and with them the town.
A fortunate few overcame this inevitability by developing other industries to balance their economic livelihood; many, however, did
not, and entered into a long twilight period. In the end they might
completely disappear, or at best retain only a shadow of their
former size and importance.

Such a melancholy fate was far in the future for the eager participant as he rushed to the new discovery. Optimism was in the air, and few had dark thoughts. The prevailing attitude was probably very similar to this report:

> I do not deem it necessary at this time to speak of the extent or richness of our mineral veins. That we have them of extraordinary value both in gold and silver is now, I believe, a well established fact. . . . This city [South Pass, Wyoming] will soon take rank among the magic cities of the West.[5]

One of the first things that had to be done was to provide at least a rudimentary government for the mining district. It became the accepted practice to rely on a miners' meeting to delimit the size of claims and to set the procedure for filing a claim. Sometimes the miners would hold a meeting even before they reached the site to adopt laws to govern the district. One classic instance of this was when the first large party traveling to Alder Gulch, Montana, later Virginia City, agreed to certain rules governing claims before reaching the area.[6]

Out of these meetings developed the early governments of the mining districts. In the urban setting of the mining rush, some law and order was needed quickly; government could not develop slowly in the evolutionary process of previous frontiers. The immaturity of the settlement might magnify the problems, but experience had taught the people that in this situation the individual acting alone was not sufficiently strong. Communal government was the best available answer. All their lives the majority had submitted to some form of local governing authority, and the cosmopolitan nature of their backgrounds provided a rich heritage upon which to draw. There were also some men who had worked in other districts and had experience in drafting crude mining codes. From this reservoir the California miner, the Midwesterner, and the European emigrant collaborated to produce the framework of government.

The mining district provided the logical basis for a governing organization, because it superseded the mining camp, and was often the only basis available. The individual in Idaho, Colorado, or Montana in the early 1860s found no local government whatever and a weak territorial administration. This situation would change drastically in the next twenty years throughout the western United States. Territorial or state government, and in most cases even county administration were organized and functioning. Still, the establishment of local administration remained a problem for the early settlers.

The laws of the mining districts were the first attempts to control the problems of the mushrooming urban community. Examination of the codes of a series of these mining districts reveals many similarities. The district boundaries were defined, the claims described, usually in some detail as to number, size, and procedure for filing, and finally, district officers' duties were prescribed. The number of officers was normally limited to the barest minimum: a president, recorder, and perhaps a sheriff or judge. No bureaucracy or expensive government was desired or needed. The miners' court represented the tribunal of justice, administered by either majority vote or the jury system. With the development of the district the government became more complex.

In this earliest government, democracy, under the leveling influence of poverty and a fresh start in a strange land, reached a zenith. Normally everyone of a suitable age, usually from the mid-teens on up, who actually resided in the district was recognized as a voter and prospective office holder by the miners' meetings. Then, paradoxically, as urbanization increased, voter qualifications did likewise. Generally, property restrictions came first, followed by increased residence requirements. Age became a more important factor, and finally race entered into consideration. It was tacitly understood, following the prevailing custom, that women could not vote, for no effort was made specifically to disenfranchise them.[7]

In the initial struggle for shelter and wealth, democracy flourished. With the changing situation, some people becoming wealthy and many having vested interests to protect, conservatism in granting the franchise became accepted practice. The democracy of general poverty had passed, to be replaced by a more traditional attitude.

The miners often held their meeting near the few tents and log huts which would in time become the mining camp. This yet embryonic community was under the district's laws. In the boisterous rush to organize a government, town development received little attention. The camps were left to grow as they would, where they would. With more time and foresight, later conferences produced a few guidelines. Generally, it was stipulated that at least the plat of the village be recorded with size of blocks, lots, and streets carefully marked.[8] This proved a minor restraint for a generation of speculators and town promoters. Ambitious plats of stillborn towns, cradling the dreams of these Americans, remain as a symbol of their abounding optimism.

The rapidity with which at least the framework of government appeared typified the mining frontier. After this initial flurry, there was a time lag before the development of organized municipal government for the mining camps. The mining district laws, concerned principally with the preservation of property, evolved into a more general code with the later addition of criminal statutes. Supported by district or territorial government, they formed the basis for jurisdiction in many of the earlier camps. By the middle of the 1870s this situation had been modified to the extent that some of the new camps developed an autonomous position within the first months of their existence.

The camp was growing along with the district. From a haphazard collection of tents, brush huts, wagons, and perhaps caves in the side of a hill, it evolved into a community which, in the eyes of its inhabitants, deserved the title of city. To the Easterner or European who visited, the contrast with a real city was appalling. The following two quotations illustrate their dismay; both of the camps in question were about ten years old:

> Narrow and dingy as is this mining town [Black Hawk, Colorado] its people are making a brave effort to give it a look of comfort. . . . Scarcely a tree or shrub is to be seen, or even a flower, except it be in some parlor window; but as we drove up into Central [City], we came upon a very pretty conservatory, attached to a neat cottage. It was something strangely cheering, yet touching, in the universal dreariness.[9]

> Virginia City [Montana]. Good Lord! . . . A street of straggling shanties, a bank, a blacksmith's shop, a few dry goods stores, and bar-rooms, constitute the main attractions of the 'city'. A gentleman had informed me that Virginia *City* contained brownstone front houses and paved streets, equal he guessed to any eastern *town*. How that man did lie in his Wellingtons! The whole place was a delusion and a snare.[10]

The local people, unabashed by such opinions, went on viewing their camp as a booming community and were not hesitant in the least about naming any small cluster of buildings a city.

Around the camp were the miners' cabins, most located near their claims or at some nearby convenient location. They were utilitarian in all ways, from the construction material to the furnishings. A miner wrote about his dwelling, "Our cabin outwardly presents the appearance of a Missouri stable, being built of rough logs," but he concluded it was warm and tight for winter and cool in the summer.[11] These miner-prospectors, although one of the key economic and social factors of the camp's life, were considered as part of the greater mining community, not of the camp proper. Their dwellings might have been the original camp, but with increased growth and the arrival of other people who made their living in the community, they became much more than just a collection of miners' cabins. To be sure, there were always those men who lived in town and worked in the mines, but they quite often were a different breed from the original miner-prospector.

One of the earliest worries of many mining camps was the In-

Early 1865 picture of Helena, Montana, with a wagon train parked in the main street. The wagons might have been carrying goods to Helena or leaving to supply nearby camps. *Historical Society of Montana.*

Helena in 1874, nine years later. Note the changes in architecture and building materials in this now mature community. *Historical Society of Montana.*

dian problem. As the "Emigrant's Song" stated, "We'll lay on the ground and sleep very sound, Except when Indians are howling around." From the Sioux in the north to the Apache in the south, the Indian menaced the mining frontier. Isolated mining communities and prospecting parties were in danger of being raided, especially in the years before 1880. Indian scares drove miners into the camps for protection, disrupted communication and transportation with the outside world, and created problems for everyone concerned. Actual raids meant the loss of time, property, and often one's life. Some camps, in fact, found their growth retarded until the Indian menace was removed or abated.[12]

Normally, the frontiersman turned to the federal government and the army to solve this problem. Sometimes, when the government was unable to respond or was too slow for the local people, they organized their own forces. Home guards or local volunteers offered the show of protection, if not the substance. These groups were probably as much social and political as military. Some, like the Butte, Montana men in 1877, actually went into the field against the Indians; others more nearly fit the humorous description that the miner-newspaperman, Richard Hughes, wrote concerning the Custer, South Dakota home guard, "The statement was ventured that the reason for dubbing the organization 'Minute Men' was that it never went so far from town that it could not get back in a minute."[13]

Occasionally, the trouble would continue over a period of time without apparent relief, and the tempers of the people would grow increasingly warmer. The government and the army would be correspondingly damned for dereliction of duty and protests would be lodged by sending memorials to Congress. The citizens of Silver City and Grant County, New Mexico, for example, became so disgusted with the failure of government attempts to stop raids that they subscribed to a fund to be employed to pay for Indian scalps and to maintain a scout constantly on patrol. They further resolved to protest solemnly against paying directly or indirectly any tax to support Indians on reservations from which they could raid white settlements. Fortunately, such strong statements were not backed by action.[14] This impatience, this willingness to tamper with military operations reflected typical frontier attitudes, not solely those of camp residents.

The ever-moving mining frontier caused many problems for the government in relation to its Indian wards, for the miner respected neither treaty nor Indian rights in his quest for wealth. This situation kindled numerous local conflicts which were not resolved until the Indian was removed or eliminated. Perhaps the best known example of the effect of the mining frontier on Indian policy occurred in the Black Hills in the 1870s. This area had been guaranteed to the Sioux by the 1868 treaty ending the struggle over the Bozeman Trail, known as Red Cloud's War. The Black Hills retained a special significance for these Indians, because they were the sacred home of Sioux deities. Rumors of gold had long been circulated before they were confirmed by the Black Hills expedition of Lieutenant Colonel George Custer in 1874.

In the months that followed, a steadily mounting number of prospectors and miners tried to enter the Black Hills, while the army attempted to keep them out. The government found itself in an awkward position, for the peaceful relations with agency bands were endangered and all the Sioux threatened reprisals for this invasion. Negotiations failed to produce the desired sale, and in 1876 a military campaign to compel non-agency Sioux to enter the reservation resulted in the annihilation of Custer and part of the Seventh Cavalry at the famous Battle of the Little Big Horn.

The tragic events of that campaign brought to a quick termination the negotiations for the Black Hills. The government had not brought on the Sioux War of 1876 to obtain possession of the gold fields—far from it.[15] The rush into the area furnished an excuse and justification for both sides to end a truce which had not proved satisfactory. The events of 1875 and 1876, however, marked the opening of the last chapter of the American Indian's struggle against the oncoming whites. The mining frontier helped perpetuate this struggle and provided many of the problems which had to be overcome if it were to be finally resolved.

Indians were troublesome and could be dangerous, but roads were an even more immediate worry. One of the key factors in the success or failure of a given camp and region was the type and quality of transport arteries which served it. Through them flowed in goods, capital, and manpower essential for development, and out went the wealth of the mines. Inaccessibility was always the great fear of the camp. Wrote one worried editor concerning the urgency of the question of local roads, "On this more than anything else the immediate future depends." [16] Many communities languished until transportation in some form finally overcame the barriers and distance to provide a connection with the markets. The effort expended by the people was large; the results varied. Some of the roads have become the basis of the modern highway system; others are only lines on old maps. At one time, all served the same purpose: to provide avenues to maintain the camps and mines.

The earliest miners might follow an Indian path if one was available; generally, however, they opened their own trail in order to reach the mineral sites. Rocks, trees, and bushes had to be removed and streams bridged as the road wandered up mountain and canyon. Primitive at first, they became, with use and need, well defined and common thoroughfares. The almost unintentional result was a network of trails and roads throughout the entire Rocky Mountain region.

These were not enough; each camp felt it needed the shortest, fastest, and best possible routes for transport. At the beginning the main requirement was roads, but soon a camp could not be satisfied unless it had a railroad connection. The value of roads to the camp and district was recognized by the people, as is shown in early records. Minutes of district meetings frequently referred to the problem. To promote good roads, the miners' meetings paid for surveys, regulated widths, appointed supervisors to see that roadways were in good condition and, despite a reluctance to tax themselves, even went so far as to approve special maintenance taxes. Often, rather than paying money, a citizen could work off his taxes at a specified rate per day. Some districts used any local fines collected to maintain the roads. Money was a recurring problem, and many devices were used to finance and build a road: a general turnout of the people to work on the project, a subscription drive for money or material, or a tax to underwrite the cost of the endeavor. At times, after the project was completed, the townspeople would work to repair the road or clear obstacles such as snow from it.[17] Communal effort was one of the keys to solving the early transport problems.

The other key was the toll road, which was favored because its construction and maintenance did not require public funds. Private companies took the risk and hoped that revenue would provide enough profit to make the venture worthwhile. To stimulate construction, local residents subscribed to stock by exchanging labor or offering cash, materials, or interest in lodes. There was a great deal of interest in toll roads, particularly in the 1860s, and in western Colorado during the next decade, when this type of roadway was relied upon extensively. On paper, as Mark Twain humorously described it, the gamble was slight and the prospect of profits stunning:

> When they [Nevada Legislature] adjourned it was estimated that every citizen owned about three franchises and it was believed that unless Congress gave the territory another degree of longitude there would not be room enough to accommodate the toll-roads. The ends of them were hanging over the boundary line everywhere like a fringe.
>
> The fact is, the freighting business had grown to such important proportions that there was nearly as much excitement over suddenly acquired toll-road fortunes as over the wonderful silver-mines.[18]

In those places where the territorial government had not reached such a degree of political development, or was not as active, miners' meetings granted charters. In order to secure such lucrative prospects, each company had to agree to perform certain duties and obligations. These might be purposely vague or carefully delimited, involving questions of destination, rates, repair, length of franchise, right-of-way, and penalties for failure to abide by the agreement. Construction itself was a difficult task, but it paled beside that of constant repair. Nature alone created havoc on the roadbed, without the wear and tear of use. Capital was not available and Eastern investors were not interested in waiting for future profits when valuable claims were to be found. The high initial cost stopped many shaky, speculative ventures before they got off the planning board and drove others to bankruptcy before the project was completed. With these financial and engineering problems overcome, there still existed no guarantee of a profit for the investor.

The fickle public, which had desired the road, just as quickly resented what it considered to be high tolls, poor roads, and general inconvenience. Protests appeared: "It is a lamentable fact that one can hardly travel twenty miles in a mining region without being confronted by the toll gatherer. Free roads are great incentives to patronage." [19] Toll roads existed only as a relatively transitory feature on the mining frontier. The trend moved rapidly toward public highways, with the toll roads coming under the public domain through purchase, neglect, or franchise cancellation. They had been a stop-gap measure when nothing else was available, nevertheless serving a definite purpose of providing a means by which the mining districts could be reached.

Some of the northern camps were located near rivers which provided natural highways. Generally, however, the rivers running out of the Rocky Mountains were not navigable for a steamboat within hundreds of miles of the mountains. The major exceptions were the Columbia River and the Missouri, which was a more important artery to the mining regions. Although not in the category of a present-day pleasure cruise, the trip up the Missouri was the safest and most comfortable transportation to Montana. The dangers were

great on this always treacherous river, but the rewards for the ship-
owner were also great, with one voyage possibly producing a profit
over and beyond the original cost of the boat and the trip's expenses. The significance of the mining camps to the river trade is
reflected by the number of boats operating. On the Missouri, in any
year before 1865, the greatest number of arrivals at Fort Benton had
been four in 1862 and 1864. Starting with 1865 the number jumped,
reaching a high of 39 two years later. It has been estimated that this
represented over 12,000 tons of freight and 10,000 miners transported
by steamboats in 1867. Not all of these supplies were destined for
the camps, because the army employed the boats to supply its posts.[20]

Competition was limited initially to slow wagon trains which
passed through Indian-infested country. The river boats easily met
this challenge with lower rates and passenger fares and their other
advantages. Still, some people remained unconvinced. The factors of
delay, uncertainty, and the possibility of but one yearly communication with the East produced doubts. Merchants had to rely on a
single investment for the entire year's stock. The major disadvantage
involved the seasonal nature of the river route. The boats went up
river in the spring with high water and down again before the low-
water season. For the remainder of the year the Missouri maintained
its unnavigable course.[21]

On the Columbia and Missouri Rivers, ports developed; here the
goods were stored until the arrival of freighters which transported
them to the camps. Not unlike their counterparts on the Mississippi
River, these towns were in the economic orbit of the inland settlements. Their life span was limited by the productivity of the mines
and the coming of the railroad. The rivers carried but a small fraction of the total of passengers and freight, which decreased as the
years passed. The coming of the railroad to Montana in 1880 ended,
for all practical purposes, this aspect of transportation on the mining
frontier.

Solving the important Indian and transportation questions was academic beside the all-encompassing question of whether the mines were good producers. The merest rumor of mineral wealth was almost enough to have someone start a camp in the vicinity. That the future of the settlement depended on its mines had to be constantly in the minds of those who chose to live there. While the specific relationship of the camp to its mines is beyond the scope of this book, the connection should be kept in perspective by the reader, for much of what occurred in the community was in some way related to the mines.

Before going on to the story of the first years of a camp's existence, it would perhaps be well to attempt to define just what a mining camp was.[22] In some ways it is easier to describe what it was not. It was unlike an Eastern village or town, for example, in orderliness and stability. Its birth was typically quicker, its life shorter, and its decay more rapid than those of its Eastern counterpart. In and around these settlements was a vitality, intensity, and expansiveness out of proportion to the actual number of people involved. The closest modern parallel to this is found in a town going through an extensive boom period. Normally, but especially in the earlier period, the camp served the needs of a large surrounding area, its business and social districts appearing to the visitor to be beyond the needs of the immediate community. The camp was cosmopolitan and its population transitory. It reflected the frontier traits of independence and adaptiveness, yet it was an urban community in the true sense of the word.

These characteristics made it different from earlier and later communities. The mining camp stands almost alone as a phenomenon of frontier America. In the United States other boom communities existed similar to it, but never in such large numbers or with such significance to American history. It is unfair to call it just a boom town, for it was more than that. Permanence came with the settlement, even if the original camp disappeared. It is hard to define the camp specifically, for it had many ingredients, both borrowed and original. The reader and scholar must keep this in mind when comparing the camp to other communities, in order to avoid distortion.

The camp is gone, and with it the conditions which made it. Never again will its like be seen. It is a part of the American heritage, and its intensity can perhaps best be described in the words of one who knew these communities intimately:

> It surprises me to see how rapidly this country improves. . . . I shouldn't have the patience to count the business places but can say that the market is so well stocked that all necessaries and many luxuries can be obtained in the stores. Recalling that only eighteen months ago this was a 'howling wilderness', or rather a howling desert, . . . truly truth is more wonderful than fiction, . . . but truth and the marvelous go hand in hand when Young America finds a good gold gulch." [23]

Five

Boom Days

Aﬁ€R the birth of the district and its own nativity, the camp was ready to swing into its first boom. The time pattern varied from camp to camp, but if the mining community were going to amount to much, the period of boom activity had to occur. Hurry was the slogan of the day—hurry to get in on the ground floor, hurry to get the choice lots, hurry to receive the new merchandise, hurry to build the first substantial building. There were great profits to be made for the skilled and the fortunate; but for the unwary, the gamble was almost as high as that of searching for a rich claim in the surrounding district. The old warning, "haste makes waste," applied very neatly to the situation, but this adage was far from the minds of most people. The object was to get there, acquire a share of the profits available, and *then* consider such other factors as permanence.

In this first rush to the camp for purposes of mining the miners, all types of people appeared—the saloonkeeper, who knew he had almost a sure thing if he could be the first or among the earliest to establish his saloon; lawyers who came and waited for the inevitable trouble to develop over claims or vein rights; and the merchant, whose venture was perhaps more of a gamble, for he not only risked his stock but might have to face stiff competition almost from the moment he arrived. The prostitute, the fancy madam, and the girl of the line could hope to make money in the masculine society by plying their trade. The mining speculator schemed to

59

make his fortune from mining property, but speculated on town lots as well. Among the first to appear were the salesmen who came to sell their wares and then move on to another lucrative market. All had relatively the same idea in mind, although the methods of approach varied considerably. They set up the camp's first business district and its earliest commercial center of relaxation and pleasure.

Of these early arrivals, one of the most important in the saga of the camp was the merchant. Less colorful and exciting, perhaps, than many of his companions, he made significant contributions. He, too, dreamed of wealth, but wealth that came from trade rather than mining, a more conservative, stable income. While the profit motive lured the storekeeper, he realized that the greatest profit would be secured from a permanent, prosperous community, not from the fleeting fame of the rapid boom-to-bust mining cycle. It was to his advantage to promote law and order, schools, community improvements, and better means of transportation, for each of these would stimulate economic growth and thereby increase business.

While his neighbors worked feverishly at mining or its related industries, the merchant set up his tent or flimsily built frame structure and opened for business. The result might or might not resemble the typical building of more settled regions. One Pike's Peaker described a store he saw constructed of three tents, each differing in form and size, with many signs "telling of the variety of occupations carried on within, and what is offered for sale." The signs, he concluded, were "literary curiosities." [1] This observation points out a very interesting fact—the merchant was more than just a storekeeper; he served the community in numerous capacities. For example, he might be the town postmaster, the banker, and the insurance and real estate agent; he probably would dabble in mining by grubstaking prospectors and help start local industries such as lumbering. His place of business was typically a general store, especially in the younger camp, which had no need for specialized shops. When the camp matured or mines proved to be exceedingly valuable, then all types of businesses would appear, but the general merchant remained the backbone of the business community. The miner and other residents could purchase or order almost any article needed in this store. This nineteenth-century department store carried dry goods, groceries, clothing, medicines, hardware, notions, liquors, agricultural implements, and mining equipment, all crammed into one or perhaps two rooms. The selection remained small, but few customers left without finding at least a portion of the items for which they had come. To meet the demands of the time the general merchant sold wholesale as well as retail.[2]

To succeed in the fluctuating economic cycle of the camp, the merchant had to be skilled, farseeing, and a bit speculative. He had to be willing to work hard and experience the discomforts of the raw urban frontier. Like his customers, he was probably transitory, appearing in several camps before settling down or leaving the frontier. None of these individualists should be called typical, but a case study of one mining camp merchant, Horace Tabor, indicates certain characteristics of this kind of man.

Tabor was born in Vermont in 1830 and migrated to Kansas in 1855, where he met with indifferent success. Joining the rush to Pike's Peak in 1859, he arrived in June with his family at the scattered collection of huts known as Denver. Looking upon himself as a pan handling man, Tabor left immediately for the diggings. Despite his optimism and hard work, the fortune he sought eluded him, and the next year he followed the rush to California Gulch which was within a few miles of the later site of Leadville, Colorado. Tabor staked claims with poor results, but here he and his wife started a store. He combined this endeavor with a post office and an express office, while his wife opened a boarding house. These various enterprises returned a modest fortune for the family. The camp, however, declined and the Tabors migrated across the range to the more promising camp of Buckskin Joe. The story of their previous experience was repeated, except this time the store barely provided a subsistence. To supplement the family income, Tabor served a term as the county superintendent of schools.

Seven years passed before the Tabors abandoned Buckskin Joe to return in 1868 to California Gulch. Here again, the now-familiar store and boarding house were opened. Tabor branched out, cutting ties for a prospective railroad with no profit in the end for himself. With the discovery of silver at Leadville, he opened a branch store in the new camp and in July, 1877, moved his family there. Finally, after all the years of searching, Lady Luck dealt Tabor a winning hand, and before long he owned "the whole damned town" and a great deal more as well. With fair regularity Tabor grubstaked prospectors in hopes of finding a rich mine, yet nothing of importance was discovered, and he found himself poorer, but not willing to give up. Then on a May day in 1878 his grubstaking was rewarded with the discovery of the Little Pittsburgh Mine. Almost overnight the long-sought fortune materialized. It seemed now that almost everything Tabor touched turned to silver.[3]

Tabor the merchant became Tabor the silver millionaire. His subsequent riches-to-rags story is well known in Western folklore and history, and need not be repeated. What is of interest are the earlier years when Tabor followed the lure of gold and the dollar from one camp to another.

By 1878, with hard work, the Tabors had been able to accumulate a small savings and property of some value. The census of 1870 had listed for him $5,000 real estate valuation and $3,000 in personal property. This, together with experience and memories, was the total reward for nineteen years spent on the Colorado mining frontier. It was a modest enough achievement, considering the effort and privations involved. Both Tabor and his wife were nearing fifty and could look forward to more years in the camps with little prospect of betterment. Conditions, over all, were improving but the wealth Tabor desired eluded his every effort.

Three contemporaries, writing at the end of the 1870s, have left an interesting picture of Tabor just before wealth and his subsequent divorce wrought a change in him. They described him as having a native talent and business aptitude, a gambler to the ex-

Interior of a boarding house in Silver Reef, Utah, in the 1880s. *Utah State Historical Society.*

tent of outfitting numerous prospectors with a grubstake, generous and a "rare good fellow," [4] although he was generous to the detriment of business profits.

Tabor's restlessness reflects the mobility of the mining camp merchant who hoped to find the golden wealth at the end of the rainbow. Combining merchandising with mining, to the degree Tabor practiced it, was not common. The multiplicity of occupations along with the store (to make ends meet) was typical for the day and time. The family store, with little or no outside help, prevailed, particularly in the smaller camps. How many other men like Tabor had a capable and resolute wife behind them, who served as a stabilizing influence and kept the family going through hard times, is not known. Augusta Tabor's role was extremely significant, not only as a wife and mother but as a businesswoman.[5] Certainly she was typical of many.

During the rush and early boom periods, one of the most lucrative businesses was that of providing room and board. Rooms of any kind, let alone decent ones, were hard to find. One newspaper reporter, after spending several sleepless nights in a hastily built rooming house, commented that hearing all whispered secrets, the loves, the hates and gossips of his neighbors was the "nicest fun," but he humorously concluded that "Good men and women are leaving this city every day simply because they are sleepy." Construction failed to meet the demand, which resulted in halls partitioned by cloth into bedrooms, saloons offering floor space for a price, and other means devised to provide the bare essentials of shelter and a bed. The results, as can be imagined, were trying. Episcopal Bishop Daniel Tuttle, on his first visit to Virginia City, Montana, in 1867 (four years after the initial discovery) found rents high and lodging primitive, especially when having to share a double bed with a complete stranger.

Conditions in newer camps were correspondingly worse. Large tents were partitioned with canvas into sleeping rooms which contained bunks made of rough boards covered with loose hay and gray blankets. Such refinements as wash bowls, sheets, and pillows were conspicuously lacking. For women, few special arrangements existed. To the Eastern visitor this lack of privacy with few conveniences, even in separate rooms, proved the environment crude and undesirable. Such handicaps had to be accepted until the situation improved and construction caught up with demand.[6]

Alongside the general store and boarding house appeared the saloon. It was considered as essential as the other two, and no camp was worth its name unless it could boast of several. Visitor and resident alike left testimony to the ubiquitous nature of the saloon, from the rush of 1859 through the close of the 1880s. Alexander McClure's description of the placer mining camp of Blackfoot, Montana, was a typical reaction. When he visited it in 1867, the camp consisted of two rows of cabins along a single street, with half the cabins "groggeries," McClure estimated, and about one-fifth gambling saloons. The saloon was the apex of masculine society and the epitome of its culture. Here congregated the miner, the merchant, the single man, and the family man in the companionship of his friends.

Inside the building a man could play cards, relax, have a drink, lunch, often on free food, conduct business, or do well-nigh anything within reason he desired. It was the man's castle. It was almost an essential stop for the outlying miners on their visits to the camp. Like the other buildings of the town, the first saloons were built of any material available, but as the situation improved, the saloons took on added trimmings and even social status. However, they retained their original position in the community throughout the history of most camps.[7]

It was important that a camp or district have at least one newspaper. Consequently, the newspaperman appeared early, although normally not until the mines were established and the camp on its way to becoming a metropolis. The paper could provide many services for the camp, including publicity, promotion, and helping to create an air of permanence. These were essential, if needed capital was to be found and growth insured. Not all camps had a local paper, but a surprising number did, at least for a time. Some presses were taken from camp to camp and before the end of the frontier had been used to publish several different papers. A few communities circulated their own paper but had it printed in some other town. The rest had to get along as best they could with neighboring gazettes.

The majority of the papers were locally owned and edited, and for this reason produced an individualism unmatched by modern publications. In spite of this originality, their purposes and plans, as often set forth in the first edition, were strikingly similar:

> to publish a journal devoted to the interest of the people now inhabiting and who design to remove to this new and soon to be the most important Territory [Montana] of the United States. . . . The interest of the miner, the agriculturalist and business man, will be carefully looked after . . . And finally, it being our object to publish an independent (not neutral) paper, we shall leave it to our readers, as to how we shall fulfill the promise.[8]

> We don't believe that our mission is to make or unmake nations, hence shall not dabble in politics. Believing that all our miners and prospectors are fully supplied with religious reading, we shall preach no sermons. Thus we will have nothing pressing upon our time or space to prevent our giving full and complete reports from this and adjacent mining districts.[9]

> The *Herald* bids the people of Yankee Fork good morning. It has no apology to offer for locating at Bonanza City, the centre of this great mining region. A paper is needed here, and we believe the camp is abundantly able to support one. . . . A newspaper is a necessity here, for many eyes are watching the advancement of the locality, . . . The paper will be devoted to the interest of the Yankee Fork section in particular, and the Territory of Idaho in general, leaving politics to the politicians and party issues to those who delight to make them.[10]

All were promoters and boosters of their locality. While they might piously state they planned to refrain from political embroilments and sermons, they were, fortunately for historians, unable to do so for any length of time. The main task was to report local, state, and national news with international items when available; national and international stories were normally copied from larger newspapers or gathered from some other news agency. If the paper amounted to much, several columns would be devoted to local items. Generally, the sign of a declining newspaper and camp was an increasing percentage of news cut from other sources.

The reporter's work might be complicated also by his contact with the public:

> The life of a news-gatherer is beset with considerable woe. He is jawed for what he doesn't know and kicked for what he does, if he tells it. He is compelled to laugh at mossy jokes and sympathize with imaginary ills. If he refuses an item he makes an enemy, and if he prints it he makes two. He is cursed until his suspenders burst—he is thankful he wasn't licked, and he goes on looking for the next fellow whose mother-in-law has come to stay for the winter.[11]

Unpaid subscriptions and renewals continually plagued the paper; it was hard enough to make a success of the enterprise without this added handicap. Editors advised their wayward patrons to settle promptly or be cut off from receiving the paper. From the frequency and universality of the comment, one may question just how much good the warning produced.

To start a newspaper in a camp required great effort and a gambler's instinct. The owner and editor, possibly the same person, had to have faith initially that the town and mines would grow sufficiently to support their newspaper and perhaps a rival. If they decided that a newspaper could be supported, then the problem of securing equipment and having it transported to the camp had to be overcome, which took time and money. Unlike other parts of the Trans-Mississippi frontier where the newspaper might come first and build a town, the mining frontier discouraged this type of speculative venture. Yet the urban nature of the frontier needed a paper as much as it did a church or school. The newspaper was the spokesman of the community, its gadfly and its advocate.

While the problems faced by the editor remained great throughout this period, the 1860s were perhaps the worst. Until the coming of the telegraph and railroad, the life of the newsgatherer could be hectic, especially during the winter months when the roads were closed. Then the editor was left to his own devices until the roads were opened again and he could get news from the outside. If he were really unlucky, the supply of paper might give out before a new order arrived, or the press might break down with no surplus parts available. Under such circumstances, some papers in smaller isolated communities appeared at increased intervals and in decreased size during the winter months, when mining was slow anyway and local news scarce.

Perhaps the greatest problem was finding enough news items. Articles from other papers and journals and selections from books could fill part of the space and enlighten subscribers. But the reader wanted local news, so "in violation of a rule of physics something was manufactured out of nothing to fill a vacancy when the facts were lacking," as one editor stated. All stump speakers became "eloquent orators" and "profound speakers"; local produce was some of the best the editor had ever seen (with a long description following); "rich, new" strikes were reported in glowing terms; and all "maidens" who married blossomed, by aid of cold type, into lovely and accomplished brides.[12]

If a newspaper was unable to survive in a camp despite valiant efforts, the editor would just move on to another; other times he felt the prospects were better elsewhere and simply left on his own. In either case, it was a sad day for the community, for it had lost something which could not be replaced except by another paper.

The freighter brought the editor his equipment, the merchant his goods, and the saloonkeeper his whiskey: mundane tasks but essential to the continuance of the camp. With the first rush, freighters and packers arrived simultaneously, over roads barely passable, the freight they carried almost as valuable as the minerals sought by the miners. Of the two methods, wagons had the advantage, since pack trains carried fewer goods at a higher cost. The ability of the pack trains to go where the freight wagon could not retained for them a continuing share of the business. To transport the supplies and haul the ore was not an easy or fast job, particularly in the mountains. Many problems, including bad roads, the weather, breakdown of wagons, and isolation on the road, made it that much harder. Some men became itinerant freighters, drifting throughout the West wherever their cargo took them; most, however, operated on a fairly basic pattern within a region. The scale of operation ranged from the single individual with one or two wagons to large companies with hundreds of animals and numerous wagon trains.[13]

The business was limited by the climate in mountainous regions to spring, summer, and fall. In spring, the busiest season, the freighters hauled merchandise to restock winter-exhausted stores. Lucky, indeed, the merchant whose shipment came early, and he could well thank the freighter for giving him a jump on his competitors. The winter months offered few problems in the southern camps, but for the rest it meant isolation, or at best, a few shipments carried by sleigh or laboriously freighted over snow and ice. To provide transportation of ore, some mill owners offered to pay higher rates, but the winter difficulties and dangers remained too great.

Despite his almost indispensable hold on the camp, the freighter was not one of the community's favorite sons. People grumbled when shipments were late, especially in the spring, when the inconvenience was most keenly felt, but seldom to the point of hunting up old pieces of carpet and gunny sacks and striking out for the hills to mingle with the natives, as one mining camp wit suggested. Freight teams blocked sidewalks and streets, littering the area with manure and straw, much to the discomfort of those who had to wade through the resulting mess and confusion. These were relatively minor inconveniences, though, compared to the real issue at hand—rates. The complaint was voiced that exceedingly high rates resulted in unneeded increases in the cost of commodities. The disgusted public thought they had uncovered the real cause for this outrage—greed on the part of the freighters. In answer, the freighters blamed high tolls, poor roads, and the soaring cost of feed for the high rates, not very valid reasons to the irate housewife forced to pay the final bill as it was passed on by the merchant. Each side stubbornly held to its contentions, and what galled the residents most was the realization that little could be done unless railroad connections were secured. Demand also influenced the situation. In the boom days, when the need was greatest, there never seemed to be enough teams and wagons for the required hauling—reason enough to increase the rates.[14]

A fact which must be considered in viewing the question of rates objectively is the balance of trade. It remained decisively against the camp with more goods brought in than taken out, leaving empty wagons on the return trip. This resulted in an increase in rates as compensation. At the same time, the freighter must have understood that the market was not inexhaustible, and in order to acquire enough income to pay for the large investment, he took advantage of a temporary situation which favored him. After the boom passed, the rates tended to go down to a more reasonable level. Despite the initial advantage enjoyed by the freighter, his situation was precarious. The decline of the mines and/or the coming of the railroad meant a sharp reduction in his business. He had no choice then but to retrench and become a feeder from the railroad to the camps which had been bypassed, or move on to another area.

Within the camp itself, the freighter was a transitory figure, since only those companies actually operating from the town had permanent connections. Participating only in those activities which interested him or related to his occupation, he stood outside of much community life. The people depended on his service, but at the same time generally relegated him to a low position in the social strata.

As in all boom situations, the camp went through a period of inflation. This inflationary spiral was reflected in the sale of real estate. Houses and buildings were always scarce during this time, and no matter how rapidly they were constructed, they never seemed to saturate the appetite of the community. So serious could the situation become, that, as one wag reported, "let a man take a pick and shovel and begin grading a vacant lot and in less than half an hour someone surely will come along and try to rent the house to be built there." Inflation was conducive to speculation in real estate as well as in mining claims. Land which the federal government could not *give* away as a homestead, suddenly was offered by the foot to prospective buyers. Lots which the season before had gone begging at $25, increased 50, 100, and even 200 percent in value over the winter as the camp boomed. In some of the larger and wealthier camps, even greater increases than these were recorded.[15] Land was purchased and held as a speculative venture, the owner hoping that the town would grow in his direction and that the lots would be on the main thoroughfare. The fortunate few who guessed right only encouraged others to try. For every success there were numerous failures, but to these budding entrepreneurs nothing seemed impossible.

For those who had buildings to rent, the investment might return 100 percent within a year, or in some cases ten percent per month on the capital invested. For prime locations, rents of $400 to $1,500 per month were not considered out of line with the prevailing situation. Office rent in Leadville, Colorado, was reported to be higher than rent in New York City. For those lucky ones who had buildings on good locations, the return on their investment was one of the best that could be found in the camp.[16]

People were willing to pay high prices for several reasons. In this type of boom situation, a skilled merchant could make a great deal of money. Every day's delay, waiting for a building to be constructed, meant lost profits. When a blacksmith could clear $300 in two weeks or a merchant average $1,000 per day in sales,[17] it was better to make profit now and if necessary build later. Construction costs were high and had to be added to the initial price of the lot. For the man who looked ahead it was obvious that this situation could not last and that prices and rents were bound to fall, along with profits. Yet if a man had made his money during the flush times, he could easily afford to build, buy, or even continue to rent if he did not care to make the investment.

This abnormal situation generally did not continue beyond the first year or, at most, the second. Real estate prices seemed to decline earlier than rents. While the camp was booming, these terms might have been accepted even if not desirable; now, however, protests started to arise. This "suicidal policy," warned the *Helena Herald,* was hurting the mercantile community and helping to cause an economic slump.[18] That growth could be retarded by this policy was one warning which need not be repeated to the growth conscious community. Eventually, rents would come down and the condition would be leveled according to demand. By this time, too, construction would have caught up with the need, and it was not improbable that within a short time vacant buildings would be in evidence. Overbuilding was a typical reaction, and eventually almost all camps faced this problem. It was considered not as a sign of progress, but rather as one of stagnation or even decline.

A question which clouded many a camp's early history was ownership of the townsite, and consequently, the legality of property titles. Mining camps mushroomed without much thought of who might be the real owner of the property. The promoter's dream of town plotting usually came *after* discovery, not before. By the time the idea of a camp became established, there were many people already squatting on the site. The high value of the property, plus the uncertainty of ownership, encouraged lot jumping. This form of criminal activity was fairly widespread. Usually, a show of force was sufficient for the owner to reclaim his property, but violence resulted if neither side was willing to retire.[19] Lot jumping created considerable bad blood and anxiety among the property owners. They might band together for mutual protection against jumpers. If it became widespread or flagrant, then demands would increase that something be done to prohibit it and to establish legal ownership.

Occasionally, the original settlers formed a town company at the very start of the rush in hopes of securing profit or in order to validate their lots. Infrequently, the site would be plotted and opened to all at a minimal or no charge. In either situation the problem of disputed legal ownership was avoided. Generally, however, the camp was not so fortunate.

The easiest way to secure title was to go to the federal government for a town patent or request a government or private survey to solve contested ownership of property. It might be left to the city government to provide a survey and register each lot on a town plot. This cost money, and the local inhabitant probably found himself paying the bill, whether it was done privately or communally. Probably a few registered complaints at this high handed intrusion into their wallets, but all stood to gain by it.[20]

If the first inhabitants made no effort to establish title to the land, trouble could develop for the city. Such was the case in five-year-old Alta, Utah, when, to the astonishment of the citizens, they found themselves occupying land claimed by a speculative company. It seemed that some ambitious and shrewd Salt Lake City merchants claimed the land and secured a patent by virtue of an Indian treaty. They promptly offered to sell the lots back to those who had assumed they owned them. The residents were distressed, but were in favor of paying a nominal sum to the patent holders to avoid becoming involved in a costly suit to contest the patent. The local paper lamented: "We trust this matter will be amicably settled. It hangs at present like a pall over Alta, preventing improvements in building, and in other ways retarding the growth of the city." [21] Another similar, but less frequently encountered problem, was that of a camp's location on or near a placer discovery whose claims might supersede the town site. This situation could more easily be resolved between the two owners of the lot.[22] As the newspaper suggested, the result was bad in either case for the community, and had to be decided as quickly as possible.

Town companies also could give the property owner a headache. The earliest arrivals would get in on the ground floor, to the dismay of those who followed. Dissatisfaction might lead to a court case to contest the company's possession. This was expensive, clouded the individual titles, and could depreciate the value of property until it was settled. The struggle could drag on for several years until one side or the other finally conceded.[23] In the meantime, the reputation of the community was damaged or at least marred, to the consternation of many who were trying to promote it.

Life in the mining camp has frequently been pictured as adventuresome and exciting. The first months or year of a community's existence probably justified this description. The excitement of new discoveries, the great plans for the camp and district, the general optimism, the stimulation of boom times all blended to create a bright illusion. Men and women were caught up by it and swept along, happily hoping the end would be as rosy. The camps were a beehive of activity—people moving in, prospecting parties coming and going, buildings and houses constructed, new stores opening, saloons and dance halls going full blast, a little criminal activity, and perhaps the stir of local politics. All the adventure, the zest of opening up a new frontier were rolled into one small area, where all could watch and participate. The urban camp became a kaleidoscope of the settlement of a large segment of the Trans-Mississippi frontier.

To the inhabitant of the camp, perhaps, this adventure was not so exciting, for he was involved in his own work and often had little time to spend enjoying the sights. The winter season could be especially dull in the isolated camp, cut off as it was from normal communication and transportation. Mining was slow during the inclement weather with many out of work or working only part time.

The dreary days of winter passed slowly. Nathaniel Langford, a Montana resident from the early 1860s, wrote that old newspapers went the rounds until they literally dropped to pieces and every type of reading material was in constant and unceasing demand. Card games such as euchre, poker, and cribbage were resorted to until they became "stale, flat and disgusting." To the south in Colorado, Matthew Dale wrote home that he had nothing of interest to report except that the days jogged along quietly and monotonously, seldom stirring from a uniform dull routine. The few events which served to arouse the miners to anything like excitement were the weekly arrival of mail, the weekly meeting of the lyceum, and the numerous political confabs.[24] Spring brought to the young camp a revival and a spurt of activity.

Life in the mining camp was exciting in another sense. It was a continual speculation concerning the unanswerable question of the length of the prosperity. Everyone, from the laborer who hoped the cost of living would decline and his wages remain high, to the merchant, who had brought into the settlement an expensive inventory of goods, gambled that the economic cycle would remain on the upswing. In this first period, before the worth of the district became established, hope and optimism could be easily substituted for realism. Even against the optimistic background of the whole mining cycle this remains the highpoint. Never again would hopes be so high, with only the sky as a limit. Few of the participants were completely immune to the air of confidence and even visitors were caught in the spell. A person might ask himself how long this could continue, but caution was not a characteristic to be long debated in the face of prosperity and promise.

Architecturally, the camp left something to be desired. Construction which was cheap and fast was demanded. Logs, boards, canvas, and perhaps adobe were utilized. The style was left pretty much to the individual's taste, depending upon his finances, the materials available, and the size of his lot. As the camp matured, the architecture reflected its growth and change. Substantial wooden buildings began to replace the older ones and brick and stone were used more in construction. As the camp attained stronger economic footing, greater effort was taken to improve individual dwellings. Paint, for example, was used more liberally. Few new architectural styles were devised. The theme, if one may call it that, had originally been simplicity. It changed little except where wealth intervened.

The accepted practice was to copy and imitate Eastern patterns rather than to develop something new. Victorian gingerbread style was apparently quite popular, for examples of it are still to be seen in the remaining camps. Quite frequently the wealthy mine owner would leave the scene of his fortune to move to some larger city. San Francisco and Denver both had their millionaires' section, where the new wealth was ostentatiously displayed by the owners' mansions. Here individual taste was satisfied within the accepted tradition and pattern of the day. Most of these early buildings are gone, either torn down and replaced by better planned and constructed buildings or burned down or destroyed by nature and time. A few still remain; others have been reconstructed. Two of the best existing examples of a more modest nature are the older sections of Helena, Montana, and Central City, Colorado. Here are the second and third generations of mining camp architecture, refined by time.

A characteristic of the camps during the first months was a great explosion of population. This was followed by an up-and-down fluctuation until a general level was reached. Rather than following a normal growth pattern, the size of the camp reflected the mining conditions, unless, of course, the settlement was not solely dependent upon mining. For example, a Midwestern farming community such as Sandwich, Illinois, displayed a steady but not spectacular growth. Sandwich had a population of 952 in 1860, and thirty years later had reached 2,516. By contrast, Central City, Colorado, expanded from 594 to 2,360 in the 1860s. By the next decade it gained less than 300, and the population was decreasing by 1890. This was better, however, than Silver City, Idaho, which slipped from an estimated 3,000 in 1866 to 593 in 1880, or South Pass, Wyoming, which by 1890 had become a virtual ghost town. Silver Reef, Utah, within the years from 1880 to 1890, went through its boom, declining from 1,046 to 177. Into these few hectic years the mining camp crowded its entire existence, magnifying the problems of life by the sheer velocity at which it was traveling.

Six

Growing Pains

THE newborn camp had become, in its own estimation, a booming metropolis. Nothing could quite compare with it—or with its problems. All urban communities suffer through what might be termed growing pains, when, for example, the older section of town becomes too crowded or earlier planning proves inadequate for later expansion. Overcrowding did not concern the denizens of the mining camp, unless they found their town hemmed in by natural barriers, but planning was conspicuously lacking, and the result was a multitude of problems.

The growing pains of the mining camps involved such varied problems as civic government, definition of rights of way, and clearance of obstacles from the streets. One of the most pressing was lawlessness in all its assorted forms. There is a certain glamor, a derring-do, associated with this aspect of the American frontier. The story is familiar.

Amid the thunder of hooves and the sharp echo of the blazing six-shooter, a thousand Western movies and books have ended. The scene has the well-known dusty cowtown, the beleaguered marshal, the confident gunfighter. Shrouded in dust and smoke, the gunsmoke and gallop frontier has ridden into the great American saga. Adventure, excitement, and lawlessness are blended with enough sex, danger, and fatal violence to create an epic story for the public's benefit. While there is certainly a grain of truth in this approach, the romantic West was only a thin veneer covering reality.

In the process of time, the reality has come to be hidden behind a curtain of historical fiction.

The mining camp has never caught the public's fancy or the author's eye for a Western setting as did the cattle town, because many of the basic ingredients are lacking. The cowman, the farmer, the Indian are absent, although the railroad is there, but not as on the Great Plains. The saloon girl, gambler, and storekeeper are stock characters in both settings. The sheriff or marshal, however, has a less glamorous role, since there were not many gunfighters in the classic sense, no range wars or rustling, and few murders or stagecoach robberies (with the possible exception of Deadwood). Instead, mining camp lawmen faced claim jumping, ore stealing, and assault and battery, which, although sometimes dangerous, were comparatively tame. Nor does a struggle between two mining companies over land seem as exciting as a similar conflict between two cattle barons or between the rancher and the nester.

Mining communities have received a small share of the lust-and-blood yarns, for occasionally they are still used as the setting for a Western, and one can always find short stories of this nature about the camps; but before the turn of the century, the lawlessness of the mining frontier received almost equal billing with that of other Western areas. The *Harper's Weekly* of February 2, 1878, reviewing the history of Helena, Montana, noted, "It passed through its reign of terror, having extirpated the gamblers, 'road agents,' and cutthroats who infest all new mining towns, robbing and murdering at their own bad will. . . ." The big camps like Leadville or Deadwood rivaled the best of Dodge City or Abilene with their sin and wickedness. Certain segments of the American reading public followed them with eager anticipation of some new spicy tidbit or morbid account. Then with the decline of mining, the camps slipped into oblivion and the West of *The Virginian* came to consume the readers' and viewers' attention, because it was broader in scope, more imaginative and versatile than the mining frontier. Mining, with all its drudgery, was already known to the Easterner, while Indian wars, ranching, and the general Western frontier were at least a generation removed if, indeed, they were ever experienced.

The original conditions under which the camp developed were conducive to an unstable situation. The overwhelming drive for money, the lack of social cohesiveness, the newness, and the weakness or lack of local government combined with the lure of easy wealth to produce a climate in which lawlessness thrived. Undesirable elements were attracted by this situation, especially to the larger communities where size gave cover to their schemes. Conversely, these factors made it harder for the law-abiding citizens to organize community protection and relief.

It should not be surprising, then, that criminal activity became one of the earliest growing pains of the camp. An examination of newspaper articles and other records pertaining to unlawfulness reveals an astonishing breadth. The omnipresent brawl, whether of the general or saloon variety, created enforcement problems. It can be doubted that much serious bodily harm resulted; in many instances, words and scuffling took the place of more serious physical attacks. Petty thievery, likewise, continually annoyed the public and was hard to stop, as repeated complaints by disgusted victims indicated. The irritated editor of the *Helena Herald*, for example, on December 26, 1867, notified the "infernal thieves" who were keeping warm at the expense of his wood pile that they were running the risk of finding blasting powder placed in some of the logs. Drunkenness was commonplace, and bred numerous pranks and disturbances which angered more than they damaged. Illegal stills contributed to this condition, but they were only infrequently uncovered. In many communities gambling and prostitution were unlawful, but were winked at and accepted as part of life.

More serious was criminal activity which threatened life and property. Lot jumping could lead to grave trouble, while horse and mule stealing was one of the worst offenses. Robbery of individuals or businesses caused excitement when it happened, yet banks, apparently, were left alone. Of course, many camps did not have a bank, but utilized the best safe in town to store valuables. Violence against individual persons in the form of rape or murder made front page news; the people never became so callous or these events so common as to arouse little or no reaction to this type of crime. Claim jumping and ore stealing were carried on outside the town, but usually involved some local residents. Forgery, confidence games, bogus gold dust, and stage robberies were other forms of activity which harassed the community.[1]

The local police force in any one camp would not have been confronted with all these forms of crime. A view of almost any camp would have been nearer to that reflected in a sampling of the police blotter in "wild" Leadville, which disclosed the following arrests: committing nuisances (not specified), drunkenness, resisting an officer, vagrancy, carrying a concealed weapon, and discharging a weapon.[2] Except in the case of firing a gun and perhaps the concealed weapons these ranked as comparatively minor offenses. No one had been killed or harmed; the cause of most of the arrests probably could be traced to too much celebration with the bottle. With less frequency than perhaps reported by the Leadville police, these forms of law-breaking took place during the average year in any community. The unusual, the bizarre, however, was what attracted attention.

Major crimes were rare, especially in lesser-known and smaller camps. In two communities, Caribou and Lake City, Colorado, a murder was exceptional. During Caribou's thirty-five-year history only one person died violently, while Lake City, in its first boom, 1875-1877, had "only one man for breakfast." Nor are these isolated examples. Even in Deadwood, which acquired a reputation for lawlessness, the editor of the *Black Hills Pioneer*, June 23, 1877, noted that crimes and murders had been committed, "but usually such as occur in affrays and broils liable to happen in any community." Especially considering the drifting population, and the fact that scarcely "one house in ten has a lock upon its doors," he felt property had generally been respected.

Regardless of the amount of unlawful activity, any of it was a menace to the individual and a blot on the camp's record. Whether it was just a case of breaking the peace or whether, as one lady wrote, "There are times when it is really unsafe to go through the main street . . . , the bullets whizz around so . . . ,"[3] something had to be done. Almost from the very beginning of any mining excitement, certain groups within the community actively worked for law and order. The rapidity with which they proceeded, and the success of their efforts, limited crime in this initial unsettled period. In every case they eventually triumphed. In the decade of the sixties, and even into the seventies, the public often depended upon miners' courts and secret organizations to stem the crime, finally turning to regular territorial and local enforcement agencies to control it. The struggle to secure and maintain order, one of the strong undercurrents in any camp, reflected the permanence and stability which were important qualities of this urban frontier. None of these organizations, however, could be effective until they received strong civic support.

The very urbanization of this frontier magnified the available temptations and the criminal activity faced by the early settler and miner. In one respect, the lawless element had an advantage over the general public—operating individually or in small groups, it had little or no need for organization. In attempting to organize against the criminal element, sponsors found themselves up against the frequently voiced attitudes of minding one's own affairs and not caring to become involved because this was simply a mining camp, where as soon as one made his stake, he planned to return home. The rugged individualism tradition of law enforcement on a new frontier, which specified that an individual should and would protect himself from others, was a further hindrance toward collective security. To gain respect from one's peers meant to fight and win without asking quarter.[4]

To overcome the inertia created by these attitudes ranked as one of the major problems which had to be solved before a camp could reach its full stature. Yet to do anything took time, which could barely be spared from other pursuits. Lacking any strong government or established legal system on which to rely, particularly in the 1860s, those people interested in obtaining justice turned to the simple expedient of the small, tightly-knit organization used in the California camps—the vigilance committees, or more popularly, vigilantes. There seemed to be nowhere else to turn. The scholarly newspaper editor, Thomas Dimsdale, in his well-known justification of vigilante activity, *The Vigilantes of Montana*, commented, "Under these circumstances it becomes an absolute necessity that good, law-loving, order-sustaining men should unite for mutual protection and salvation of the community." [5]

Secret and extralegal, the vigilantes moved to correct the imbalance in law and order. They might advertise their intentions by posting warnings or notices in the paper. "TO THE PEOPLE OF MONTANA. The ends of justice shall be carried out in the FUTURE as in the PAST. Justice and mercy are our watchword. Be just and fear not," read one such announcement in the *Montana Radiator*, April 7, 1866. Or they might strike against the lawless element in an attempt to rid the community of a few undesirables, and intimidate the remainder. Montana and Idaho, during the first half of the 1860s, witnessed the most concerted action along this line, as this announcement stated. Vigilantes ended the career of the notorious Henry Plummer gang with a series of hangings, after Plummer had infiltrated into the legal system to the point of being elected sheriff of Bannack, Montana. Over 100 victims fell to the gang before it was broken. After this episode, warnings proved as potent as action, if the situation had not gotten completely out of hand. Order was eventually established in these two territories, but the vigilante idea did not die. It spread, gaining converts seemingly wherever legal means failed. Although never again used as much as in the 1860s, it remained always a threat. Indeed, the movement became one of controlling through intimidation and reputation, rather than by direct force. As late as the 1880s, warning notices appeared in newspapers, but by then the need for vigilance action had passed. Activity had rapidly declined in the 1870s and for all practical purposes died by the 1890s.[6]

The purpose of the vigilantes, to put down the lawless and prepare for a more orderly existence, meant more than just a few hangings or a warning in response to open violence or murder. In the more refined year of 1880, for example, in Globe, Arizona, a vigilance committee was organized to suppress all unlawful and uncivilized acts, which included discharging firearms within the town, using obscene language in the presence of ladies, giving or selling liquors of any kind to Indians, reckless horse riding through town, jumping town lots, and finally, playing cards in the street.[7] The intention was the same, but the scope much different from the earlier Montana activities.

Vigilante justice was fast, final, and without appeal. George Locke, a Montana miner writing to his sister, described one episode involving a robber who had lately been captured. The man was held for trial for five days, while the victim was sent for to identify him, during which time the robber's friends made an attempt at rescue but failed. The vigilantes, finally forced to build a log fort, defied them, and "that night our man from Helena came and we proceeded to trial by selecting a judge, jury and council for and against the prisinor [sic] found him guilty and hung him the next morning it took 13 hours to try him."[8] The lack of punctuation does not lessen the grimness of the situation nor the resolute nature of the men involved. For his part in this, Locke was indicted by a grand jury but was acquitted.

Controversial in their own day, vigilantes left behind a mixed legacy. At their best, their watchwords were justice and mercy. At their worst, however, they masked naked, mob vengeance. As a general axiom, it may be said that the further one advances from the mid-sixties, the less idealistic and more questionable became the vigilante organizations. The American trait of reliance upon recognized legal procedures served as a check upon this form of activity.

So, too, did the abhorrence of using violence to suppress violence in a civilized society. Nothing could be less a sign of the desired stability than citizens' taking the law into their own hands. As early as 1865, an Idaho newspaper editor wrote,

> A general lawlessness prevails through all these territories [Montana, Idaho, Colorado, and Utah], resolving itself in the form of these organizations; and everywhere they have brought trouble upon the community which tolerates them. The remedy for the existing evils is greater than the evil. . . .[9]

Two classes of men invariably secured control of the vigilance committees, the editor concluded: fanatics who used them to revenge their own personal wrongs, and those who used them to cover up their own crimes. While the statement was perhaps too sweeping, the editor made a valid point. The committees could become like "an assassin stealing in the darkness of its crimes," which resulted in "the breaking up of society—the destruction of public confidence —the ruin of the material interest of the town or section."[10] Tragically, this too often happened, to the discredit of the community and any person who supported the action.

Tragic, too, were those cases of error, such as mistaken identity and guilt by association. Too hasty action which led to the death of an innocent person could not be undone. Amends of a sort could be made to those who were unjustly punished, but even this restitution could not pardon or condone the original action. How many people suffered under such circumstances is not known, but each such case detracted immeasurably from the appeal and reputation of the vigilantes.

Criticism such as that voiced by the Idaho newspaper editor aroused angry retorts by those people who had been closely connected with vigilante actions. For years this subject could not be objectively or impassionately discussed. After Dimsdale's account, that of another vigilante, Nathaniel Langford, best describes their position. He wrote, "The early Vigilantes were the best most intelligent men in the mining region. They saw and felt that, in the absence of all law, they must become a 'law unto themselves,' . . . What else could they do?" Langford differentiated here between his group and those that followed. Limiting his comments, as he did, to that group of men who formed the Virginia City vigilance committee, he presented a strong case. Some of the outstanding leaders of early Montana history took part in this movement. There can be little doubt that the activities of Plummer's band had been so bloody that stringent corrective methods were needed to counteract them. Not only was this the zenith of the vigilantes' activity, but it was also one of the most justifiable examples of it. This group disbanded after its work was completed, and an attempted revival of activity in the same area two years later displayed less commendable characteristics.[11]

The type of activity represented by vigilantes did not originate in mining camps. Prototypes occurred throughout American history well into the twentieth century. Few innovations developed in the basic pattern that the committees copied from California examples. Some had a clearly defined organization with elected officers, a constitution, and by-laws. Others were little more than spontaneous demonstrations or action by a select few. It is noteworthy that in Montana and Idaho, where Californians were more numerous, vigilante action proved more popular. Certainly previous experience weighed heavily. Violence bred violent reaction, whether in Virginia City or any other camp, yet once the group lost its original, impartial, conscientious motive, public revulsion soon followed. Vigilante law—quick and harsh—did not conform to the more basic frontier trait of justice, unless in a dire situation. The secret nature of the movement, cloaking varied motives, and the possibility of error repelled many. Considering the entire period, vigilante action did as much harm as good, if not more. But in a sense, the reputation acquired by vigilantes served a useful purpose. The threat of the formation of a committee was often enough to curb excesses before a tense situation could erupt.

A fine line existed between mob action and the vigilantes. "Judge

Lynch" made certain inroads, particularly in situations involving heinous crimes, when legal procedures were thought to be too slow. But this was the exception. An incident with less fatal results is relayed by one miner who reported joining a mob to destroy a rum shop where a man had been drugged. The owner was summarily given an escort out of the district and promised the rope should he chance to return.[12] Whatever semblance of justice might be found for this type of action, none can be shown for the lamentable mob harassment of the Chinese and the destruction of their property.

Yet another form of frontier justice existed, the miners' court. The companion of the miners' meeting as an instrument of government, these courts were forerunners of the judicial system. Relying upon a combination of past experience and any legal talent available, the miners' court dispensed a rough and tumble form of justice. This system was most popular in the 1860s, although isolated instances, as in the Black Hills, appeared later. With the eventual organization of a territorial judicial system the need for miners' courts passed.

Provisions relating to these courts are found in the records of early mining districts. Some districts established thoroughly detailed procedures and rules to govern their courts, which showed the fine hand of unknown frontier lawyers. Specified terms, court regulations, oaths, jury selection, and duties of the clerk were carefully delineated. Jurisdictional power, frequently the same as the equity and law jurisdiction granted by United States courts, received its support from the consent of those who willingly subscribed to its formation, rather than from any inherent coercive force. In many districts, however, the system did not display this formal organization. Here a president or judge was selected and the miners assembled to act as jury. The sessions were usually held on Sunday in cases of no immediate exigency, for this was the most convenient day. Richard Hughes witnessed a Gayville, South Dakota, miners' court in action and left a revealing description. Since there was no building in town large enough to hold the crowd, court was held in the street. The case involved a murder and the crowd was closely divided into two rival factions, which engendered a great deal of bitter feeling. One side was determined to hang the defendant, the other equally steadfast in its determination to set him free. Despite the opinionated atmosphere, the judge and jury were elected by a voice vote of the crowd. The trial lasted all day and into the night before the jury returned a verdict of assault and battery! The evidence seemed to prove that the actual deed had been done by someone else. Since the verdict was practically one of acquittal, no attempt was made to impose a penalty. The prisoner was thereupon escorted out of the area.[13]

Simplicity and economy were desired, since time was of the essence for everyone involved. None of the tedious, expensive, legal technicalities, such as "pleading, adjournment, amendment, demurrer" were allowed. Great faith was shown, consequently, in the intuitive, honest nature of the participants, for the emphasis was entirely practical. One participant remembered that it was agreed that there would be no long arguments; each party and his respective witnesses would give their evidence in a plain, straightforward manner. Depending upon the seriousness of the offense, the guilty party might be banished, flogged, or hanged. Prisons and escape-proof jails were almost totally unknown, so possible sentences were severely limited. The trend gradually moved from corporal forms of punishment to fines which could be worked out on public projects, if the party did not have available funds. Criminal cases represented only a portion of the court's docket; the majority involved civil matters, primarily mining disputes. Out of the local precedents established in these cases evolved the basis for the detailed and complicated mining law of the nineteenth century.[14]

The question of legality remained moot with the evolution of miners' courts into the territorial system, which accepted their established precedents. Serious doubts arose, however, in the Black Hills in 1876, when the mining tide swept over land guaranteed to the Indians within an organized territory. Being trespassers on Indian land, the miners could not appeal to any government for legal protection. The establishment of a provisional court system, following a brief attempt at using miners' courts, partially solved the problem, although its jurisdiction remained limited to petty offenses. Two local residents, Seth Bullock and Richard Hughes, disagreed about the effectiveness of the system. Bullock described it as an improvement over the miners' court, while Hughes pointed out its obvious weakness—no standing in law. Until the government cleared the Indian title and a Federal judge appeared, the situation remained unsatisfactory.[15]

The near failure of miners' courts in the Black Hills should not imply an overall defeat. The courts, overseers of civil rights, property, life, and justice in a world where an individual might, too often, decide right or wrong, provided legality and jurisdiction for mining camps and districts. Until Federal authority could be imposed, their existence granted a permanence to the district. With decisions based upon common sense, experience, and majority vote, rather than on legal precedent, the verdicts were not free from error; the trial of Jack McCall for killing Wild Bill Hickok is an outstanding example of a miscarriage of justice in a miners' court. McCall was found not guilty, having pleaded self-defense, although he had shot Hickok in the back. Fleeing from the Black Hills, he was later tried again in a Yankton, South Dakota, court which found McCall guilty and hanged him. The court ruled that the miners' court had no legal basis, thus denying McCall's contention of double jeopardy. How many other less serious errors were committed becomes insignificant when compared to the benefits derived from the application of judicial practice in a manner acceptable to the average citizen of the mining frontier. It remained, however, a temporary expedient, one which could not provide a permanent solution. This awaited the arrival of the duly constituted legal system, including a law enforcement body.

While the majority of the people were concerned about their mining investments or property, and ways to protect it, some were thinking further ahead to providing municipal government. One way to promote the desired stability and legality was to establish legal government, but the major drawback was the cost. On paper it sounded feasible, but in actuality it was known to be expensive, or so argued those who opposed this step. Something had to be done, for the camp could not continue to struggle along with extemporaneous governing methods. This was especially true in the larger communities. One of the camp's obvious growing pains was evolving a solution to this question.

There were, of course, other numerous reasons why the inhabitants coveted city government. The newspapers ranged themselves in the forefront with articles and comments like this:

> Park City [Utah], the most promising mining camp in the West, has been running along for years without a city government, with an inadequate police force, with bad roads, and all modern inconveniences. Is it time a change was made? Are you willing to help make it? [16]

An increase in lawlessness, without adequate safeguards, especially aroused the citizenry to action. The need to regulate streets, sidewalks, buildings, general nuisances, and to protect general health became more pressing as the months passed. The matter of providing a water system, or any of the other problems which faced a growing urban community, might also be sufficient to activate a movement for organization. Fire, the ever present danger in the hastily built wooden structures, prompted many people to consider city government favorably. When volunteer efforts failed, then the community as a whole had to provide some protection if it wanted to prevent this scourge. Nothing else hung over the mining camps like the dread of fire.[17]

Commonly, the first step was taken by a few interested citizens, who discussed the idea among themselves and then called a general meeting or perhaps called a meeting initially and opened it to a general debate. The speed of action and the time of initiation varied from camp to camp, as the comment about Park City illustrates. Some communities acted within the first year or two; others waited for sufficient development or interest. Opposition always appeared, for this step touched the extremely sensitive pocket nerve. Others, perhaps less forthright, argued that the camp was not ready for this development, or that the present situation suited them "just fine."

If the meeting agreed to create a city government, then work could start in earnest. An obvious first step was to petition the territorial or state legislature, or go to the county supervisors, if such a body existed, for an incorporation charter. In the legislature, a certain amount of political lobbying usually was required to obtain the charter. The local paper carried a very important burden in this struggle, for its wholehearted support was essential to help convince the legislators, and if necessary, the reluctant local citizenry. A committee of eminent townspeople might be sent to the capital, supported by letters from others who could not go. In the end, with the success of their plea, the people turned to the actual formation of the government.[18]

Most commonly, the mayor-council form of city administration was used, or a variation of it, in which a board of trustees or town board elected one member to be the president or acting mayor. In the history of any one camp both forms might be used, with the latter frequently evolving into the former.[19] It must not be assumed, however, that all, or even most of the mining communities chose to have a city government. Many were not large enough or did not survive long enough to need formal government. They got by as best they could or utilized open meetings to discuss whatever problems arose. In some camps, a group or committee of interested residents might attempt to provide the needed rudiments. No doubt there were camps where the question of government never came up, and little or no damage was done by this fact.

Those camps which decided to have municipal government took but the first step before the inevitable quest came for money to pay for it. How and where could these funds be raised? What degree of authority should be given to the municipal authorities? Just how elaborate was the municipal government going to become? These questions and others had been discussed, but now came the time for an answer. Tentative steps could be taken, but experience and practice would secure the best answers.

An obvious and vexatious growing pain, which could be felt and recognized by resident and visitor alike, was the condition of the roads within the community. Typically laid out in a haphazard manner, they were not improved until the situation warranted, or some civic-minded person acted on his own to try to mend the situation. The streets were not only poorly laid out, but were often undefined, with the result that cabins and stores were built in what constituted the right-of-way. Stumps and rocks apparently were left where they were in hopes that with use they might be worn away, for nothing was done to remove them in many camps. To make matters worse, mud holes developed which were a risk to man and animal, as one editor pointedly but humorously described:

> One of the most prominent citizens while crossing main street commenced sinking in the deep mud which filled the street like a river. Preparations were being made by bystanders for pulling him out when happily he struck bottom. Had the mud been a few feet deeper, he would have met with the most horrible death on record.[20]

Roads were a disgrace, an obstruction, and a source of potential trouble.

Initial attempts to rectify the situation were begun on an individual or group basis, perhaps by local merchants who felt that a better constructed main street would bring more business. In some cases, the county commissioners took the situation in hand until the city government assumed its responsibility, for it was the final responsibility of this body. Road improvement was one thing on which the citizens agreed, for everyone was aware of the problem. Hard feelings developed when a building had to be removed or torn down, to straighten the street or open the right-of-way, but even at these times the reluctant had to give way to progress. When money became available, digging and blasting cleared the large obstacles from the street and grading was then possible.[21] The council, however, could never seem to get ahead of this civic disgrace. It came back to haunt them again and again, as irate people wondered where their tax money was going, whether it might be sinking out of sight in some bottomless hole which could not or would not be filled.

While wrestling with this problem, the public was acutely aware of another and more dangerous one—fire. The threat of fire was one of the prime reasons to organize a city government. "Young America" might have been doing truly marvelous things on the frontier, but they were in continual danger of undoing everything by a carelessly caused conflagration.

Mining camps were extremely vulnerable to destructive fires. The closely built, hastily constructed buildings, dried by wind and weather, sat like tinder awaiting the spark. Sooner or later the inevitable happened—due to an overheated stove, a poorly built chimney, arson, or any one of a hundred possible causes. Aided by breezes which played around the camps, the blaze spread rapidly, destroying all in its path. Unless efforts were quickly made to stop it, the entire village would be threatened. Rare, indeed, was the camp which never suffered at least partial destruction by fire.

In spite of this ever present hazard, many camps were woefully unprepared for any such emergency. Newspaper editors, in article after article, tried to warn their readers about the peril, but the advice went unheeded. Meetings were called concerning fire protection, only to be indifferently attended, even by the merchants who stood to lose so much. Lethargy seemed to be the prevailing spirit. The pivotal point was finance. No matter what was to be done, it would necessitate the expenditure of funds. A few did not care enough to invest, while most remained either too optimistic or too shortsighted to be concerned. It usually took a fire to awaken them from their apathy. Hopefully, it would be a small blaze, but too

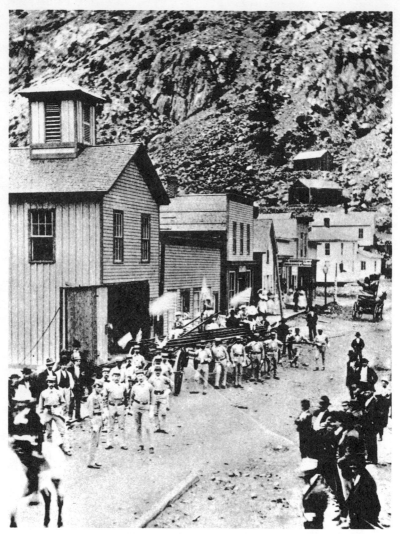

The Star Hook and Ladder Company, Number 1, and fire station of Georgetown, Colorado. *Denver Public Library Western Collection.*

often it was sizable, and a great deal of damage was done. After the disaster, a meeting would be hurriedly called, with accusations as to why something had not previously been done. Plans then were drawn and a committee appointed to carry them out. The public-spirited could return to their occupations with easier consciences. What happened further depended a great deal on the motivation of the people and the committee.[22]

Efforts to provide a solution branched in several ways. The obvious method, and probably the best, was to organize a fire company, on either a voluntary or paid basis. Less effective but less expensive was purchasing buckets, hoses, and other equipment, then storing them in a well-known location from where they could be used to fight fires. An early warning was important, and some camps hired a watchman to patrol the streets, to give the alarm, and to put out the blaze before it spread. Similar duties were required of the fire warden, although he had the additional responsibility of enforcing fire ordinances. Those camps which had city government normally passed a whole series of acts dealing with the prevention of fires by careful regulation of possible causes. Public wells and fire hydrants were looked upon as good protection, but could provide a sense of security when none in fact existed. Fireproof buildings placed at strategic points acted as a break among the surrounding wooden structures, yet they did nothing to prevent or put out fires. They worked well if a building was located on the opposite side from the fire, or if the fire did not jump the break or sweep around it. Unfortunately, false economy might dictate what would or would not be done to provide a semblance of protection, which then proved inadequate.

Not all camps remained so lax about the fire danger. In some, commendable efforts were made by the residents to provide protection, usually in the form of volunteer companies. Meetings were held to arouse interest, and various means, such as dances, were used to provide money for equipment. Some of the volunteer organizations became very selective in membership; others had carefully drawn up constitutions and by-laws. Most, however, did the best they could with what they had. A larger and wealthier camp could afford to go to great lengths to prevent fires. Leadville, Colorado, besides having a very efficient fire department, installed a fire alarm system similar to that of New York and Chicago.[23] Even in camps where a concerted effort was made, too often public interest lagged, in time, and the system declined. The newspaper would sadly take note of the state of affairs, but by now the camp might be past its prime, and little could be done to reverse the trend. The older the camp became, the more vulnerable it was to fire. The fate that awaited many of them was total destruction by fire.

A fire in a mining camp almost defies description. Once started, it burned furiously and rapidly with intense heat and dense smoke. Jumping from building to building, scattering burning brands throughout the whole community, the flames relentlessly advanced. To stand and fight took courage, for not only did the usual dangers exist, but explosives were often stored in the buildings. Water might be scarce, especially in the winter season, when the fire danger reached its peak. Against this danger were arrayed buckets, hoses, shovels, axes, and even snow, if nothing else were available. To build a fire break, buildings were sometimes dynamited. The description of a fire in Virginia City, Nevada, in November, 1875, illustrates clearly what it meant to be a participant:

> Going to the door I saw the thick black smoke coming rolling over the hill. . . . The fire was then just fairly getting underweigh [sic] and firemen had abandoned all hopes of staying it by the ordinary methods. No rain had fallen for six months, everything was like tinder. . . . The streets were filled with flying people, furniture brought out of the houses was burning on the sidewalk, . . . loose horses from the stables were dashing madly to and fro seeking to escape, with the hair all burned from their backs. . . . The flames came tearing on with a front 200 yds. wide and 200 ft. high.[24]

The fire burned until it consumed all available fuel in its path, or the firemen and volunteers succeeded in stopping it. Then the people would come back to discover their losses and visit the charred remains of what had once been their town, their home.[25]

After a fire the people displayed remarkable pluck and recuperative powers. The community would rebuild quickly; tents and rude shelters appeared the next day. It was not unusual to see substantial buildings rebuilt within two or three days. Wreckage would be cleared, and everyone would set to work to produce an even better camp than the one so recently destroyed. Newspaper editors were fond of using flowery phrases as they observed the work being done around them. "Their [the residents'] buoyant spirits and unconquerable energies will rise above the accidents of fortune, and their manhood and untiring energy are bound to command success. . . . Let us not repine about the past. . . ."[26] In a short time it was again "business as usual"; within a season the worst had been pushed aside in the expectation of a better tomorrow.

Tragic as this devastation was for the camp, many times it served a valuable purpose. A prosperous community was reflected by its resiliency in recovering. The new town which emerged very often differed from the old in many respects. Gone were the wooden structures, replaced by buildings of stone and brick. Order replaced expediency in planning and construction, and when all was finished, the camp had about it a more permanent and settled air. "Young America's" dream had been revised, but continued on its progressive march forward.

All mining camps went through this period of growing pains. Their problems and reactions differed, but each faced certain fundamental questions. The answers depended on the people involved, and, to a great degree, on the wealth of the district and mines which supported the camp. In the long run, the future of the camp at least partially rested on the decisions reached. A camp which presented a lawful, governed image was more likely to attract permanent business and residents than one which did not. Finally, this type of community helped in promoting its mines, for it gave an air of permanence and stability which was noticed by potential investors.

Seven

Maturing in Spite of Itself

As the mining camp whirled along, expanding and adjusting to its newfound status, certain signs of stability appeared, at first over-shadowed by more spectacular developments, that indicated the community was maturing. The growth of the business district, which provided a center around which the community could build, was one of the earliest of these signs. Another indicator was a legally constituted law enforcement agency to replace the temporary expedients used earlier. Pushed even further into the background, two pillars of the established community, the school and church, struggled to gain acceptance. Perhaps more sophisticated cultural activities would also appear, although they would not be as popular as the entertainment provided by the saloons, dance halls, and red light district. Other indications appeared as well, and all pointed in the direction the raw camp had to travel in order to pull itself beyond a temporary settlement.

Not everyone in the camp felt that stability was necessary or even wise. Mining society, transitory in the sense that the next mountain or gulch seemed to hold out more promise of wealth to those who had not discovered their bonanza, did not encourage it. Why should they bother to expend the time and energy to stabilize a temporary home? The precarious, the unexpected, typified the economy upon which the camp relied, and colored the attitudes of all who came into contact with it. This attitude helped support, for example, the physical entertainment media of the community. At the same time

99

it hindered development of those features which produced the durable community. Any drive for money or support, be it for fire equipment or a schoolhouse, encountered this barrier. To overcome it took initiative and patience.

Those who did not adhere to this attitude, or at least felt the camp was worthy of development, pushed ahead in spite of the odds. In the forefront stood the newspaper editor, whose motive was not completely unselfish, since his success depended upon the growth and continued prosperity of the camp. His standard was raised on behalf of all. With him ranked the businessman, who also had a great deal invested and would continue to profit only in a progressive community. The merchants, however, did not present a united front, for some were as transitory as the men they served. Behind them came a motley array of people with different backgrounds and reasons for wishing to stay. There were miners and mine owners who had made their strikes and wished to settle down. Owners of transportation and freighting companies faced fewer expenses and steadier profits in the established community. Those men and women with families, who were tired of moving, hoped to make a success of it and establish a permanent home. The settlers outside the camp proper, like the farmer and the lumberman, depended on the settlement for an available market and source of supplies. Though he had no direct influence on developments within the camp, the wholesaler who supplied the goods also had a vested interest in continued growth. With mixed motives and goals these people joined to promote and improve their camp.

The business district, the heart of the community, mirrored the hopes and aspirations of all residents. The growth and prosperity of the camp were shown here as nowhere else, for empty buildings, for rent or sale, displayed visual evidence of over-optimism or of decline for all to see.

No two camps' business districts were alike, although certain similarities may be observed in all. Spaced on one main street or scattered along several different avenues stood the hotel and boarding house, restaurant, saloon, grocery, meat market, blacksmith, stage and express office, assay office, livery stable and corral, and the ubiquitous general store. Varied patterns of these establishments formed what might be described as the nucleus of the business community. As the camp grew and prospered, the more specialized stores, selling hardware, drugs, dry goods or clothing, and baked goods, emerged. With bonanza wealth such as was unearthed at Leadville, Colorado, most of the businesses found in any large Eastern city appeared, to help the miner spend his earnings.

Each of these stores had a definite part to play in the development of the camp. Faced with problems of isolation and transportation, and relying upon economic conditions based on a future unsure at best, the businessman gambled as much as anyone in the camp when establishing his concern. With an optimism and faith which would do justice to any miner, these men and women pioneered the business growth of the mining frontier.

Typical of all mining camps was the general store. Here the miner traded for almost any article needed. This nineteenth century department store carried a variety of goods, including dry goods, groceries, clothing, medicines, hardware, notions, liquors, agricultural implements, and mining equipment, all crammed into one or perhaps two rooms. The selection remained small, but few customers left without finding at least a portion of the items for which they had come. To meet the demands of the time, the general merchant sold wholesale as well as retail. The activity of this emporium was not limited to consumer business. Often the miner could sell his gold or silver bullion, and the farmer could find a market for his produce. As a profitable sideline, the store might also serve as the local bank and post office.[1]

Rivaling the general store were the more specialized shops, such as the drug and clothing stores. Some of these were quite similar to their modern counterparts. The drug store closely resembled its twentieth century descendant, selling such varied products as paints and liquors, as well as dispensing drugs. A dry goods store, how-

A booming mining camp tempted the prospective buyer with a variety
of goods, as this picture of the Virginia City, Montana, business district in the 1860s illustrates. *Historical Society of Montana.*

The business district of Alta, Utah, in 1873, included a drugstore,
Chinese laundry, restaurants, and a brewery. *Utah State Historical
Society.*

ever, might be joined with a grocery, which usually sold more than just food stuffs. The bakery often merged three businesses—brewery, saloon, and bakery. This diversity was a typical characteristic of the younger camps, where the merchant had to have his hand in several lines in order to provide an adequate income. In the larger and more established communities, with their greater clientele, the distinction between trade lines tended to become more rigid, and combinations outside the general store fewer.

In each mining camp, besides the merchants, individual tradesmen served the public in other ways. Laundries, often owned and operated by the Chinese, unless racial discrimination effectively prevented it, were essential. The barber shop retained its importance in the masculine society of the camp, although the bathing salon was conspicuously rare. This absence caused the editor of the South Pass, Wyoming, *Sweetwater Mines*, of July 14, 1869, to ask, "Is there a man in South Pass who has enterprise enough to start a bath house? Such an institution would pay handsomely, and would be a great benefit to the community at large." No doubt such an institution would have benefited every camp! Boot and shoemakers, jewelers or watchmakers, tailors, dressmakers, gunsmiths, and photographers also frequented the mining regions, settling where the economy could best support their specialized services.

The real estate and mining agents, with the insurance salesmen, settled in varying numbers; the former were especially prominent during the plush boom days. The undertaker found employment, and as one advertised, "[coffins] kept constantly on hand and made to order on short notice."[2] Business was seldom brisk enough to ply this profession exclusively, so the ambitious mortician combined his profession with, for example, a furniture store. The traveling salesman, an institution in the camps, represented something different and even worldly. If his sales pitch included a show or lecture, so much the better, for it provided entertainment. In affluent times, few more profitable stops could be made than in a mining community. Novelties were also attracted by the lucrative, or gullible, market. One advertisement speaks for itself: "Mrs. A. Johnson. Clairvoyance gives descriptions of mines, ledges and sampling of ores." [3]

An amazing variety of more mundane merchandise was sold in the camp stores. When one considers the time and work necessary to get supplies into the isolated mountains, the variety seems even more remarkable. A brief glance at any local newspaper reveals a large sampling of standard necessities, such as all types of meat, groceries, vegetables, clothing, furniture, household goods, and mining equipment. Other items offered for sale included drugs, patent medicines, toys, tobacco, liquor, out-of-town newspapers, guns, and seeds. In the luxury line, the merchants advertised perfumes, accordions, oil paintings, canaries, gold and silverware, artificial flowers, and jewelry. Of course, the variety of merchandise depended somewhat on the development of the particular camp, but even in the less prosperous ones the refinements offered for sale, if one had the money, helped ameliorate austere frontier conditions.

To augment the budding maturity displayed by the business district, the businessman turned to other outward expressions of permanence, the school and the church. These institutions would attract more people, which among other things meant greater profits. Such crass motives alone would have indicated little real faith in the camp. The businessman and those of like mind realized that these two things could provide something for the camp which nothing else could provide—cultured refinement and the semblance of Eastern respectability. Mining camp culture to the Easterner might mean the "wild West" image with all its attractions, but to the Westerner it was not enough. He was striving for something better, something similar to what he had known earlier or heard described by those who had been East.

The church had come West with the first miners in 1849 and 1859. It was not, however, new to the region, for the Spanish conquistadores had brought the Catholic faith with them three centuries before. The Catholic friars carried the word of God throughout the Southwest in the years that followed. Farther north, in what would be Montana and Idaho, missions had been established by both Catholics and Protestants during the 1840s. When the mining hordes inundated the entire area, these humble beginnings failed completely in coping with the changed conditions. The ministers and priests who served the mining communities came with the miners and after them.

The mining camp environment was not conducive to the church's activities. It may be said that the community existed for one major purpose, to make money. It was a materialistic society, certainly not unusual for that day and time, which had little time for spiritual matters. The primitive rawness of life on the frontier emphasized personal traits and conduct opposed by Christianity, and the transitory nature of the settlers presented further obstacles. These circumstances had to be considered by any denomination before it sent a minister into the camps. Of even greater significance to the endeavor's success or failure, however, was the attitude of the people themselves.

Episcopal Bishop George Randall sadly commented that "unbelief prevails among the multitudes," after visiting Colorado camps in the mid-1860s. This situation had come about, he felt, for two reasons—the engrossing nature of the mining business, and the absence of the restraining influence of home and former associations.[4] Bishop Randall's opinion might seem extreme, but others reported similar views. Describing the miner, James Chisholm, a Chicago newspaperman, wrote, "He has generally laid out for himself one broad rule for guidance through this life to the next, which has no element of faith in it. Usually he is a skeptic. You will rarely find an out-and-out orthodox man among what I would designate as the *thinking* population of the hills."[5] Not all laymen and ministers held so pessimistic a view.[6] Still, even the most hopeful of ministers had to realize that interest was lacking. To overcome this and stir any latent Christian fervor became their primary responsibility.

By far the majority of these people had been reared in the religious tradition of the Western world, but this did not guarantee that each individual would accept the tenets of Christianity. Those who came to the camps with any doubts whatsoever were encouraged by the environment to go their own ways. The social bonds and pressures of Victorian Christian morality were weakened. Gone were the home ties and the influence of the established church. In their place the individual could substitute as he chose, within reason, without risking the disapproval of his fellows. Nor were these the only factors which helped separate the man from the church. A few, such as the press of work, have already been discussed; others will be examined, particularly the role of the Sabbath in the life of the community.

Despite what might, at best, be described as a lukewarm religious environment, the church managed to take root and grow. The immediate problem which the Eastern home denomination had to combat was the chronic shortage of clergymen willing and able to go West. Even when they arrived, they found the task so spiritually and physically fatiguing that many returned home. Wrote Bishop Randall, "If this rising empire is to be rescued from the dominion of the devil, there is to be a long and severe battle, and there must be soldiers to fight it." [7]

The minister or priest was the single most important factor in the success or failure of a church. The spiritual shepherd had to adapt to the life of the community; failure to do so meant rejection and the scattering of his flock. In this respect the camp molded the image of the church, not the church that of the camp. Writing to his wife from Virginia City, Montana, the young Episcopalian, Daniel Tuttle, piously examined his own shortcomings and touched upon the traits he felt a minister should cultivate.

> But when I came to the sermon, I tried to make it too impressive, I think. I was thinking of myself too much, of God's truth and men's souls too little, and I don't believe I preached as I ought. I was cold and self-critical, and wanting to see the effect on the

audience. I know if God will send me the grace to be really humble, and faithfully prayerful, I can accomplish more for him and
for souls than by all my highest flights of eloquence.[8]

Tuttle learned his lesson well during that winter of 1867-68, becoming one of the most popular and leading churchmen of Montana
and Idaho. Another Episcopal minister, Ethelbert Talbot, stated
that it was of vital importance to be a man among men with the
qualities of good fellowship, sympathy, and fraternity. He advocated a "personal gospel of service combined with patience and a
capacity of loving men." These, too, were important for the frontier pastor. To minister to the camps was physically demanding
work. It required, especially in the first decade of the 1860s, traveling
long, hard miles in all types of weather to visit the various congregations in the parish. For maximum effectiveness, the minister established himself permanently within one camp or a short circuit.

The Reverend Joseph Machebeuf's itinerary to visit his Colorado
mountain churches in the summer of 1867 consisted of a journey of
350 miles, encompassing twenty-two days with five special lectures,
almost daily mass, confessions, and sermons. To meet all emergencies he used a heavy buggy in which he carried his vestments, bed-
ding, provisions, and grain for his horses. Sometimes he set up a
small altar on the rack at the rear of his buggy and offered com-
munion outdoors.

Many could not stand this physical strain. At least in these years
it was better for the man to be single, in order to follow the mi-
gratory instincts of the miners. Preparation and services had to be
given without books and church materials. The minister had to be
industrious and ingenious, for money was always a problem, and
improvising and substituting the only alternatives. To overcome
the indifference, he needed deep and clear religious convictions, yet
he had to be tolerant of others' opinions. In a few words, the mining camp minister had to be intelligent, willing to go to the people
and share their life, and preach the gospel understandable to all.[9]

Obviously, not all measured up to these requirements. Many types of men preached on the mining frontier, some of whom were not a credit to their calling. This group did a great deal to undermine the work of the church, far out of proportion to their numbers. One disgusted miner wrote home that he had met only one true Christian minister; the rest seemed more interested in taking collections than in ministering. The money, he felt, was used to pay gamblers or "something worse." George Parsons commented that "It is from politeness to my maker that I attend church at all here, where numbskulls and broken down ministers have charge of spirituality." [10]

At the other extreme stood the highly capable and popular ministers like Tuttle, and Colorado's John Dyer. Between these outer limits the great majority were found, dedicated laymen and ministers now forgotten and unsung, who used their lives in an attempt to better the lot of their fellow men in the mining camp.

On coming to the community, the missionary or minister found himself gaining support from several groups. The local newspaper probably gave the most public assistance on practical as well as religious grounds. The businessman held similar views. Families were very influential, for they made up the body of the permanent congregation. Increasingly, as the mining frontier spread, the family appeared earlier and more frequently. At the same time, respectable women arrived in ever increasing numbers. These factors help explain why the decade of the 1860s was the low ebb of religious influence in the camp, while a steady upswing followed. Not all men forgot their Christian background, and there resided in each camp a corps who willingly supported almost any church. Yet another group gave at least financial aid, although its members were not openly accepted into the fellowship; these were the denizens of the brothels, dance halls, and saloons. It was fine that they contributed, but to attend church remained another matter. This shocked the more staid members; one, apparently forgetting Christ's teachings, wrote in his diary, "plenty of loose women who left church for the saloon, [I] don't see their object in attending church." [11] These were the people, from saint to sinner, the wealthy and the poor, who in their way encouraged the establishment of the church in the mining community.

The church was not the picturesque structure of rural Currier-and-Ives New England or Mississippi Valley fame. Any building or room which happened to be available for a meeting served the purpose. Services were held in courthouses, theaters, carpenter shops, dance halls, deserted stores, private homes, and schoolhouses. Even saloons were converted, with the faro tables making convenient pulpits. Particularly adaptable, with seats and a stage in the front, was the theater. A very good justification existed for such practice. It was not thought wise to erect a church which might be deserted in a year or two, if the camp was abandoned, especially if there was no resident minister. Notice of a service would be given by word of mouth and printed announcements, and at the appointed time the worshipers gathered. With the limited facilities of a small community, this was the best that could be done. It really did not matter where the service was held, as long as the congregation had a worshipful attitude. An English visitor, used to the formality of the Anglican church, still found himself able to adjust to a theater setting, with the choir placed in the orchestral seats and "sitting in the conventional sofa of the stage was my Lord Bishop. . . ." [12]

A certain amount of pressure always existed to build a church, for it was the outward sign of progress. If a minister could be found who would be willing to undertake the task, then the next step was to secure enough money. Normally, members and even nonmembers joined to help construct the building, furnishing materials and labor to keep the cost down. It was helpful if the minister was a carpenter, architect, and organizer, for often the needs were many and the laborers few. With the completion of the structure, the dedication service was held, but the church was not really complete in some people's eyes until an organ and bell were acquired. They hoped as much as possible to have the traditional trappings in this more primitive setting. In far too many cases, however, the problems presented during this period were only the beginning. A church edifice did not solve the other pressing problems of Christianity.

The origin of the church in each camp varied. Possibly it was organized by a layman or minister sponsored by a home missions society, or a national church, or an itinerant preacher. It might have been a spontaneous revival of religious interest in a small group of local people. Some congregations started as Sunday Schools, evolving into an organized church body. A community could ask a neighboring minister to preach to them, and then become part of his charge.

Many denominations came into the religious void that accompanied the establishment of the camp. Universally found was the Catholic Church, which went into every territory under discussion and into almost all communities with either a church or visiting priest. The Methodist Church was the most prominent Protestant denomination. Reminiscent of the circuit riders, Methodist lay preachers, ministers, and missionaries rode from camp to camp within a region, establishing small congregations where they could. After these two, the Presbyterian, Congregational, and Episcopal churches were most commonly encountered. Episcopalian centers were located particularly in larger camps, although members were scattered throughout the region. The last major denomination, the Baptists, had active laymen and itinerant ministers but fewer established churches. The Mormons naturally dominated the Utah scene, although the camps adhered to accepted Christianity. Mormon missionaries appeared in the surrounding states, but secured few converts in mining communities. Some talk of a countermissionary movement into Mormon country ensued. Albert Richardson, who toured the West in the mid-1860s, visited Salt Lake City. Unimpressed by what he saw, he pointedly wrote that the problem might be solved as soon as Utah filled up with mining men, for "The miners are iconoclasts; and human nature will triumph." [13]

The popularity of some churches over others resulted from several factors. Many of the settlers came from the Midwest, bringing with them loyalty to their home church. The Baptist and Methodist had been traditional frontier faiths, moving West with the pioneers. Methodist appeal can be partially attributed to Westward movement as well as to a very active lay and official church body. An inducement affecting church affiliation related to how actively the church supported its workers in the field. Wavering Christians often shifted their allegiance to whichever denomination started services in their community, or if it were the only one available, they had no choice. Immigrants from England and Europe strengthened the Episcopal, Methodist, and Presbyterian churches, although all had strong American traditions behind them. In the final analysis, the older churches predominated, and no new religious movements developed exclusively in the mining camps.

It must not be imagined that each town had two or more Protestant denominations active in it. Especially in the smaller camps, the community church predominated. Supplied by a visiting pastor, or if fortunate, a permanent one, this house of God served the needs of all the Protestants of the area. The choice of the minister's denomination depended upon who might be available and the general preference of the congregation.

The same people who supported the church generally gave their aid to education. The minister often led the fight, for the church was one of the leading educational agencies in the community. It was not unusual to see church and school sharing the same building. The intent of these two institutions was somewhat similar— to provide a cultural and intellectual uplifting among the young and old. In comparison to new agricultural regions, mining camps had little immediate need for schools. The presence of families and children, in the early days of a camp's existence, remained the exception. Such a situation did not last long once the community became settled, when almost spontaneously an educational system blossomed in its simplest form.

The first school would most likely be of a private or subscription nature rather than public. This was considered desirable because of the lack of tax revenues, and disinterest in having taxation of any sort. As a result, the financial burden was placed on those families who had children, where it could be least afforded. As the years passed, this pattern changed with the growth of territorial and state educational systems. By the decade of the 1880s public schools were more common, even from the very beginning of a community's existence.[14]

Private schools, started by an individual or organization, were never so popular as the subscription school, which gained popularity by combining aspects of both private and public schools, and seemed to meet the needs of the community. Parents paid a fee for each child per week or month, and frequently the county or camp helped underwrite the endeavor with whatever funds were available. The training provided differed in quality, and a parent could never be sure whether the school would be in operation the next year. Nor was the burden evenly distributed by ability to pay, for the larger family paid a greater cost. Unfortunately, incomes did not rise proportionately with the cost of education. At best, the subscription school was just an expedient with obvious shortcomings. For these reasons, with the American ideal of free education, agitation soon started for a public school system.

Although initiated by interested individuals, the campaign to open a public school became a community project. Public opinion, however, was never unanimous concerning either its desirability or its necessity. A correspondent of the *Owyhee Avalanche*, of April 28, 1866, wrote: "Amid the hurry and excitement of money-making in new places—the education of the rising generation is too much neglected. Parents cannot leave their children so rich and valuable legacies as good education and habits of industry. . . ." Horace Hale, early Colorado teacher and superintendent, and later president of the University of Colorado, concluded that the gold seekers had little overt interest in education. Under the surface, he and others thought they discerned at least an awareness of the importance of good schools. Yet time and time again civic complacency hindered or prevented construction of needed buildings. Once a school had been started, encouragement and support could decline disastrously. Fortunately for the sake of the young people, such inertia generally would be overcome with hard work.[15]

Public funds other than taxes were lacking or insufficient. To solve the dilemma required some ingenuity, for materially the school promoters had nothing from which to start. Temporary expedients, such as renting rooms or houses, were utilized, but these were soon outgrown as the population increased. Funds for constructing a suitable schoolhouse were only the initial expense. Then came the outlay for equipping the classrooms, which was estimated by one school board at $1,400, a sizable figure for that day. Not all communities were so thorough in providing educational tools such as maps, blackboards, books, and desks, but still the essential materials did have to be purchased. The operating costs depended on many variables—the number of teachers, salary, fuel, supplies, repairs, and length of school year. It is doubtful that many schools had a budget of less than $500 in this category. The burden for these expenses fell on the permanent residents, around whom the remainder of the transitory populace ebbed and flowed. The most equitable solution, a school tax in the form of a special or regular mill levy, was supplemented by special projects, such as purchasing a site and constructing a building by issuing bonds redeemable with tax money. Opposition arose, and on occasion became so heated that special elections on the question resulted in defeat for the measure. The struggle was futile, and eventually a school system based upon taxation was devised. For the moment, this was satisfactory, but then came the problem of delinquent taxes, particularly as a camp started to decline. Nothing could more quickly undermine the entire system than this.

Various devices served as stopgap measures to tide over the school budget until a sound financial basis could be conceived. For example, concerts and programs by the children raised money for the fund. Balls and suppers provided some help, as did contributions from individuals. Fines for violating ordinances were yet another source of revenue. The Colorado territorial legislature passed a law requiring that the third claim on each lode be vacated and recorded for the benefit of education, to be sold later. Needless to say, this scheme never proved popular with those who had the third claim. Taken all together, these measures did not begin to provide enough to help offset school expenses. The problem for the community was considerably lessened with the organization of a school district and the stabilizing of the local economic situation. In scattered cases, however, public schools had to be closed because of lack of funds. In the final analysis, the benefits derived overrode the objections. The whole community received a far greater return than the actual value of money spent. The school system, "this grand and enduring fruit of public liberty," provided sorely needed educational opportunities. Indeed, one editor wrote, "Nothing speaks more loudly for the enterprise and permanency of a new town than a well-regulated public school." [16]

The physical plant of the school varied considerably. In the early days almost anything which could be reasonably acquired or rented was brought into service. The result reflected the primitive condition of the camp. For example, a young woman who taught school in Bannack, Montana, in 1863 found herself working in a crude house, plastered inside and out with mud, with a dirt floor and roof.[17] Unable to stand these conditions, she moved the school to a room in her own house. In the more mature camp, the typical wooden schoolhouse was built, either separated into several rooms, or just one large room accommodating all the students. In some of the wealthier communities, multistoried brick or stone structures became the ultimate in school buildings.

Inside was gathered a heterogeneous assemblage of young scholars. The graded school remained the exception, for usually ability or age predetermined what the student was taught. Most of the schools were organized on a system roughly corresponding to the modern elementary-junior high concept. The ages varied considerably, from five or six to the early twenties. One school board laid down the regulation that no child under six would be allowed to go to school. The members stated that to send them earlier "just to get the children out of the way" imposed a great annoyance upon teachers and could harm the children. School terms were flexible, running anywhere from three to ten months. Nor was there an established period of the year when they would be in session, since both summer or winter terms were used. Education was hampered further in the mining community by the need for boys' labor, and also their own desire to start working by the time they reached their teens. Some of the larger camps provided a high school education for those who were interested, but the cost and increasing public apathy generally prevented acceptance of this idea.

The problems faced by teachers, pupils, and parents have a somewhat modern ring. Overcrowded classrooms and heavy teacher loads were typical complaints, as was the need for an enclosed playground to prevent injury to the little folks. Books were scarce, particularly in the 1860s, resulting in the students' bringing whatever they had. This produced a varied assortment, and was a decided handicap to teaching. Equipment like maps was nonexistent or in short supply. With the later improvement of transportation and the increase in settlement, the quantity and quality of books and equipment showed a steady improvement. Truancy, that perennial problem, occurred with disturbing frequency despite rules and regulations against it. This was not just a problem caused by the students, but by the parents as well, who winked at or encouraged their offspring's reluctance to go to school. Under such handicaps, the teachers struggled to provide at least the rudiments of the three R's for their pupils. The result depended on the students' willingness, the teacher's ability, and community support.[18]

A progressive note was sounded in a few camps which provided night schools and what might be termed adult education classes, which offered such subjects as composition and penmanship. Sometimes English was taught for the benefit of foreigners living in the community; or, at the request of a minority group, such as the Germans, their native language might be placed in the regular school curriculum. Generally, these special courses were privately taught and each person paid his own tuition.[19]

Initially, the school system required little supervision. As it grew and necessitated more expenditure, local control entered the picture. At first a simple arrangement of a committee appointed by the city council or their fellow citizens was thought adequate. Then the elected school board or board of trustees became a permanent fixture. Eventually, with the formation of a district and association with the state system, the standard school administration of the day evolved.

The schoolhouse was one of the most important activity centers of the camp. Student programs and exhibitions ranked as a very popular feature of the year. These came usually at the close of a term or around a holiday period such as Christmas. Here was an opportunity for the teacher to display his pupils' talents, not to mention his own success, and a chance for proud parents to observe their children's accomplishments. Meetings of all sorts were also held in this building, as were community parties. In the often isolated condition of the camp, such community gatherings were long anticipated and heartily enjoyed events.

In retrospect, the mining camp school and its problems were little different from those faced by any frontier community in the nineteenth century. Isolation, financial worries, securing good teachers, overcrowded conditions, and primitive equipment and buildings were common dilemmas. The public displayed certain reservations toward the idea of public education, relating in particular to financial questions. On the whole, however, a lively interest was shown in education, either pro or con. In the final analysis, while the quality varied with the teacher and the camp, the opportunity was offered to acquire educational skills and to transmit the cultural heritage of the American people on to the next generation.

No greater service could have been rendered by these mining camp schools.

Other activities which may be defined as educational and cultural made their inaugural appearance in the camp, lending a semblance of maturity to the scene. The traveling theater company arrived on the mining frontier within months after the miners. With no regular season at any one community, they followed the circuit to many. The lecturer also took to the road. Few camps had the privilege of hearing such a noted personality as Horace Greeley at the threshold of their existence, as did Central City, Colorado, but most had the opportunity of listening to some speaker within their first year. It did not matter who spoke, really, for the occasion provided a chance to break the monotony of the mining existence, to view something besides their own small world, and be entertained or perhaps educated. A brass band made up of local people provided a similar outlet, besides serving to associate people of similar interests. This

The brass band of Black Hawk, Colorado, in 1862. *Denver Public Library Western Collection.*

last point should be kept in mind, for it symbolized the start of social cohesion which every urban community must have to survive. Originally, the camp was made up of strangers, there for the purpose of making money. Yet it took more than this to produce a community. A start was made when the law-abiding citizens organized to promote their common interest. Now with people joining to start a church, the school, or a band, they were becoming acquainted and beginning to realize that they had common aspirations and even plans for their camp. When this occurred, something intangible happened to the entire community; it became more than just a temporary working habitation.

One of the interesting developments revolved around the efforts to organize a library. Books were a scarce commodity on the frontier. For practical considerations or lack of interest, the miners, in their rush to gain the gold field, left behind such luxuries. Once arriving at the new discoveries, those who had been accustomed to the enjoyments of reading found the void hard to fill. One Eastern visitor noted that the typical library of a miner consisted of a pack of cards, a copy of the "Mining Code," and perhaps a well-thumbed copy of a book such as Mark Twain's *Roughing It*. Nor was he more impressed by one camp's entire library, which contained Byron's poems, a novel by Dickens, Shakespeare's plays, and an old *Harper's Magazine*. The scholarly Matthew Dale, who went to Colorado in 1859, wrote that same year: "Everything is readable these long nights and [I] would give a pension had I one to spare for my text books . . . and every scrap of music is sought after with the avidity of gold hunting." Not all miners shared his literary tastes. Magazines and newspapers were more eagerly sought after than books, although many an old-timer later remembered the pleasant winter evening spent with a novel in some secluded cabin. The desire to keep abreast of the outside world and help ameliorate the isolation influenced to a great extent the demand for the standard magazines and newspapers. Publications were passed from hand to hand, until they simply wore out; news, any news, even if old, was eagerly received.[20]

The quest for reading material did not reflect an equal drive for a free public library. Financially, the camps could not support one, and wealthy patrons remained few and far between. In its place developed the circulating library. Operating usually from a local store, or perhaps a rented room, it was open to those who were willing to pay the monthly or yearly dues. The number of acquisitions remained small, probably in the low hundreds, and the variety depended on the group or individual ordering the books. They generally included, however, the standard historical, classical, biographical, and fictional works of the period. Books could be rented or borrowed by the week or month; some circulating libraries offered free use of their volumes to anyone, if they were not taken from the reading room. Support of these libraries varied, reaching a peak during the winter months. Not all camps offered even this type of library; the only collections in the community belonged to private individuals. Others were slow in starting and faltered when the camp declined.[21]

To provide a library of any sort in the camp meant that the sponsors had to overcome not only the financial problems but the transient tendencies of the residents as well. Enthusiastic adherents might move, undermining the program if other interested persons did not replace them. If and when the camp declined, the situation became worse, because the burden of support fell on fewer and fewer people. The most practical solution, the subscription library, did not need so many supporters, nor was it reliant on public financial aid. It provided a reservoir of books and sometimes magazines, which although neither extensive nor broad in coverage, met the needs of the camp. It was a practical compromise.

To be on a stagecoach line was another step in the camp's maturation. To the editor of the *Yankee Fork Herald*, of September 25, 1879, it meant living "No Longer in the Wilderness." This was

Stagecoaching in the Rockies was a treacherous experience, especially in the winter. *Harper's Weekly, February 8, 1868.*

his headline to a story which read: "Whoopee! There's the stage, direct from Blackfoot, on the Utah and Northern Railroad. How are you, Challis [Idaho], and the balance of God's country? You're a liar if you think we ain't got a stage road in Bonanza." Excitement and romance combined when the stage rolled into town. For young and old alike, it was the highlight of the day, unfolding a drama, a glimpse of another world, in the eyes of a young girl in Deadwood, who wrote that there was something intimate about the wooden coach and horses which could not be matched by the train.[22]

Without the stage, an ingredient was lacking in the community's existence. When connections were finally secured, the public seemed unhappy until daily trips could be scheduled, although many camps had to remain content with bi- or tri-weekly arrivals. The nonappearance of a coach became a matter of concern. Robberies, considering the number of lines operating, were rare, but accidents of various types now and then delayed the trip. For the owner of the stage line, a route among the mining camps had highly profitable potential. Accidents were only one of the problems he faced, however. Way stations had to be built, then maintained; equipment constantly needed repair; bad weather was a worry; provisions for the animals in a nonagricultural region took money and time. Passenger fare alone failed to provide enough income, and the government mail contract frequently supplied the main item of revenue. Its loss to a rival was a serious blow and might mean selling out or changing routes. Carrying bullion also was profitable, although dangerous. In some areas it was necessary to hire an extra man to ride shotgun in order to provide protection. The situation became so bad on the Deadwood run that a specially constructed coach was placed on the line to transport the bullion.

Concord coaches generally seemed to be the most popular type of conveyance, although wagons, buckboards, and sleighs were utilized to meet different conditions. For the passenger, the journey became a test of endurance, as Mark Twain revealed in his account

of his trip to Nevada. A ride to a mountain camp was equally laborious and more exciting. The pace, though slow on the upgrade as the horses strained to pull the coach, swiftly changed once the summit was reached. Passing a freight train on the narrow mountain roads was an experience long remembered, especially with the prospect of going over the edge because of a miscalculation. Dust and heat in the summer, snow and icy winds in the winter added to the passengers' discomfort. Food at the stops might or might not be palatable, depending on the owner, and the customer's taste. Having survived the ordeal, the passengers reached the camp in a whirlwind of excitement and were unceremoniously deposited on the main street to be objects of curiosity for the residents.[23]

The glamor days were numbered, and by the mid-1880s the great era of mining camp staging had passed. To be sure, stages were still going into isolated camps until after the turn of the century, but with much less grandeur. The appearance of the railroad was the principal cause, although the times and needs of the public were changing as well.

To police the maturing camp took more than just a miners' court or vigilante action, which had outlived their usefulness. Depending on the size of the camp, the residents turned to the organization of a standard law enforcement agency—either a one-man operation or a regular force. In the larger camps the force might be quite large, consisting of a chief and several patrolmen, while a small camp was fortunate to be able to afford a two-man staff.

In spite of oft-told tales, it was not a glamorous job full of adventure and danger. The task of maintaining the peace and tranquillity of the community and enforcing city ordinances was the same for town marshal, constable, or policeman. Specifically, the deputy or patrolman was expected to patrol his beat and not enter public drinking or gambling houses or a house of ill fame unless in the line of duty. The city marshal or chief of police supervised all police activities, had charge of the jail, and served in such other capacities as street supervisor and dog catcher. Drunks, petty lar-

ceny, breaking city ordinances, stray dogs, and other assorted activities took up most of his time. The salary varied, but was never
very high: that of a marshal might range from $900 to $2,000 per
year, less for the rest of the force. It was not unusual for the police
to receive part of the collected fines or a set fee for all arrests to
supplement their income. Some camps even insisted that the men
furnish a uniform at their own expense, while the town provided
only the star, club, and whistle. For this reward the taxpayers expected a virtual superman, on the spot wherever trouble occurred,
and available at all times. If the community failed to provide
enough money to support two shifts, either the night or daytime
remained unpatrolled. If circumstances warranted, private subscription might provide at least a night watchman to supplement the
police. The limited size of the force continually made the task
that much more formidable when the situation demanded close
surveillance.[24]

Once the boom period passed, the problem of lawlessness declined, becoming similar to that of any country village. For the
time and conditions, the protection provided was at least satisfactory, if in some camps not so efficient as the townspeople would
have liked. The basic problem, as in all governmental operations
of the camp, was money. Far too often the public exhibited a tendency at the wrong time to be penny-wise and pound-foolish. Nor
was community support always what it should have been. Certain
people were willing to wink at infractions of the law if it meant
profit, no doubt to the point of providing graft when needed. The
well-known breakdown of law enforcement in Leadville and Tombstone cannot be blamed on the police any more than on the general public. Without public support, the law enforcement officers
were powerless to stem the criminal element. Law and order had
to come to the camp; it came, and a part of the frontier epic slipped
away.

Eight

Magnet in the Mountains

WHILE the camp struggled to gain a firm footing, the residents were aware of what was occurring around their settlement. The miner and the merchant were not the only ones attracted by the wealth of the district; two particularly lucrative doors opened for the ambitious. The community offered a market of great potential, for self-sufficiency in food production had not been achieved, and better and faster means of transportation were in demand. The company or man that supplied these struck his own gold mine. As a result, the farmer appeared and then the railroad; both developments augured favorably for the future. The mines and the camp could not, and did not, hold out the promise of permanent settlement in themselves. Mining is self-liquidating; on only a few occasions did a district last for more than a generation. Thus, if the mining frontier was to leave a tangible heritage, a balanced economy had to be forged, permanent settlers attracted, and a transportation network devised connecting the region with the rest of the country. The role of the camp and mines, for the two cannot be separated in this case, consisted of providing a profitable market, which was most important, promotion, and even capital. The significance of the results went beyond regional boundaries to the national scene.

The popular musical *Oklahoma!* whimsically suggests "The farmer and the cowman should be friends," which reflects the legendary antipathy of the cowboy for the sodbuster. The miner, on the contrary, welcomed and encouraged the farmer to come and settle.

The urban mining frontier needed agriculture, and the camps provided a ready market of a scope unknown to previous agrarian frontiers. The farmer's and the miner's labor complemented each other without serious conflict. The farmer, often part of the rush, stayed to settle and cultivate the land long after the miner had gone.

The Great Plains, renowned as the "Great American Desert" since the days of the Pike and Long expeditions, had served as a barrier to settlement. So convinced had some Americans become of this fact that they were willing to turn the whole region over to the Indians as their permanent home. The pioneers rushing to Oregon and California tarried only briefly in their crossing. They had neither the time nor the inclination to plant a crop and wait a season for the harvest. Gradually settlement crept onto the eastern fringes, and doubts arose in some minds about the desert concept. Even as late as 1866, however, General William T. Sherman wrote in his annual report to the Secretary of War: "These plains can never be cultivated like Illinois, never be filled with inhabitants capable of self-government and self-defence. . . , but at best can become a vast pasture-field. . . ." He noted in the same report that agriculture was being "pushed with an energy and success that promises the best results" in the territories of Montana, Utah, Colorado, and New Mexico.[1]

Before the miners came to the Rocky Mountains, farming had long been practiced in the region. In the upper Rio Grande Valley, the Spanish and New Mexicans toiled for over 200 years on their small plots. They were antedated 700 years by the Anasazi ancestors of the Pueblo Indians, who had even practiced rudimentary irrigation. In New Mexico, which bordered on a truly desert region, and where grazing was easier than farming, agricultural development remained almost stationary, tentatively reaching into southern Colorado only in the nineteenth century. The Mormons deserve the credit for conclusively proving the richness of the soil, when water could be found. With hard work and intelligent planning they had turned the arid Great Basin of Utah into a fruitful irrigated garden.

Starting settlement in the mid-forties, they were established just in time to receive the full benefit of the California rush, as a way station on the overland route, and because of Utah's proximity to the markets of the gold fields. Scattered settlements throughout the rest of the region supported the conclusion of the Spanish and Mormon experiments. It remained, however, for the miner and the farmer who came with him to break down completely the desert idea in and along the mountains.

That the camps were lucrative produce markets had been understood for years. The *Niles Register*, May 16, 1835, had noted:

> The laborers at these mines afford a valuable market to the producers of corn, pork, etc., in the parts adjacent which do not produce gold—but in general, it is as profitable to supply the diggers, as to dig for gold.

The comment referred to the mining regions of the Southern states. Even in these settled areas with relatively small mining operations, local farmers had profited. If this were true concerning competition from a large farming area, it would be more so for the man who settled in a new area protected by 600 miles of prairie or mountain ranges from the nearest agricultural settlements. He took a calculated gamble, but rich rewards beckoned. Person after person testified in the 1860s that farming was a "decidedly good business" in their country, better perhaps than mining.[2]

It was a recognized fact that if the camps hoped to survive, farming had to be developed to furnish fresh meat, vegetables, grains, and fruit. The long supply lines, vulnerable to weather and Indians, did not insure a steady supply of staples, let alone perishable foods. With few second thoughts about the "Great American Desert" idea people swarmed out of the Midwest in 1859 to go to the Pike's Peak region, and then a few years later into Montana. They were not professional miners, but farmers, merchants, and laborers who found economic conditions poor enough at home to encourage them to venture westward in hopes of bettering their fortunes. Reaching the gold fields only began their problems. Mining, hard and tedious, did not bring the envisioned wealth, especially since the best claims had already been staked or required techniques beyond their capabilities. Many, disgusted, returned home; others cast around looking for some different occupation, and farming was a natural possibility. High food prices and rich meadows in watered valleys along the foot of the mountains induced many to turn to farming.

These early miner-farmers faced unknown factors in their pioneering venture. A woman in Montana wrote home that gardening would pay extremely well if anything could be raised, for no one knew with any certainty whether there were any nights in the year free from frost. Experiments had to be made first on a small scale to test the soil and climate. Finding implements and seeds presented a problem, because few had been brought by the miners. Of a particularly vexing nature was the continual Indian menace to the more isolated farmers who settled away from the camp. Those fortunate ones who possessed the courage and tenacity to stay found ready markets and high prices. William J. McConnell, later prominent in Idaho politics, located a farm in April, 1863, on one of the tributaries of the Payette River. Starting with about two gallons of onion sets, which grew well and sold for $1 per dozen, he and his partner prospered. McConnell and those like him found themselves in the enviable position of having a seller's market. This allowed the farmer to secure a foothold and gain time to master the different environment.[3]

The camps did as much as they could to encourage agricultural production. Often during the initial years of settlement, the newspaper virtually advertised for farmers: "This is what we want— open up farms, boys and you will be richly repaid for the little labor required."[4] Everything, from verdant soil to high prices, which might induce the farmer to come, received praise, occasionally beyond what the facts warranted. As the years passed and agriculture became an established part of the economy, the papers took great pride in local produce, especially the first crops or outstanding yields. As new camps developed, they likewise encouraged farmers to settle nearby, and the cycle continued. Each became, in its own eyes, one of the best markets of the region. Papers took it upon themselves to act as local agricultural experts, editorially advising farmers what to grow, with diversity as a key theme. The public was reminded to encourage the development of agricultural resources, to put an end to the necessity of importing high priced staple supplies. Not to be caught remiss, the town councils did their share to stimulate farming. No business license was required in many camps for the local farmer selling his own produce or home manufacture. Ultimately, it was hoped that all this effort would produce a mining community which relied on its own resources for balanced prosperity. The majority failed to achieve that status, yet the striving aided permanent settlement.[5]

The extent to which mining stimulated agriculture went beyond the immediate area of the camps, which were only a nucleus for an ever-increasing cycle of activity. This development can be clearly traced in Colorado and Montana; other areas followed similar patterns, varying under regional conditions. Although the original market decayed and possibly disappeared, the agricultural settlements lived on—monuments to the frontier which had passed.

Farming appeared in eastern Colorado almost simultaneously with mining. On April 23, 1859, the new *Rocky Mountain News* recommended that territorial farmers stay at home rather than rush into the mountains. Stock and produce would gather their share of all the gold that would be mined in the coming summer, it predicted. During the remainder of the spring and summer, comments appeared in the paper about land under cultivation. The Midwestern farmer who pictured himself as the dashing miner frequently returned to the plow from the pick after observing mining reality, or, with more accurate knowledge, did not bother to go to the camp at all, settling instead along the streams which rushed out of the mountains. Such a man was David K. Wall, who settled on the site of present Golden (west of Denver) in 1859. Until almost ruined by grasshoppers three years later, Wall had steadily increased the extent and yield of his farm. For him, the rush to the gold fields and the high price of foodstuffs produced a comfortable fortune. Understandably, he made money, for his farm was located near the main route to the camps. With prices high in Denver but almost doubled in the mountains, Wall found himself surrounded by available markets. A visitor to the region in 1860 reported seeing large numbers of haymakers at work in the Boulder Valley cutting grass for the mountain camps. He was surprised to find the greater portion of the valley settled by farmers. Prices remained high for several years, encouraging more people to switch to agriculture, as mining became expensive and complicated. For the miner, the predicament of high prices and depressed mining conditions from which the Territory suffered produced an intolerable situation. One, writing home after trying mining without success, concluded that farming decidedly was the best business in the country.[6]

Mining could not stagnate long, however, before it affected farming, and in the 1860s Colorado was suffering in all respects. But a foothold had been gained, and with the mining resurgence in the late 1860s and 1870s, farmers could supply the demands of the new camps. A change had come over farming during the decade, with diversified operations replacing pioneering agriculture. Dairy products from local herds appeared on the Denver market in 1860. Registered beef cattle arrived in large numbers after the conclusion of the Civil War, and soon the cattle industry was launched on the plains. Fruit trees, grapevines, sugar beets, and bee colonies were introduced during the decade. The first thresher arrived in 1861, and ample wheat was grown to keep at least one mill busy the next year. By 1866 a total of 100,000 acres was cultivated, with roughly 70 percent used for wheat and corn.[7]

Irrigation was the key to much of the success enjoyed by farmers during these years. The early enthusiasm generated by prolific yields in what had been considered a desert soon subsided, and farmers began to realize the commercial advantages of the region's agricultural resources. Prices generally went down from the initial highs, but the markets expanded with the opening of each new mining region. During the 1860s the question of food for incoming settlers was solved through local production of staples and establishment of mills. The people lived simply without the luxuries available farther east. The arrival of the railroad ended this period, for new markets opened for Colorado cattle, the demand for food luxuries increased, and the entire home market changed. To meet this, the tempo of agriculture quickened.

Here are all the major ingredients for the permanent agricultural economy of Colorado. Irrigation on valley and plain opened thousands of acres of crop land on which were raised vegetables, fruit, corn, and wheat, where the idea of doing so would have produced serious doubts twenty years before. The camps no longer remained the sole market; the railroad brought within reach a multitude of possibilities.

Western Montana was a land in many ways more hostile to agriculture than Colorado. Gold was found here in the early sixties, and the rush began. Many of the early settlers had an agricultural background, but they found the season, altitude, soil, and amount of moisture strikingly different from what they had previously experienced. Unlike some of the Colorado camps, very few in Montana were located where agriculture was possible. Another factor, that of more accessible gold deposits which could be successfully worked by simpler methods than those used in Colorado, discouraged desertion of mining for farming. High produce prices finally broke down this reluctance, and by the year 1866 the influence of farming had become noticeable in the Territory.[8]

Alexander K. McClure, editor, writer, and politician, who spent half a year in Montana in 1867-68, saw many homesteads which failed to impress him. The problem, he thought, was created because the farmer or rancher held claims and merely farmed to live until his "slumbering wealth" was developed by someone else more capable. Most of the ranches had been improved in a most temporary and indifferent manner, and the abundant crops were derived from the fruitfulness of the soil rather than the skill or care of the farmers. Only in the Gallatin Valley, he concluded, did farming seem to be regarded as a legitimate business.[9] McClure's observation of the temporary nature of farming reflects a characteristic of early Montana and, to a smaller degree, Colorado. The lingering temptation of sudden wealth by mining prevented some people from changing completely to agriculture for a living. The vision of opportunity in the settlements and the lack of working experience with the climate and soil helped keep alive the golden hope. Once farming and markets had been established, the transition from miner to farmer became much easier. In later mining camps the ex-farmer appeared less frequently than in the early 1860s. By then, if he migrated, he looked for land to cultivate rather than turn to an entirely different way of life.

Little was heard in the 1870s of the myth of the desert. John Tice, on a journey combining mining and agricultural examination, reached several interesting conclusions. He felt that the plains along the mountains were admirably adapted for raising all kinds of stock to supply the wants of the mountain settlements. This land, near an abundance of water and blessed with a far milder, more equitable climate, as well as contiguity to the "only real market that will ever be there," appeared more desirable and valuable than the more remote land to the east. The mountain valleys were well adapted to growing oats, hay, and garden vegetables, all of which, Tice noted, found ready sale at "highly remunerative prices" in the camps.[10] Both Tice and McClure understandably judged Western agriculture by their experience in the East. Their view was perhaps too narrow, too harsh. The Great Plains and mountains necessitated new approaches to farming. The early pioneers lived in the transitional period, their successes and failures paving the way for those who came later. In time, the Colorado farmer would cross the Continental Divide, following the miner onto the western slope. In this new and growing land the farmer found markets and, relying upon previous experience, moved ahead rapidly. Farther out on the plains, ranching and then farming flourished to an extent not foreseen by Tice. In Montana, farmers expanded into the western valleys, turning to supplying the numerous military posts as well as the camps. In both states, so firmly rooted did they become that when mining declined, they survived the trying times without serious damage.

The cattleman played a role in the camp, although it was not as significant as that of the farmer. Cattle and oxen brought by immigrants and miners, the first domesticated meat available in the camps, soon were replaced by regular beef cattle. The markets opened by settlement provided one minor incentive for the great expansion of the 1870s and 1880s. A few of the camps, ideally located near range country, became supply centers for the ranches. Globe, Arizona, merchants, for example, in the late 1870s relied on the ranch trade to tide them over during the lean years before mining prospered. Silver City, New Mexico, passed rapidly through the mining period to become the social and trade center for a cattle range. At least one Montana rancher, Nelson Story, made a sufficient stake by mining to purchase a herd and drive it up from Texas to his ranch.[11]

Geographical factors prohibited large ranches near the mining districts, except in the southwestern states. The miners had not been cattlemen, nor did they have cattle available to establish ranching. The rise of the camps, however, led to a chain reaction which created several developments favorable to ranching—a large influx of population, urban communities, demands for protection, the coming of the army, and finally, the creation of Indian reservations. Each provided markets for cattle. Indirectly, encouragement was given through the evidence that cattle could survive northern winters on prairie grass. The effect that cattlemen had in the camps beyond providing beef was transitory, but Tombstone stands as the one outstanding exception to this generalization. The wild reputation acquired by this settlement resulted as much from cattlemen as from miners. Mining had less impact on sheep raising than on cattle ranching. A report of sheep being driven from Utah to Montana in the winter of 1863-64 is one of the earliest recorded incidents of this nature. The sheepman only slowly appeared; the market was not extensive and the range belonged to his rival, the cattleman.

The effect of mining on an already settled area such as Utah intensified economic opportunity. Utah farmers had an ideal location to supply nearly all the camps between the Rockies and the Sierras, which they energetically exploited. The money which flowed into the territory provided a source of cash income and a means to balance the economy in what would otherwise have been strictly an agricultural community in the 1850s and 1860s. Some conflict arose, but the producer and the consumer naturally gravitated together, helping to overcome the animosity, but not alleviating it by any means. The editor of the *Park Record* (Park City, Utah) wrote:

> They [Mormons] also forget that Park City, Alta, Bingham, Silver Reef, Frisco and all other mining camps give employment to large numbers of their subjects besides furnishing the best markets for their produce and fruits and pay them *cash* for it. . . . Every farmer in Utah knows that to encourage mining means to enhance the value of real estate and furnish them at home with a good market for their produce.[12]

The mining camps and the businesses which they sustained, staging and freighting, furnished a continually expanding market for agriculture. The significance of the combination mining-farming frontier was manifold. The steady progression which characterized Midwestern settlement became one of rapid, almost instantaneous settlement no longer contiguous to older regions. In the early years farming possibilities did not lure the people West; gold brought them there, then other conditions influenced their decisions. Environmental obstacles, the Indian and distance, which could have hindered settlement for years, seemed less formidable before the opening markets. Almost on the heels of the miner-farmer came communication and transportation revolutions which limited pioneer farming to a short interval, when compared to the settlement of Illinois and Kentucky. Evolutionary experimentation gave way to immediate trial and error in selecting seeds and cultivation methods. The three essentials of previous farming frontiers—land, water, and wood—were now abundant land with smaller reserves of water and wood. Overcoming the handicaps was the key to success, and it meant a modification of the farmer's cherished individualism. Large-scale irrigation projects, for example, everywhere demanded cooperative effort. The successes of the decade of the 1860s, the testing period, paved the way for the succeeding influx of settlers.

The mining community stimulated agrarian settlement in the West. Not self-sufficient, the camps had to depend on an equitable geographic division of labor. Agriculture, a key development in the economic structure built by mining, has been one of the most enduring. The farmer would have come eventually, even if the mineral wealth had never been there. He would not, however, have arrived so soon, in such numbers, nor with such tempting prospects of success. The market provided by the camps sustained him through the years of adjustment and provided a source of income which insured permanent settlement.

Both the farmer and the miner needed the railroad, for it was the cheapest and fastest way to get goods to and from the outside markets. The coming of the railroad was a momentous occasion for the mining community. It heralded as clearly as anything else the end of the old frontier and the beginning of a new era. All other forms of transportation gave ground to it. The reliance on horse and wagon faded before the iron rail and steam engine. The slowness and seasonal nature of wagon and riverboat were replaced by all-weather, fast, transcontinental transportation.

Every camp envisioned itself as needing a railroad. No topic received so much universal comment as the necessity for and the possibility of securing one. No efforts or adjectives were spared to encourage the prospective lines. The building of the Union Pacific into the Rocky Mountains had started the great railroad rush, almost rivaling in intensity the original 1859 stampede. Colorado and Montana papers visualized the coming millennium in glowing terms, "every rail placed upon the prairie or riveted to the mountain side a step of the giant of civilization in his path to the West." The Indian was doomed. The cost of living would go down and with it wage scales, which meant the mines would be even more profitable (or in some cases profitable for the first time). Property values would soar, commerce improve, and Eastern capital be drawn West. The East and West would be united. The Rocky Mountain territory was indeed going to become more profitable than the wildest promoter had ever dreamed possible, and all this would occur with the connecting of the rails. The blessings were too much for one editor, who wrote, "It is too vast and infinite for human calculation." Over twenty years later the residents of White Oaks, New Mexico, saw with the coming of the railroad similar advantages. Times might have changed, but the desire for better transportation had not abated.[13]

For the individual camp, prospects were indeed alluring. Cheap transportation, "the instrument and test of civilized progress," meant the end of isolation, faster hauling, and reliable year-round service. It could provide, with proper promotion and luck, an increased influx of Eastern and European capital, new industry, development of the city and its mines, and an almost unlimited future. In retrospect, it is easy to see that the railroad alone could not do all these things, but such foresight was not granted and probably would have gone unheeded in the enthusiasm to secure a connection. In the estimation of the people, as shown by the editorials in the papers, the railroad held the key to the new era.[14] In a sense they were quite correct, for those camps located near or on the railroad line generally lasted longer and remained more prosperous than those which relied solely on wagon transportation. Of course, it must be taken into consideration that the railroad tried to reach the wealthy camps and not the marginal ones.

To obtain the desired line the public often went to great effort and expense in an all-out campaign. In Central City, Colorado, in the mid-1860s, newspaper articles began to appear, stressing the possible benefits which could be gained. Progress of the Union Pacific was followed carefully and this camp, like the whole territory, was greatly dismayed when this line bypassed Colorado. The years 1870 and 1871 witnessed a great increase in interest. Tracks of the branch line Denver Pacific by then had reached Denver, and Centralites deemed it possible to extend the tracks on into the mountains. Article after article appeared, stressing the importance of the railroad. Discussions were held over the relative merits of the standard gauge versus the narrow gauge, and the desirability of floating a bond issue. At every turn critics appeared, worried about cost and other contingencies such as the influx of cheap labor and the subsequent reduction of wages. A committee was organized to investigate, promote, and, if possible, secure the railroad. The big issue of 1871, an election to vote on railroad bonds, was approved. Now a sense of expectancy took hold as the actual construction started. The paper followed the progress with daily or weekly reports. Finally, the great day dawned and the tracks reached the district. The local paper appeared, with flowery commentary:

> It is a great leap forward, such as we have not taken in years, the *avant courier* of a new era, with a world of rich promise in the long train of events coming out to us from the East and the West, the North and the South. If there's anything on earth we need at this time it's just such a train, and the sooner it gets here and begins to peddle its blessings the better we shall like it.[15]

The train did eventually reach Central City, with the appropriate ceremony, which included speeches, toasts, and band music. Needless to say, all had a gala time at this momentous event. The means successfully used by Central City were not all-inclusive. Subscription drives were conducted to purchase company stock, and leading townsmen formed corporations to lay track from the main line to the camp. It must be kept in mind that this became a community effort. Dissenters always appeared, but they were pushed as far into the background as possible so that they would not impede progress. Interest closely followed the actual construction and anxious moments were endured if for some reason it stopped. Excitement and anticipation came to a climax the day the first regular train arrived.

The benefits of securing a railroad were not limited solely to the camp, for it presented attractions which made the community a very desirable market for the railroad. William Palmer, builder and president of the Denver and Rio Grande, explained, "A population engaged in mining is by far the most profitable of any to a railway. A hundred miners, from their wandering habits and many wants, are better customers than four times that number otherwise employed." [16] The acquisition of almost all material and merchandise to build and operate a growing town from outside sources, combined with the needs of mining, produced a transportation reality which made Palmer's statement not just wishful speculation.

The completion of the first transcontinental line in 1869 marked the opening of the exploitation of the mining frontier by the railroads, from California to Colorado. In the next two decades, dreams became realities as the tracks reached out to the bonanza camps. Each served as a stimulant for the other. Significantly, the great mining development in the Rocky Mountains came after the 1860s, yet without this mineral wealth the region would have held little attraction for the railroads. In another respect, the opportunity for railroad expansion grew with the changing mining conditions. The easily obtainable gold of Montana, Idaho, and Colorado was rapidly depleted. What remained required expensive, heavy machinery to mine and mill. This shift from pan and shovel to quartz mining necessitated safer and cheaper transportation. By the year 1890, railroads had penetrated the Rocky Mountains from the Rio Grande to Idaho with branch lines extending into the vast intervening expanse to reach the camps. Although the profit of the mining trade remained only one factor in the total construction program of the major companies, it merited thoughtful consideration.

To trace the development of the railway system in the mining frontier lies beyond the scope of this study. However, a brief examination of one road which was intimately connected with mining will serve the purpose of analyzing the effect of the attraction to these areas and the problems involved in reaching the goal.

The Denver and Rio Grande Railroad, as the name implies, originally intended to build south along the mountains from Denver. This differed from the normal pattern of constructing an east-west line through one of the mountain passes, then building on a north-south axis. The Rio Grande, advantageously situated along the foot of the mountains to tap the mining regions, by 1876 had reached southern Colorado in the vicinity of present day Trinidad. At this point, as the recent historian of the route emphasizes, the westward pull upon the main line by the attraction of the mines became irresistible, ultimately changing the direction of the entire railroad. Within the next fourteen years, Leadville, Silverton, Lake City, Ouray, Aspen, and many smaller camps celebrated the arrival of Rio Grande trains. Leadville illustrates the attraction of mining camps. At a time when Western cities were begging for railroad connections, Leadville had two railroads, the Denver and Rio Grande, and the Santa Fe, fighting the so-called "Royal Gorge War" to gain access to it. Branching beyond Colorado, the northern mining regions of Utah and Salt Lake City became part of the line. Out of this emerged the modern Denver and Rio Grande Western. The problems encountered and overcome by the engineers and construction crews in the mountains testify to both the fortitude of the company and the lucrative wealth of the destination. High passes, tortuous grades, and savage weather continually hampered operations. Manpower shortages, despite high wages offered, frequently delayed work. The problem involved not hiring the men but keeping them on the job once the tracks neared the camp and mines. This narrow gauge line fought rivals, declining mining conditions, and economic depressions to emerge eventually as one of the strongest of Western railroads.[17]

By far too much had been expected, too much promised in the coming of the railroad. Optimism, desire, and even desperation had been substituted for common sense. But a realistic appraisal shows that better transportation and traveling facilities, more comforts and luxuries for the public, and stimulation of mining did result. A decline in commodity prices and mining expenses normally followed, although seldom to the degree hoped or promised. Promotion of new industries, trade, and development of the district depended on several variables, and railroads were only one. Complaints against high rates and the threat of monopolization quickly dispelled some of the joy. Businessmen's visions of larger profits disappeared when they found themselves at the mercy of their supposed benefactors. The long awaited influx of people, which some had anticipated and others feared, did come about with greater accessibility. As might be expected, the undesirable came, along with the desirable. The result was pessimistically pictured, in the words of a Deadwood citizen on the arrival of the first train, "Well, . . . we'll have to lock our doors now." [18] Considering all the factors, the railroad remained more a help than a hindrance. At its best, it benefited a prosperous community or rejuvenated a declining camp. At its worst, it provided faster, year-round service and an end to isolation. Whether the best or the worst occurred depended almost as much on the flexibility of the camp as on railroad policy.[19]

The railroad was the crowning feature of the transportation network attracted to the mining frontier. First had come crude trails, then the toll and public roads and, in a few areas, river transportation. Over these had traveled the freighters' wagons and the stagecoach, but all had their disadvantages. The railroad, the product of nineteenth century technology and skill, furnished the ultimate answer. An immense change had come to the West. The pioneering days gave way to a more settled life, and finally by 1890 the distinct marks of a mature community had been made. Rodman Paul, in his study of the mining frontier, stated that no factor was more influential in bringing to an end the frontier phase of the mining

West than the revolution of transportation which came with the railroad.[20] The significance of the others, as well as the telegraph, must not be forgotten. One needs only to compare the 1860 figures of cost, distances, time schedules, and population with those of the 1880s to comprehend the magnitude of the change wrought by these developments. The handicaps had not been completely overcome even by 1890, for there remained areas, especially in Idaho and Montana, where the realities of physical geography had not been surmounted.

The impact spread from the Rocky Mountain region to the entire nation. Various Midwestern and Pacific Coast cities vied to tie the Western markets to themselves via improved and shorter routes. The profit-conscious post-Civil-War merchant willing to take a few risks could not overlook the potential. Naturally rivalry developed. Until the coming of the railroad many cities had struggled for dominance. The river towns along the Missouri, and the West Coast seaports, located on or near established trails, reaped the rewards. Sharp competition reigned, as each trade center of the camps tried to outdo the others. For those fortunate regions able to trade with both East and West, the bargaining position was excellent. Generally, the question was one of distance and geography, with the Midwest dominating trade along the eastern slope and California having the upper hand to the west.

The coming of the transcontinental railroads changed this alignment. Chicago and Omaha replaced river and trail towns. Chicago's mercantile interests especially profited from trade and investment in mining schemes. New York and other Eastern cities found the mining frontier open to direct shipment, and profited somewhat. A journalist wrote in 1867 that "There is a glorious harvest to be reaped in those places [mining regions]," and indeed he was correct.[21] Far more than he foresaw would unfold.

The farmer and the railroadman, both lured by the markets of the camps and mining frontier in general, changed the face of the land. The wilderness, the frontier, disappeared before the rail and the plow. The camps with their urban markets and wealth have come and gone but have left behind a more important heritage than the mere minerals taken from the ground. They encouraged agricultural settlement and construction of a transportation network which have become the basis of the Western economy. The miner opened the land, but the farmer settled it and the railroad supplied it.

Nine

Problems of Urbanization

Urbanization of the mining frontier brought with it certain inherent problems. The most fundamental was that of government. As the camp grew to maturity the issue was pressing and clearly demanded a solution. The earliest efforts toward government were stopgap measures, and in a minority of cases these were all that the community required. With the appearance of recognized municipal government in the form of an elected council or board, the barrier which separated the expedients from the permanent had been crossed. The larger the camp, obviously the greater the need, but in the medium-sized community, of 1,500 to 3,000 population, city government also was a necessity.

The concept of city government as part of the first wave of frontier settlement was a relatively limited one in American history. The forty-niners had practiced it, as Charles Shinn brilliantly described in his 1884 monograph, *Mining Camps, A Study in American Frontier Government*. While the experience of California could not be transposed to fit the entire West, as the Californians spread out they carried with them their concepts. Blended with these were those of the Midwesterner and Easterner, who had come to the mines; all these, with a dash of European influence, combined to produce a government. It was much like that of other American towns, yet different by the very nature of the surroundings. In many cases the government operated fitfully, but that it operated at all was a tribute to the men who devised it.

For the sake of simplification, a composite picture of municipal government will be drawn. The reader must keep in mind, however, that it remains only that and nothing more. A composite will not fit the experience of every camp, but will serve to give an indication of general tendencies.

At the apex of the system were the council and mayor. The real power resided in the council, which levied and collected taxes, controlled local finances, appointed all non-elective city officers, and filled any vacant post until the next election. The councilmen were responsible for all city ordinances and regulations: this was one of the most important functions. Helping to organize the police force was their duty, as well as laying out the procedures concerning it. They acted as a watchdog agency over the rest of the government to see that it functioned efficiently, economically, and honestly. Standing committees, if any existed, were appointed by the council, or by the mayor with its approval. The mayor's duties were circumscribed. The official spokesman of the council on public affairs, he presided at its meetings, although his use of the vote might be limited to breaking ties. At all times the mayor was supposed to be vigilant and active in enforcing laws and ordinances. When the occasion warranted, his honor performed ceremonial and other duties.

For their work on behalf of the community, the men who held these positions might receive some monetary compensation. The mayor frequently was paid an annual salary, although seldom very much. Councilmen were lucky if they received a set fee for each meeting they attended. Far more often they served gratis. Two possibilities might have dictated this course—a feeling that the lack of salary would attract only dedicated men, or, more likely, the prevailing shortage of funds. The amount of time spent at these tasks varied. At least twice monthly, council meetings were advisable and in larger camps, more often.

The day-to-day working segment of the city government, consisting of the treasurer, clerk, marshal, and attorney or solicitor (all of whom might be elected or appointed), performed its duties within a limited sphere. Frequently, the budding bureaucracy also included a street commissioner, engineer, city physician, and the nineteenth century version of the garbage collector—the city scavenger. For the sake of economy, however, several of the offices might be combined, like that of marshal and street commissioner. The city marshal was the enforcement agency of the council; his support and power depended on that body.

The two key officials in the actual operation of city government were the treasurer and the clerk. The treasurer kept account of all money received and paid city warrants. He prepared the reports of the camp's financial condition and collected for the council all fees and taxes. With the frequent lack of an assessor, the treasurer had to assume these duties as well. The clerk kept the city papers and documents, served as secretary of the council, and maintained an office to transact camp business. As a precautionary measure, at least one camp (Aspen, Colorado) had him countersign all warrants issued by the treasurer. Controlling as they did much of the governmental, financial, and business affairs of the community, these two officials were required to post heavy bonds, from $3,000 to $10,000, before assuming office. Unlike the council, both of these offices carried with them a salary, usually a fixed stipend for the clerk, and a fixed sum or a percentage of all money collected, for the treasurer.

The city attorney held an important position, especially in the larger camps, where his services were required more frequently. He helped draft city ordinances and other legal instruments, as well as serving in other legal capacities. To give the camp a healthy, presentable appearance was the task of the scavenger and the physician. The scavenger removed all dead animals and saw that no "swill, offal, garbage, litter or any unsound, putrid or offensive matter" was left around the camp. The job was extremely significant, but it was, unfortunately, ignored in economy drives. Sanitary precautions, when left to individual initiative, could create a situation that was a menace to health. The physician was supposed to inspect meat and vegetable markets, superintend the city pesthouse and hospital, and aid the indigent sick. Once again a good theory often fell short in practice. As a substitute, a board of health might be organized. The engineer was to make surveys, plan improvements and supervise their construction, and furnish builders with lot lines. Of all the offices, this one occurred the most infrequently. It was a good idea, but its expense made it highly impractical for the majority of camps. The practical solution combined the job with some other.

The mayor, council, clerk, treasurer, and, perhaps, attorney formed the nucleus of local mining camp government. Some aid was given by interested residents who served on standing committees (for example, finance, fire, and health), or as members of temporary bodies formed to meet emergencies or special problems. To govern this community was not an easy duty, for there existed no governmental tradition on which to test and base decisions. In the rapidly changing world of the mining camp, the pace of government must quicken or fall helplessly behind reality. To match this challenge took individuals with both foresight and courage.[1]

The overriding question in all matters was financial. Where and how could the camp find the money? Maintenance of an elaborate, expensive system was not the problem; the fundamental point was having money to meet the basic demands of the community. The city fathers found themselves facing opposition to taxation and temporary residence. Urbanization worked against the transitory nature of the mining frontier and often came out second best. Plans for the next year could not be based upon the assumption of a steady population growth. Nor did the hard-core permanent settlers care to be taxed to support the rest of the community. Property values fluctuated with the fortunes of the camp and could change almost overnight. Businesses opened and closed within a year. The assessor's problems and the resulting bookkeeping would have been staggering. This left the council with the choice of finding a more equitable tax base, one which would answer the needs but not put the entire burden on a small group of people. Several methods presented themselves; the principal one was a license tax on all businesses.

This had the advantage of catching every firm or individual business within the community, thus considerably broadening the tax base. It also hit hard certain elements which might be called luxury, or even undesirable concerns. The cost of the license varied with the occupation—if it was classified as respectable, the fee was lower. In the higher fee bracket were saloons, dance halls, gambling establishments, breweries, liquor dealers, and theaters. The cost of the license, which might extend from three months to a full year, depended on several variables. For a traveling show, a fee was collected for each performance, while a permanent theater paid a set fee. Establishments with billiard or gambling tables and bowling alleys were assessed a flat rate per table or alley. Saloons, liquor dealers, and breweries could pay a fee based upon sales, but a far easier method to enforce was a standard fee which ranged from \$50 to \$300. Protests against this form of discrimination usually brought the complainant little satisfaction.

Classified as having respectable occupations were general merchants, bakers, doctors, hotel owners, and other similar members of the business and professional community. For this group it cost from \$5 to \$50 to secure or renew a license. The other method of licensing merchants, based upon the volume of business, was never as popular, because it required far greater supervision and expense on the part of the city. Where either method was used, it was reinforced by stiff penalties for the violator. The marshal saw to it that all conformed or were arrested. As a revenue source for the camp, license taxes were extremely significant. The mayor of Tombstone stated that about half the cost of city government for 1881 was paid from these receipts. He patted himself on the back by reminding the voters that his economical administration was primarily responsible for lower taxes, but this does not dim the importance of the license fee in the operations of the government.[2]

While the chief source of revenue remained the business tax, another source, fines, augmented it. Fines were collected for varied offenses, most, as penalties for breaking some ordinance, but some simply for the purpose of raising money. In those camps which passed ordinances against prostitution and dance halls, and then tacitly allowed them to operate without interference, a steady flow of money was provided for the treasury in monthly fines. This amounted to little more than a tax on the establishments under the letter, if not the spirit, of the law. In Leadville, Colorado, for example, this became one of the most important sources of revenue.[3]

By the time the community had reached maturity a more refined and stable tax structure was gaining acceptance as a better means of securing money. This system was based upon the real property of the residents as designated by the assessor. The amount due was determined by the property valuation either on a percentage of, or on the basis of so many mills per dollar, valuation. Using either method, it was common to set a limit on the amount which could be collected for general city purposes. Penalties were imposed for delinquent taxes, with forfeiture and public sale the ultimate result of failure to pay. Special taxes were devised to provide additional income, such as a poll tax to provide money to repair roads. Maintenance of the streets, that vexing subject, required some ingenuity to solve. To avoid placing further taxes on the people, the burden was shifted to the individual property owner, who was required by law to work on and keep clean the section in front of his property. A fairer method was to require every male resident over 21 to work a set number of days per year on street maintenance, or pay the city to hire a substitute.[4]

In spite of all the effort to devise a suitable tax system, one of the chronic complaints of the camps remained the lack of money for city operation. Against the background of rapid growth, it was hard to find an equitable answer. When the situation stabilized to the point where a steady income could be counted on, then progress might be made. Unfortunately, a camp which failed to grow could quickly start to decline. This in turn presented similar problems, but now the city fathers had to retrench because of the decreased flow of revenue. Property was no longer a stable means of income, for its value declined and much was simply abandoned by its owners. Understandably, failure dogged the efforts, but what was accomplished deserves much credit.

Assuming yourself to be a taxpayer, what could you expect to receive for your tax dollar? Municipal government, with varied services, and police and fire protection are two which have already been discussed. Maintenance of the streets was another, although you personally might have had to do the physical work under the city's direction. Dust and manure were standard inconveniences, both personal and public. Some camps provided sprinkling carts and cleanup crews, but others left cleaning methods to individual initiative. Sidewalks not only dressed up the community, but served the useful purpose of keeping the pedestrian out of the mud, manure, and assorted pitfalls along the street. Along the main streets, at least, the city was expected to build and maintain sidewalks, but much depended on the financial status and cooperation of the camp. Often it was left once again to private effort, with, as can be imagined, a corresponding lack of uniformity.

A municipal water system was foremost, in the eyes of many residents. Wells or a stream served the demands of a young or small camp, but as the population expanded, impurities from mines, streets, garbage, and privies made this supply unsafe for use. The threat of a shortage of water during a fire matched that of impure drinking water. Some camps faced a scarcity of water for any purpose and had to look to other areas for a supply. Few private individuals had the money or desire to build the necessary water system, thus leaving the field open to a municipal or privately operated company. The extent of the project depended on the need and the availability of a water supply. Piping water from some nearby source or relying on water wagons were two of the most economical methods, although not necessarily the best. If, however, reservoirs had to be built, ditches dug, city mains laid, and fireplugs strategically placed, then the cost increased and with it the risk and rates. The original expense proved only the beginning, for the system had to be kept in constant repair in order to function properly. Failure to bury mains and pipes deep enough left the community at the mercy of winter freezing at the time when the fire danger reached its height. Irritation over incidents such as this aroused the citizens: "This thing of putting in pipe, paying tax, and then having to carry water four blocks is not calculated to breed harmony. The council have our permission to resign in a body or separately." [5]

The council probably did not follow this sage advice, but next summer had the pipes relaid. The water system was usually one of the first public projects undertaken during the plush days, and one of the first to suffer when the camp declined. In the boom, the sky seemed the limit; nothing was too good for the metropolis. Elaborate measures were taken to insure enough water to meet expanding needs, with a resultant heavy debt on the camp. Then came the awakening, with the camp's decline and reduced service, the same high taxes, and perhaps eventually a defaulting on the debt. Tragically in many instances, this happened at the time fire struck. "Good water and plenty of it is a necessity as well as a luxury," commented the *Montana Post*, October 15, 1864. True then as now, water was an essential without which a camp could not grow or long survive, but an essential which became a heavy burden when the community had gone past its economic and population peaks.

A crying need existed in the camps for sanitation measures. Not the cleanest places to begin with, considering the mining and general lack of planning, they became even worse after years of habitation. The problem arose in connection with drinking water, but the lack of sanitation was a general health hazard to everyone who resided in and around the community. The problem certainly fell under the camp's jurisdiction, but little of a concrete nature was accomplished. This in itself was not unusual, for Eastern cities had similar problems which had not been, or could not be, resolved. Some tentative measures were taken—for example, the establishment of a dump at an outlying spot. A sewage system was unheard of, and the disposal of waste, if, as generally happened, no city scavenger existed, was left to the individual's discretion, whether in the dump or behind his house. Ordinances were passed, supported by fines, and enforced by the police. Still the problem persisted. Too frequently many people disobeyed or ignored the law, leaving little the police could do unless strongly backed by the council and the public. The contradiction between the ideal and the reality became apparent. The best intentions were pushed aside and the resulting price paid in human lives was appallingly high.

Another contribution to the generally unhealthy situation, though less serious, was animals running loose, especially hogs and dogs. Hogs, although claimed by some to benefit the camp by eating garbage, were not considered a sign of progressive civilization by the crusading newspaper editors, who spared few words in expressing their feelings. Dogs literally overran the camps; their barking and howling ruined many a night's sleep. Endless varieties of these creatures which "miners delight to honor by the classic appellations of purps and dorgs," roamed at will. It was hard to keep ahead of the natural increase, let alone decrease the existing canines to a reasonable number. A city pound, special dog taxes, and roundup offered solutions, but not always effective ones. Legislate as they would, the city fathers seemed unable to cope with the dogs. Once in a while, some disgruntled citizen took the matter in hand and liberally distributed poisoned meat. This took stray and family pet as well, and was not condoned by fellow townsmen. Goats and burros, not to mention the family cow, wandered freely in some camps, producing further problems.[6]

Other public services were secondary in nature. The educational system was supported by the municipal government with special taxes, but operation and direct control were left to the school board and authorities. Charity did not start as a publicly supported institution; seldom did the camp become involved. This matter was left in the hands of the church, private groups, or the county commissioners., If a problem of need became acute, particularly in the winter months when work slackened, a special committee might be appointed to look into the matter, but the situation usually improved before the recommendations were acted upon.

Frequent reference has been made to municipal ordinances. To provide a framework of legislation on which law and order could be maintained and government operated was a primary responsibility. The ordinances covered a multitude of subjects, varying from one community to the next. A certain continuity in scope was noticeable with other frontier and older towns, reflecting common urban problems and attempts at solution. The ever present fire danger resulted in an entire series of regulations dealing with chimneys, flues, stovepipes, fires within city limits, storing of powder and fuel, and even construction procedures. Some merely reflected common sense, such as not taking a lighted candle or lamp near combustible material. Others, more emotional than rational, were thought to be important: for instance, forcing the Chinese into a certain section because of their "extreme carelessness as to fires." Turning in a false fire alarm was a serious matter, and the culprit, if found, was severely punished. Vagrants, a common nuisance, persisted, if one can judge from the frequency with which city statutes were passed to deal with them. Mention has already been made of ordinances dealing with the canine crisis, sanitation, and taxation—each important in its own right. The ordinances all carried fines for disobedience, with especially heavy fines authorized for violation of the fire ordinances.

Under the general classification variously known as misdemeanors, nuisances, and offenses affecting public safety were found regulations covering a multitude of sins. At the top of the list stood the bawdy house, house of ill fame, disorderly house, or any of the other descriptive nomenclature used to delineate the red-light district. Prostitutes and lewd women were strictly forbidden by word, sign, or action from plying their trade within the camp. To perform any indecent, immoral, or lewd play, appear in public in an indecent dress, or sell lewd books or pictures offended Victorian sensibilities. Ordinances were passed, which, if they had been strictly enforced, would have amounted to public censorship under broad definitions. Although few camps prohibited gambling or gambling houses and saloons, fines were levied if they became disorderly. With all these temptations available for children, it would appear logical, considering the era's moralistic tone, that some attempt would have been made to prohibit their participation. Very few camps statutorily prevented minors from going in or about saloons or other questionable establishments. One that did failed to set an age limit for a minor, leaving it, apparently, to the judgment of the arresting officer.

Other ordinances of a less sensational nature, although no less important to the peace of the camp, prohibited disturbing a lawful assemblage or congregation. Wild riding or driving within the city was looked upon as undesirable and a menace to pedestrian safety. Strict enforcement of speeding regulations, as well as ordinances against frightening horses, curbed the worst aspects. Cruelty to animals received the careful attention of the councils, resulting in ordinances to end this evil, although their effectiveness may be doubted. Public drunkenness, of course, was frowned upon, even if the saloons operated openly. Excessive drinking, along with creating any improper noise, riot or disturbance, and committing any breach of peace, was treated much as it would have been in any town, with fines or jail terms. The culprit might even be placed on bread and water for a specified number of days. Further ordinances dealt with the destruction of public property, obstruction of a street, failing to illuminate or put a fence around construction holes at night, damaging trees, fences, etc., by using them as a hitching post, impersonating a policeman, resisting arrest, and one aimed at the younger set—throwing a "stone or any other missile" upon any building, tree or other private property. To enforce strictly a law like the last one was out of the question, but it could be used in the case of serious damage and was comforting to have on the statute books.

The six-gun, without which a man felt undressed in the wild West according to tradition, gained the careful attention of newspapers and councils. However, the majority of citizens did not carry revolvers, although frequent complaints of gunfire indicated careless exhibitions by the uninhibited. Really there was no need for anyone to be so armed, for guns were not needed in the daily occupations of the camp. To cure excesses, the discharging of firearms quickly became illegal, as did the carrying of concealed weapons. Enforcement of these ordinances had the desired effect; nights became calmer, and safety for innocent by-standers better insured. The passing of this ephemeral stage of the frontier was little mourned, but rather looked upon as a positive sign of civilization.[7]

These ordinances regulated the communal life of the mining camp. Enforcement did not always measure up to the intentions of the city fathers, but some good was done nevertheless. They represented the mature aspirations of the mining community.

Since few camps were wealthy enough to afford a city hall, the best known municipal building became the jail. The jail could be an imposing structure, or any quarters which appeared strong enough to hold prisoners. In some camps after prisoners tunneled, broke, or walked out of supposedly escape-proof buildings, the jail became the object of civic scrutiny and scorn. Normally, however, it was accepted as the best possible means to confine the few inmates serving sentences, and for sobering drunks. Prisoners under such circumstances became a burden, particularly with food bills. Fines were a much easier and economical method of punishment. For those unable to pay the requested amount, work could be furnished on street repair, wood sawing, and laundering, which was particularly suited to the infrequent women guests. Some people questioned the need for a jail, but it served a definite purpose as a depository for the obstreperous members of the community.[8]

The attitude of the ordinary camp dwellers toward their local government remains obscure. Records are few, but it may be assumed that they favored it for the order and continuity provided by municipal administration. Reservations appeared, however, when it seemingly overstepped the bounds of propriety in levying taxes, whether on a local or state level. The Montanan, James Morley, wrote in his diary, July 16, 1864:

> We have a new territory now and a governer [sic] has been appointed. To-day a collector made his appearance in the gulch to 'stick' us for a four dollar poll tax, as he said, to raise $5,000.00 to build a jail. That seems to be of primary importance in organizing government in these latter days. I more than half wish, when I see such officers and scores of 'pettifoggers' going about seeking whom they may devour in the country, that Uncle Samuel would let us severely alone, for it is a fact that miners can make their own laws so as to get along smoothly with each other, better than government laws enforced by such men."

The individualism and self-confidence expressed in this entry, the spirit of his generation, came to loggerheads with the urbanization of the mining camps. Urbanization required that individualism be subordinated somewhat for the benefit of the entire community. That the municipal government did not always effectively master this conflict should not imply failure. Rather, that order was imposed with a rapidity and to an extent unknown in earlier frontier periods should be a measure of accomplishment.

Municipal government meant local politics. Politics *per se* were never far removed from the mining community or American life in general. In the early days they might have been shunted aside in the scurry to find paying claims, but political activities appeared frequently as the camp matured. Partisan lines, not rigidly drawn in the early camp contests, soon became the accepted practice. Issues arose, people took sides, names were called, and soon Democrats and Republicans tore at one another's principles. It remains a matter of conjecture whether the average citizen took much interest in politics. Evidence is very contradictory. For example, one man living in Central City, Colorado, during 1860 commented, "Politics in this country are much like whiskey, . . . plenty and most villainously mixed." [9] Another in the same camp at the same time wrote, "I hear nothing about politics out here as every body is for money. . . . We know or care but very little about politics in this country therefore I do not keep posted as I should or ought to." [10] Obviously the first writer was concerned about the political scene and reflected his interests in his writing. The second heard or saw little of the political situation, although feeling somewhat guilty for not being more informed. Such was the lure of wealth that even the momentous national happenings of 1860 did not offer a distraction. Tombstone's George Parsons, although personally active in politics, wrote in his diary the day that the news of President Garfield's death reached the camp, "Away out here on the frontier where politics are quite generally ignored and party lines very loosely drawn, the feeling is more profound than I imagined it would be. . . ." [11] Yet Alexander K. McClure, visiting Montana and Colorado in 1867-68 on a semipolitical tour, remarked about the understanding and awareness of political issues by Western audiences. Members of both parties attended all meetings and the speaker had to be prepared for any question. [12]

These quotations were written by people who chose to describe their views; vast numbers left no records. What opinions they held will never be known—only surmised. It would appear, however, that the section of the population represented in the camps was quite similar to any other group in interest and disinterest in politics. In the final analysis the choice rested with the individual and how the issues personally affected him.

Mining camp politics was taken quite seriously by at least a minority of the citizens, and, on some issues, by a majority. Newspapers would warm up to the subject each campaign season, and the battle started, especially if the camp supported two papers. The contrast between the tickets was startling. Voters, warned about the "lamentable situation," "the dirty contemptible" lies, the opposition's gang of "chronic cranks" and "political vampires," had another choice. Loyalty to the correct ticket was recommended and favorite candidates pictured as "intelligent and progressive" with "integrity and ability." Not all papers were so biased, but this was an age of no-holds-barred politics. Issues varied, and ranked as high in getting the people out to vote as did the candidates. A hot issue, combined with a hotly contested election, would attract the voters. When the results were tabulated, charges and countercharges of corruption and bribery occupied readers' attention for weeks until finally the issues and accusations were allowed to rest in peace. Then, until the next campaign time, politics could be conveniently forgotten and put away.[13]

The charges of corruption were frequent enough to warrant the assumption that many of them were probably justified. Residents of Central City and Leadville, Colorado, admitted that money was paid openly for the votes of men who gathered at the neighboring saloon and marched to the polls. People from neighboring towns and visitors voted along with the registered voters. Colorado did not have a monopoly on corrupt politics; similar occurrences happened in other camps. To end these irregularities, election ordinances and registry laws were enacted.[14] They helped, as did the gradual introduction of the secret ballot, but political morality could not be improved solely by such devices. Until that day when democracy meant more to the individual than money or partisan politics, all the safeguards devised could not really insure a fair election.

Political rallies and election day in the camps were better witnessed than described. They retained a certain aspect which has been lost in the more sophisticated twentieth century. Imagine, if you would, holding meetings out of doors on crisp fall evenings, at an elevation of nearly 10,000 feet, with bonfires for light and warmth and a wagon for a rostrum. Or put yourself in the place of the speaker who had to compete with a bar, gambling tables, and the allurements of the painted ladies for an audience and still managed to maintain his share of listeners. The effect produced on the listeners was not always favorable. After suffering through a rally outside his hotel window, Bishop Daniel Tuttle wrote, "It was sickening to see them drink whiskey and hear the profanity and blasphemy of their talk. . . . I feel sad for the country's future, ashamed of the American name." [15] Fortunately for the country, the Bishop's reflections proved less than prophetic. Oratory exhibited a fascinating combination of the rough-and-tumble along with the polished. The crowd was receptive to it. To the outsider it might be amazing, but the miner liked to be entertained as well as informed. As election day neared, the camps took on a different air, more lively in appearance, with politicians campaigning, banners posted, and cigars and whiskey passed out to willing recipients. Torchlight parades and rallies enlivened the evenings. When the day arrived, voters were offered transportation to the polls in some communities, and the local band serenaded one and all. A feeling of expectation pervaded the scene, concerning either the outcome of the election, the reopening of the saloons at sundown, or both. With the final results the victors celebrated, and if the issues and campaign had not left too bitter an aftermath, the losers joined them.[16]

Politics, as the reader can see, meant more to these people than issues and candidates. It provided entertainment and a change of pace from everyday existence. How many people went to the rallies for no other reason than this cannot be ascertained, but certainly it was a factor. Issues might be remote or local, but if the weekly paper carried little else the reader acquired an awareness of them. The roughness noticed by Tuttle and others could have been partly because politics remained strictly a man's game, although the environment of the community stimulated this type of approach as well.

In the small world of the mining camp, politics provided an outlet for men who would have otherwise felt confined by this narrow existence. These men became ward captains and the amateur speakers. A sense of importance, of belonging, in the predominantly impersonal, transitory life of the miners was created as the parties appealed for each vote. To judge harshly these political activities by any standard other than their own assumes too much historical hindsight. What may be observed here was a combination of seriousness and entertainment which marked the American political scene for almost the entire nineteenth century and in a sense remains a part of our modern political life.

City government and politics played an integral part in the life of the mature mining community. Whether the same may be said for the public remains inconclusive. Too many variables are introduced to make any precise statement. Studies of some individual camps point to the conclusion of W. Turrentine Jackson, in his examination of the White Pine, Nevada, mining district, when he wrote, "Democracy of the mining camp appears self-interested, politically passive except where property and patronage matters are concerned." [17] The same might be said of Eastern towns as well. In any case, more significant historical research must be conducted on individual camps before generalizations can be made.

Ten

The Mature Camp

THE mature mining camp epitomized the urbanization of the mining frontier. To call it mature by Eastern standards would be a misnomer. In the eyes of the more sophisticated Americans, the community was youthful—even vulgar—a place to let one's inhibitions wander. In the historical cycle of the camp, however, it had reached its full stature as a mining community. No time or place can be designated as the breaking point between this phase and earlier developments for any one camp. Maturity glided into the community much as summer followed spring. A myriad of signs foretold its coming, yet the townspeople would awaken some day to find it upon them without any great fanfare. It might be indicated by the improvement of hotels, rooms with carpeted floors, black walnut furnishings, and sheets and pillows "white as the driven snow." More seriously, a change was evident in the community itself. The great day of mining excitement was gone and with it a certain amount of optimism and fervor. To be sure, important discoveries were still possible, but the region was known, its riches had been mapped, and its wealth was held, in many instances, by wealthy individuals and corporations. To uncover a valuable claim, a long shot even in the initial rush, became a rare occurrence.

Conservatism began to have its effect on the community's affairs, although it did not dominate like that brand which swept the East after the Civil War. This conservatism arose from several sources.

Some people, having made their fortune, did not care to have it reduced or threatened by any means other than their own hand. They were not vigorously hostile to the freedom of opportunity which had characterized their initial success, but they hedged when it came to outright acceptance of this idea. A split was noticeable in the camps between what might be termed the capitalists and the laborers. The wealthy property and mine owners tended to be much more conservative in most matters than the laborers, although both could become quite radical (to Eastern eyes) when their interests were threatened. Witness for example the Western support of William Jennings Bryan in the election of 1896.

This split had ramifications in the society of the camp. The camaraderie of the earlier years receded as new waves of settlers arrived. There still existed a feeling of companionship between the old-timers, which wealth could not break, but this group steadily decreased as people moved on to newer discoveries. Society now had its "in" and "out" groups, with wealth and position the great dividers. Even into that bastion of masculine society, the saloon, divisiveness crept, as the bit and two-bit saloons helped indicate the economic status of their patrons. Even the church reflected the change, as some denominations became accepted by a certain group which would not think of being found in any other.

It must not be thought, however, that once the community reached maturity it became static. Change still was in the air; no camp could long afford to remain stationary for fear of declining. The transformation in society was just one reflection of the turmoil within the camp; others appeared almost anywhere the viewer cared to look. The hustle and bustle of the previous days continued, but it was channeled now into different paths.

Cultural activity exemplified the new atmosphere. Lecturers appeared frequently, as money became available to sponsor them. The topics varied, and entertainment remained an important criterion, but the discerning member of the community had a much better selection from which to choose. Nor were all these entertainers brought in from outside, for as the community diversified, it found among its own residents those qualified to present a program. Innovations appeared. A novelty and special treat, the talk illustrated with slides, opened to the viewer the visual wonders of the world for only a small pittance or for free.

Frequently during the winter months series of lectures were arranged with a combination of local and outside speakers. These would be sponsored by a society or a group of societies. The literary society was a natural, but churches, debating clubs, and full-fledged lyceum organizations also participated. Each of these efforts indicated a growing intellectual atmosphere within the community, not only as an outlet and stimulating association for the members, but for the public at large. Debates on predetermined topics served to while away long evenings, and, handled properly, were instructive. Free rein was given in selection of topics; the following list indicates some of the interests of the nineteenth century: "Resolved, that theatrical performances have an immoral tendency. Shall Indian claims to land prevent the march of civilization? The elective franchise should be abridged so that none shall be permitted to exercise the same unless fully able to read and write the English language intelligibly." [1] An outstanding example of a lasting intellectual organization was the formation of the Montana Historical Society in 1865 by some of the leading residents of Virginia City. These societies also sponsored social activities for members and occasionally for the public. Generally, it may be concluded that the inducements of such a group appealed to those with similar interests or pretensions. The overt influence beyond the immediate group was small, yet it testified to the fact that the mining communities were not intellectually sterile. The well-known American lecturer and traveler, Bayard Taylor, on a speaking tour of Colorado camps in June, 1866, attested to this. Unimpressed by the physical appearance of the camps, he repeatedly praised the audiences as being "attentive and intelligent," the equal to those of New England.[2]

Cultural improvement, companionship, and social outlets, not necessarily in that order, were provided by musical organizations—glee clubs, minstrel groups, and church and community choirs. Local talent performed in concerts, operas, operettas, and serenades with varying degrees of polish and success. Humorous incidents, such as a mixup in sheet music, were not uncommon. The resulting confusion between accompanist and soloist provided great hilarity for the audience. Hecklers occasionally attempted to disconcert the performers, but all these distractions only served to amuse. In a similar vein, the local drama society presented its performances. In conjunction with such activities, the evening might be capped by a dance. This type of activity also served the purpose of raising money for worthwhile causes or organizations. Local programs and professional musicians who performed at the camps furnished many hours of musical enjoyment, a taste of culture to many who would have received it in no other way.[3] Simply for the recreation and entertainment they provided, these diversions cannot be underestimated for the contributions they made to the whole community.

In the camp the opera house or theater was a mark of cultural distinction, of maturity *par excellence*. Here were presented legitimate theater, musicals, and lectures—the cultural entertainments of the respectable element of the community. The building itself could be strikingly eloquent, like the brick Tabor Opera House of Leadville, Colorado, with its dress circle, upholstered chairs, and interior decorations of white, gold, blue, and red. Or it might be a rough-hewn building, with a small stage and any type of seating accommodations.[4] In either case it served the same purpose, and was the same symbol. It mattered so much to have one in the camp that the local newspaper might take it upon itself to advertise editorially for some enterprising person to build one, as did the *Owyhee Avalanche*, May 5, 1866.

The professional groups played here when they visited the mining camps, although in the earlier years when the companies first arrived they used whatever space was available. Almost all camps had some type of hall which could be temporarily renovated for

The Tabor Opera House in Leadville, Colorado. *State Historical Society of Colorado.*

use by the troupe. The program presented was fairly standard—a serious drama followed by a shorter farce. The whole range of plays, from the popular melodrama to Shakespeare, at one time or another was performed. Variety was offered by operas, minstrel groups, and specialty acts.[5] The patrons, selective in their tastes, permitted shows which failed to meet their approval to play to empty houses. On the other hand, an actor or actress who became a favorite received enthusiastic acclaim; and it took a certain talent to become a favorite of these mining camp audiences. Training and ability were prerequisites, but something else was needed as well; the performer had to understand and appreciate his Western clientele. One of the most popular and capable of all Western actors, John S. Langrishe, typified these characteristics. Langrishe had his own troupe which toured the mining camps for twenty years, starting in Colorado in

1860 and later appearing in Montana, Utah, Wyoming, Idaho, and the Black Hills. Universally respected as a man and a performer, Langrishe might be described as the idol of the mining camps. Even ministers who frequently viewed the stage with mistrust spoke highly of him. His career spans the period of the frontier theater. While unable to establish any permanent season, Langrishe found, by moving from camp to camp, that he reached a continually expanding audience. Comedy, his forte, suited perfectly the tastes of almost all of his patrons. One who observed his performance noted that a good deal of swearing was introduced in the farces to please the miners.[6] Both he and his wife (who was a very good actress in her own right) were typical of the people who brought the theater to the mining communities. They worked under primitive conditions and to reach the camps took hard days of travel. Yet they overcame these difficulties to bring a flavor of culture and a large slice of entertainment to people who willingly patronized their performances.

The theater, then, meant a great deal to the frontier mining community. The quality varied from "insipid" to "very well rendered," according to those who viewed the performances. It also offered an opportunity to act, for in most camps local talent presented plays with more frequency than did professional groups. For the mining people, the theater provided a rare opportunity to glimpse some of the theatrical greats of the day and attend professional performances. The theater reflected social status, for the elite class could attend this entertainment without lowering its standing; the same could not be said for the other forms of entertainment. The theater appealed to those who desired culture, to local pride, and to the vanity and sensitivity of the upper crust. These people provided the money which brought talent far beyond the ordinary means of a town the size of a camp.[7]

The urban aspect of the camp provided fertile ground for the development of the theater. Its rapid growth and success may be primarily attributed to this factor. Money, interest, and people were concentrated in a small area, each essential to support the endeavor. To the Easterner, the setting and productions might have seemed crude, yet in this very crudeness was a striving for something better, something of value—an opportunity to find refinement in the rough-hewn atmosphere of the camps. In their own way the actors and actresses of the legitimate theater played an important part in taming the frontier.

The theater, the capstone of the cultural-entertainment media of the community, was a great step forward in the eyes of residents. A similar advance and one which completed the law enforcement agency was the court system. On the local level this meant justices of the peace or a police court. Depending on the circumstances, the camp might also have a territorial or state and perhaps a Federal judge. Ordinary matters were handled by the local courts with fines or short jail sentences given to the guilty parties. The first courts had been established early on the heels of the miners' courts. Any room available served as temporary quarters, including store lofts, saloons, and empty buildings. Gradually this situation improved, to the relief of the judge and the advancement of the whole system. Some of the courts were almost as rough-edged as the men who appeared before the bar, since decorum and procedure were quite different from the traditional judicial practices.[8]

The public, while amused by some of the lawyers' antics, was distressed by the frequent slowness of the courts and the quibbling legality of the attorneys. As in the modern day, attention was focused on legal technicalities and the insanity plea which made a dead letter of the statute books and, warned one editor, encouraged mob law. Although jurors and witnesses received remuneration for their efforts on behalf of justice, it remained hard to find men who would be willing to serve on juries. Not only did they lose working days, but they could not escape the ill feelings of the litigants. The editor of the *Pinal Drill* (Pinal, Arizona) consequently advocated abolishing this system and allowing the judge to handle the cases alone. The struggle to find men for jury duty had its humorous moments. The same paper noted that the sheriff succeeded in capturing 35 of the most substantial citizens for service, notwithstanding the remarkable fact that 95 percent of said persons were suffering acutely from all ills to which flesh was heir, from lumbago to heart disease.[9] Public spirited people, advocates of the legal system, too frequently weighed duty against financial loss and found the former wanting, but the mining camp held no monopoly on this characteristic.

Lawyers swarmed to the camps like bees to pollen. Lucrative prospects awaited them, for inevitably mining disputes developed, and with them fees from both sides. If in their eagerness they overcrowded the field, temporary occupations, from gambling to mining, tided them over. While needing their services, the public at the same time displayed mixed emotions about the profession. Some of the ablest and worst lawyers appeared in the West. Alexander McClure wrote that if he had been judge, one-half of all lawyers would have been in jail before the first day of the session had been completed and the remainder probably stricken from the roll before the end of it. A radical anti-lawyer attitude was shown by one Colorado mining district which would not allow them to appear at any trial unless they were personally involved.[10] At their best they represented educational and professional competence, both desirable for the community. Some became outstanding experts in mining law, while others used this early training as a stepping stone into politics. Dishonest and inept lawyers, however, helped undermine faith in the judicial process, doing a great deal of harm to the camp and to their own profession. Whatever their skill and contribution, they appeared everywhere, becoming as much a part of the mining camp as the merchant.

Among those people whom the *Pinal Drill* pointed out as difficult to secure for jury duty were the merchants. As the camp matured, the merchants found the business risks declining, but quick profits were not so easily gained as competition appeared. An expansive profit potential still existed, but it stabilized along with the community. The farsighted businessman, who visualized the potential and rode out the ups and downs, found that his income remained high despite the changes.

To generalize concerning the profits of a mining camp merchant is risky in the extreme. Unfortunately, many of the records which could shed light on this question have not been preserved, but the following serve as an indication of the business volume and profit margin. Isaac Rogers, a clerk in a Virginia City, Montana store recorded in his diary the amount of gross income per day. He wrote on January 12, 1865, "only moderate amount," $153; a month later, "tolerably good," $191 and "a very fine day" $208. He also described a "very dull" day, $54 and "very poor" $38. James Miller, working as a clerk in the same town, noted on September 22, 1865, that sales for his firm totaled $41,386.93 for the past 41 days, averaging slightly over $1,000 per day. Other businesses displayed equally lucrative trade. The receipts of a first-class restaurant in Leadville in June, 1879, averaged $150 per day. A blacksmith recorded that he and a partner cleared $300 for two weeks' work. Laundering, despite stiff competition, was equally productive.[11] The figures quoted refer to camps which were going through a period of prosperity. Of these transactions, those mentioned by Rogers probably reflect more nearly normal trade activity than do those of Miller, which were taken at the height of the busy summer season.

More conservative figures appear when the camp passed beyond this stage. For one of the two major general stores of Caribou, Colorado, trade amounted to approximately $70,000 annually during a six-year period, while another business (cigar-newsstand) in the same town averaged $5,000 to $6,000 in trade per year over three years. A firm with stores in two camps did slightly better than this, netting $39,000 over a nine-month period. The net profit, for example, on the sale of most commodities ranged from 10 to 25 percent.[12] While these firms made money, other companies made little or no income and were forced to suspend operations. What made one man successful and another a failure depended on a combination of business acumen, work, and luck.

To make a success of his venture, the businessman had to surmount an assortment of difficulties. Securing the goods and freighting them to the camp only served as a starter. The market fluctuated seasonally, late fall and winter (except Christmas) being the slack periods and reflecting the nature of prospecting and mining. Prices vacillated sharply at first; as Jerry Bryan, an Illinois prospector in the Black Hills in 1876, noted, "Everything fluctuates here except Whiskey and Labor. Whiskey is at the top notch and labor at the lowest." [13] They leveled as the supply caught up with the demand. Still the merchant had to be careful to prevent overstocking and glutting the market.

Business rivals and cutthroat methods seriously challenged the merchants' prospects. The alluring dream of wealth brought businessmen in large numbers to the camp, often beyond justification and need. Too much competition served to eliminate the more unstable firms, but also weakened those which remained. This happened to the lumber industry around Leadville. Lumber, always a needed commodity, was in particularly short supply; this situation resulted in 30 sawmills, employing about 1,000 men, by early 1879. Increased production and competition had driven the price of lumber down from fifty dollars per thousand feet in March to eighteen in June. By then one-third of the mills were standing idle, but the remaining owners confidently predicted an upswing in business.[14] "To the victor belong the spoils" guided and justified the actions of these nineteenth century entrepreneurs.

In this climate of local rugged individualism, each merchant matched his wits against his neighbor's to secure customers. Various promotional schemes were tried. Offering discounts for cash purchases and catch-phrase advertising, such as goods "all at bottom prices" and "quick sales and small profits," proved two of the most popular and lasting methods. Stores remained open seven days a week, doing a brisk trade on Sundays. Rival firms launched price wars. To attract the public, raffles offered everything from sewing machines to billiard tables as prizes. Occasionally, an owner used this method to raffle the entire stock of his store. In a slightly different approach—to cut down overhead and thereby lower prices— merchants collected accounts at the end of each month.

The bane of existence to businessman and tradesman was credit and credit buying. Business could be conducted on this principle, cash and carry, or a combination of both. The second guaranteed a stable income and less risk, but in the speculative nature of the mining economy, credit prevailed as a fundamental condition. Miners might be paid once a month, purchasing on account until payday, or those who worked their own claims might not hit pay dirt, necessitating credit to continue operations. Mining companies ran up bills while waiting for richer ore or more money from the stockholders; the merchants themselves used the system to stock their own stores. If these debts could be collected at the end of a month or within an allotted time, the creditor suffered no loss and had to an extent stimulated economic growth. If, however, a mine failed, or the debtor simply decamped without paying his arrears, the merchant found himself saddled with a loss. The normal practice of carrying a debt on the books for months, while the storekeeper collected a portion of it, and the debtor in turn received more goods on credit, only made matters worse. The creditor found himself in a dilemma. He could continue to extend credit, hoping finally to achieve payment, or he could stop it and face the possibility of losing the tardy customer with the debt still unpaid. A final recourse remained—placing the account in the hands of a lawyer for collection—but by then the merchant had accepted the unlikelihood of total or even partial payment.

Businessmen were certainly well aware of this situation. Notices appeared frequently in the newspapers, requesting all people in debt to a certain firm to come forward and settle their accounts. Overextension of credit weakened a firm seriously and could push it into closure. The question of competition within a small area of limited population persisted. If one merchant offered credit, the rest, out of necessity, had to follow. To the buyer, the life of the mining frontier was to an extent based upon credit and there seemed nothing wrong with the system.

The problem received frequent comment in the newspapers, both in editorials and in letters from merchants with suggestions and plans to avoid it. The buyer was reminded that debts build up and was encouraged to endure present inconveniences and temporary deprivations rather than to suffer the embarrassment of too many liabilities. The effect of credit buying on prices was damaging, for the merchant increased the price to allow for expected loss. The blame for the system was placed realistically by the merchants on themselves. Ways to avoid the worst features were plentiful, including thirty-day limits, black lists of "bilks" sent to other camps, and organization within a camp against "lame ducks." The frustration of the merchants and the magnitude of the problem appear clearly in the following newspaper excerpts:

> As business is conducted here today probably one-fourth of all the customers are a loss and a burden to the dealer. If he could assume to rid himself of their favors his business would at once assume a healthier and better shape. It is not individuals alone who belong in the dead-head procession. There are some calling themselves businessmen and some call themselves mining companies who are just as much entitled to a place on the 'black list.' [15]

> Probably no more unfortunate business system could be introduced into a mining community than that of general credit—or more properly 'jawbone'—for that is what it amounts to in far too many cases. Nothing so completely clogs the wheels of mercantile prosperity as credit. . . . Its demoralizing effects can be seen at every turn. It is the parent of extravagance, profligacy, indolence and peonage.[16]

Protest as they might, the merchants were unable to stem the tide of credit, for primarily it reflected the speculative and optimistic ideals which underlay the economic philosophy of the mining frontier. Credit in all its aspects, from mining stocks to grocery accounts, provided capital for development.

A handicap in the commercial world of the mining frontier was the failure of a banking system to develop as rapidly as the rest of the community. Banks would have been a stabilizing factor, particularly in the chaotic 1860s. The primary function of the bank, that of providing a source of credit, was not what the miner necessarily wanted his bank to be. Credit could be found elsewhere. He looked upon a bank as a deposit-exchange establishment, since earlier the store was an exchange for gold, and the safe was a depository for valuables. The bank was also considered a status symbol for the community. Eventually banks were established, but usually only after one to several years. Bankers seemed unwilling to venture into the financially unknown and raw frontier situation of the 1860s. An outstanding exception was the private mint and banking firm of Clark and Gruber in Denver, which opened in 1860, and had an excellent reputation throughout the West. With the further development of banking establishments in cities such as Denver, Boise, and Helena in the late sixties, the situation improved.

When a bank did appear, usually in the larger camps, it rendered typical services. These included purchasing gold and silver, accepting deposits, making loans, serving as a discount house for foreign currency, and as a clearing house for drafts on banks throughout the United States. Some went further and served as stock brokers, real estate agents, and even had their own assay offices. Anyone who borrowed money faced a high interest rate, particularly during the boom period, when fluid reserves were small and demands great. Reportedly, rates reached 25 percent per month, although a more common rate was 10 percent. At least one bank went so far as to charge its customers one percent per month on all gold dust deposited in the vault for safekeeping.[17]

For both the banker and the depositor, risks existed in this day before Federal insurance. With little or no regulation, some banks started on a shoestring almost as a speculative venture, while others were victims of foolish banking practices, such as speculative loans. Even what seemed to be a very sound loan to a well-established mining company carried with it a certain amount of speculation not found in ordinary banking transactions. With this instability in the background, banks were vulnerable to runs, which, if prolonged, inevitably compelled the closing of their doors. Once the rumor of short funds started, it spread at a panic rate among depositors who had no guarantee to protect their money. It took a person of steady nerves to resist the temptation to take his money out, just in case. Bogus checks threatened the banker, and this threat was partially responsible for the practice of discounting a certain percentage or in refusing to accept those drawn on unknown banks.[18]

The businessman, whether banker or merchant, made a noticeable contribution to the success of the mining frontier. Besides being a community leader, he encouraged the development of the entire region. William Andrews Clark, later one of Montana's copper kings, made his early wealth in merchandising, investing wisely in Butte property which he helped to bring to prominence. Horace Tabor aided Denver and other less-known towns when he invested money in property and various civic schemes. Personal motives drove them, certainly, but the public benefited. From the earliest months almost to the very end, the businessman was actively involved in his community's existence, a rock around which much of its history swirled.

For the businessman and his fellow citizens, rapid communication with the outside world could mean the difference between a successful and an unsuccessful venture. The matter came to a head early in the isolated camps in the 1860s. The most desirable solution, a connection via telegraph, could be secured relatively quickly.

The telegraph reached the West in the 1860s, providing the best method of all-weather communication. The newspaper and commercial interests immediately gained by the completion of the line. The importance of this type of communication was readily shown by the speed at which the camps acquired it; for example, Virginia

City, Montana, secured a line in November, 1866. To induce a company to construct the system, stock was subscribed or money advanced by the local residents. Methods similar to those used to attract a railroad were employed, and despite the fact that the monetary requirements for a telegraph were less, the problem of collecting pledges frequently delayed actual work. Lamented the editor of the *Black Hills Pioneer*, October 14, 1876, "Shame! Shame! citizens of Deadwood, to think that so great a boon is near and inertia should prevent you from seizing it, and that you hold tight your purse strings against public enterprise. . . ." When the project was finally completed, a celebration served as a fitting climax—a chance to demonstrate the new device and promote local pride. Relatively easy to construct, the thin telegraph line spread over mountain and desert, helping to unite the region.

The telegraph, according to its most enthusiastic promoters, would readily enhance the prestige of the camp.[19] If that were true, what would happen if that most modern of inventions, the telephone, were installed? Less than a decade after Alexander Graham Bell's experiments produced a working model, the telephone reached the mining frontier. With alacrity the camps, realizing its usefulness, accepted it, perhaps for the sheer novelty, or simply to get a step ahead of the Easterner. Early efforts were made on a small scale to install lines from mine to mill, or from town to mine. Arousing much curiosity, the phones were further promoted by public and private demonstrations. Agents then circulated throughout neighboring districts to encourage similar lines. Eventually, if the town prospered, telephones would be placed in other mines, stores, and finally in homes.

In the year 1880, three of the 148 telephone exchanges listed in the United States census were located in mining camps. This did not represent a very large percentage of the total, roughly one-fiftieth. Considering, however, the fact that two of the camps—Leadville and Deadwood—had been in existence less than five years and the other, Park City, Utah, less than fifteen, and all three had smaller populations than most of the other cities being served, the accomplishment was remarkable. The novelty of the device produced many interesting experiences for local people, including concerts from one or several points for all those who cared to pick up their receivers and listen. Keeping the lines repaired in the face of severe mountainous winter weather tested the endurance of the linemen. Yet telephones continually gained in popularity, for they were one of the best ways to end the isolated existence of the scattered camps and mines.[20]

The telegraph and telephone represented permanence, the advance of civilization, and modernization to the inhabitant of the mining community. Modernization, particularly, meant progress, for the Westerner did get a jump on the Easterner. With the coming of these two innovations another segment of the frontier passed away. The communication revolution, for instance, changed business methods, mining, and law enforcement and indirectly, if not directly, affected the everyday existence of the people.

Community self-respect was enhanced by the mature status the camp had achieved and the forward steps being taken. The newspaper and local leaders were not willing to allow such progress to be hidden and unabashedly promoted their camp. The lengths to which they went to publicize its virtues rivaled those of a modern chamber of commerce. Civic pride demanded it, but an element of necessity was involved. A camp had to promote itself and its mines if it hoped to continue a progressive existence; otherwise newer and seemingly richer districts would lure away money and settlers.

The best illustration is to follow the efforts of one camp. Caribou, Colorado, was isolated against the backbone of the Rocky Mountains, twenty miles from a railroad. To encourage investment and publicize its attributes, the residents used several promotional techniques. Almost from the first year of its existence, Caribou ores were displayed at territorial and national fairs and exhibits. Samples sent to the 1876 Centennial Exhibition in Philadelphia won awards for two of the mines. Perhaps one of the better publicity

stunts staged by any camp was devised for President Grant's 1873
Western tour. When Grant alighted at the entrance to the Teller
House in nearby Central City, he found the walk paved with
Caribou silver bricks. Tourists were invited to come enjoy the
scenery and benefit from the "pure and invigorating" air of the
10,000 foot elevation. It greatly worried some of the residents that
for much of the camp's life it had no newspaper. Scarcely, it seemed,
could they be known abroad without this voice, yet they had to get
along as best they could without it.[21] The success or failure of all
these ventures cannot be measured, yet all helped to publicize the
region and in this respect had a certain lasting effect.

The blessings derived from this type of activity could be mixed.
Misrepresentation brought discredit to the town and the district.
The stigma attached might permanently injure development, and
continued and overuse of hackneyed praises rendered them empty
and meaningless in the public's eye. The risk of deception had to
be run in the skirmishes between mining districts to promote their
own welfare.

Competition of this sort produced a natural rivalry and jealousy
between camps. Local papers derided other camps and were answered in kind. The polemics which ensued intensified as threat
followed counterthreat. Accusations and disparaging remarks were
thrown with abandon, as the following sample shows. Each quo-
tation reflected the feeling toward the new bonanza queen, Leadville.

> has a man murdered for breakfast daily, and has only three or four
> paying carbon ore deposits. Leadville has turned out just as we
> told you it would. (Deadwood)
>
> 'home to let' seen on every street and at every turn. (Park City,
> Utah)
>
> Ouray [Colorado] can crow about her weather and mines if she
> cannot boast a population of 12,000 and a murder every week.[22]

These comments reflect both in-state and out-of-state attitudes. Rivalry within a state or district probably involved more combative-

ness when both political and commercial rivalry came to a head. Sarcasm, untruth, and slander were utilized, depending on the editor and issue. Competition between camps—dormant for years— might be quickly awakened when one threatened the other. Any district was markedly sensitive when its population was being drawn away to a newer and richer strike. In defense of the life of the community, any means seemed justifiable.

Aroused emotions and damaged civic pride were not the only results of these antagonisms. At times the newspaper war turned into an outright struggle for survival. Consider, for example, when Virginia City, New Mexico, challenged its neighbor, Elizabethtown, for dominance. Virginia City represented a promotional attempt by (among others) the Governor of the Territory, Robert B. Mitchell, to secure profit from the miners' trade, real estate sales, and eventually to dominate the district. Its presence was resented by Elizabethtown, which was older and nearer to the mines. Although hopeful reports were published in Santa Fe papers about Virginia City's progress, its rival clearly forged ahead, finally forcing the complete abandonment of the site.[23] Not all struggles ended in such a clearcut victory—more often one camp emerged with a decided advantage. The conflict between mining communities could be as cutthroat as any between the great commercial rivals in other parts of the United States.

Eleven

Community Leadership

In any community certain personalities emerged as civic, social, business, cultural, and political leaders. Though not always the ones who received the publicity, they were the movers, the arousers of public awareness. In the relatively young mining camp, a virgin field opened to them, yet this very youth complicated their task. While no entrenched social or political order existed, vested inter ests pressured for favoritism. The opportunity to chart community development progressively was further hindered by civic inertia, scarcity of funds, and the transitory nature of the residents. Finally, an unseen, but real, threat lurked in the background—the uncertain future of the camp. This insecurity could be only temporarily pushed aside, despite optimistic hopes and bright promises.

The newspaper editor tried to face this ultimate worry realistically and arouse his readers to do likewise. The power of the pen and press made him one of the camp's most influential men. Short of the mining and merchant princes, few could match his potential power in directing the affairs of the community. This was the era of personal journalism in the true sense of the term. As Richard Hughes, newspaperman for many years in Deadwood and Rapid City, South Dakota, described it: "The term 'Personal Journalism' is one that has long been familiar, but it is doubtful if it ever elsewhere reached the limit it was stretched in Deadwood and between the Deadwood Papers and the Central Herald, published at Central." [1] Deadwood, White Oaks, South Pass, Pinal, any of a thousand camp newspapers displayed a similar trait. A vital part of his community, the editor would enter the lists in favor of any number of community improvements, or oppose anything which he felt detrimental. His interests were varied, but focused on the camp. An examination of the *Owyhee Avalanche,* Silver City, Idaho, August, 1865 to June, 1866, found the editor promoting better trade routes and free roads, favoring removal of the Indians, stressing the need for fire protection, and opposing hurdy houses. He wanted the streets cleaned, a theater built, good public schools, progressive teachers, a brass band, and the organization of the "elements of good society" to "make the camp home like." Reformer, gadfly, crusader were all terms that could be applied to him.

A community defender, the unofficial chamber of commerce, also described tasks which the conscientious editor took upon himself. The natural rivalry between camps could easily become a personal war between two editors. The heights and depths of mining camp journalism were achieved in these no-holds-barred fights:

> And yet this penny-a-liner of the *Herald* [Helena, Montana], a conceited hatchling scarcely yet out of the shell, . . . comes up pompously and claims to be the worthy organ of the Union People of Montana. Bah! Its egotism is only equalled by its impudence.[2]

> The *Post* until the *Herald* came along had its own way and virtually monopolized the printing business of Montana. Now this aspect of affairs has changed. . . . The consequence is, that 'Dilton' [Daniel Tilton, *Post* editor] feels exceedingly sanctimonious over the humiliation. . . . But the *Herald* with a commendable zeal and enterprise, has exerted every energy, and at an immense expense, to obtain the latest news, both foreign and local, in order to make it the *best and most* reliable newspaper in the Territory.[3]

This was personal journalism as it existed in Montana in the 1860s. Virginia City, once the principal camp in the territory but now declining, was being surpassed by its chief rival, Helena, a situation which added bitter fuel to the fire. As a community defender and promoter, the editor was allowed almost any means at his disposal, from insulting fellow editors to virtual untruths about other camps. The editor of the *Sweetwater Mines,* June 6, 1868, in defending South Pass, Wyoming, against the same *Helena Herald,* observed:

> Notwithstanding the false reports, and willful misrepresentations, which have been circulated concerning our mines in this Sweetwater country, they full come up to the expectations of all the experienced and sensible men, who have come here. . . . The *Herald* a virulent and insinuating sheet, but fortunately void of influence, . . . comes out again, its columns frought with falsehoods concerning this country. . . . We coincide with hundreds of others in predicting a brilliant future for Sweetwater and in denouncing the *Herald,* as a scurrilous sheet, hardly worthy of notice.

The mines, in fact, did not live up to expectations nor was the *Helena Herald* so bad as pictured. It was actually one of the better newspapers, but in doing its duty to Helena it aroused the ire of all competing camps.

The editor, as a political figure, on occasion became a state power, although he usually remained only a local influence. While only twelve of the papers examined stated and maintained support for one party, these being evenly divided between the Democrats and Republicans, virtually all were interested in politics. The most vocal party sheets generally were found where close competition existed. Mavericks in supporting candidates and issues, the rest might, nevertheless, lean toward one party or the other. The Republicans did better in this respect than their opponents. The papers made their influence felt by campaigning fervently for favorite issues or men. As the only paper in the camp, its reporting and editorializing played a major significance in shaping public opinion. Such actions carried with them a certain amount of risk. Irate candidates just might take their feelings out directly on the person of a criticizing editor. Subscription cancellations were another form of retaliation against the paper.

Constant surveillance over the community kept the editor in continual controversy, yet it was good for the camp. He had to expect this as part of his job. It could lead to threatening letters

or more dire personal consequences. Legh R. Freeman, editor of
the *Frontier Index,* had his office burned by a mob in 1868, and
David C. Collier, editor of the *Register* (Central City), was attacked by the city attorney after criticizing that gentleman.[4] Hard
work and long hours made up their daily existence. On the smaller
papers, the editor's duties encompassed writing much of the copy,
reading proof, and probably aiding in the work of printing each
issue. Besides politics, a variety of community affairs, such as the
school board and local committees, enlisted his available spare moments. Probably he joined a lodge and took an active part in it.
In the course of a lifetime, at least one move to a more promising
location was undertaken to improve the financial opportunities.
Nor was it unusual to work at other jobs to make ends meet during slack periods.[5]

The rewards for these services varied. Monetary considerations
were supplemented by certain fringe benefits from local merchants,
including Christmas turkeys, cigars, ice cream, and assorted liquid
refreshment. In return the donor expected and usually received a
nice compliment in the paper concerning his business. Of a more
intangible nature was the satisfaction of being a part of taming
the frontier, of building a community and guiding developments
therein. Those who enjoyed wielding the power of the pen and
helping to influence the course of events found a promising outlet
in mining camp journalism. Some had too narrow vision, while
others dreamed for far too much. The mining West, nevertheless,
was a better place for their having been there.

The same statement may be made for the minister and teacher,
although neither was the public figure that the editor was. Both
worked behind the scenes; the minister was generally more influential than the teacher. For the minister, arrival at the camp and
the gathering of a congregation was only his first task. Socially
and culturally, he needed to make his church one of the camp's
progressive centers. A ready-made opportunity existed for the members of a congregation to wield a solid front for community and

individual betterment. The active church and minister stood in the forefront of reform, be it for better schools or closing the red-light district. Seldom have more obstacles been placed in the path of a minister in seeking these goals.

Many obstacles, but particularly finances, hindered the minister. The work of the church could not be carried on without money. Difficult as it was to raise funds for the minister's salary, it was even harder to find it for other demands. Collecting the pledges, so easily given, meant a long day's work with indifferent results. Colorado's Reverend Joseph Machebeuf resorted to locking the doors of one of his churches following mass and letting no one out until the question had been settled. George Parsons, collecting for his minister in Tombstone, wrote in his journal, "All on my list must pay or be denounced and scratched by me unless for good reason." Interestingly, a visiting minister could often secure a better offering than the regular man. Salaries, low at best, failed to meet living costs, and it was not unusual to find the pastor supplementing his income by working at another job, such as mining —at least part of the week. In the end, the program of the church was curtailed and limited by the amount of money available. A sad commentary on the nature of a congregation occurred when, as a last resort, at least one pastor, in order to procure his back salary, had to sell the church and lot upon which it stood.[6]

Although foreign to modern fund drive methods, lotteries were found to be a useful device, thus reconciling gambling and Christianity. Combining social gatherings and money raising functions, the church sponsored choir concerts, fairs, ice cream sociables, and bazaars. Money was thus acquired less painlessly, while the donors had a pleasant time.[7] More important in the long view, these activities provided accepted outlets where young and old could gather. The church played a major role in providing entertainment and sociability in opposition to the saloon-red-light district. Its attention had to be continually focused on the youth in the hope that, along with the family environment, enough guidance and pressure could

be brought to bear on the children to keep them from the "prim-
rose path," to use the Victorian phrase.

Sunday, traditionally the day set aside for worship, was the high
point of the Christian's week. The minister encountered problems
even here, at services, both from within the church and without.
Interruptions could be expected from babies or perchance someone's dozing off in the middle of the sermon. But drunks, cats,
dogs (individually and together), and even a deer distracted services at one time or another. One disruption of a worship service
is aptly shown in a description of the misadventures of one Big
Jake, who sadly mistook the church for some other establishment:

> Seeing the ladies and gentlemen present, he stepped into the door
> just as Father Antonio said 'Now we will sing.' This was con-
> firmatory of Jake's first impressions and he sang out 'Sing, sing!
> I'm better than a raw hand myself on the basso, but you just wait
> till the dance begins and I'll make you know that there hain't no
> feather weight in Arizona that can hold a candle to Jake,' . . . at
> the same time executing a double shuffle that made the house rat-
> tle. The astonishment of those present can better be imagined than
> described. Jake wasn't long in comprehending his mistake, and
> suggested that firing him out wasn't among the necessities as he
> would go out himself, and he didn't want no check from the door-
> keeper neither.[8]

More serious in the long run, however, was the fact that Sunday
was not the Sabbath *per se* but a wide-open, business-as-usual day.

> Today showed me an entirely new phase of life. There was noth-
> ing visible to remind a person in the slightest degree that it was
> Sunday. Every store, saloon, and dancing hall was in full blast.
> Hacks running, auctioneering, mining and indeed every business,
> is carried on with much more zeal than on week days. It made me
> heartsick to see it.[9]

Thus did James Miller describe Sunday, June 11, 1865. Nor was it
much different in later years. According to the *Pinal Drill,* February 26, 1881, the number of people at the race track outnumbered
the worshipers by about twelve to one. Outsiders came into town,

thus providing a larger possible congregation, but the attractions were many and the noise of the day could be distracting to the service itself. An evening meeting confronted similar problems, although entertainment now replaced business as the prime preoccupation. Against these almost universal conditions the churches made little headway. Sunday closing movements were tried but failed, since volunteer agreements were unable to withstand the pressure of a profitable day's trade. Legal restrictions against saloons operating on Sunday proved more successful, but did not really touch the root of the trouble.[10] This lack of observance of, or perhaps respect for, the Sabbath helped convince many visitors that the mining communities held very little regard for religion.

Even more than the minister, the teacher's influence was directed to the youthful segment of the camp's population. This was primarily a woman's occupation. Teaching at this time did not have the status it has since acquired, nor the salaries to tempt men to enter it in large numbers. Far too many of the teachers taught only as a temporary occupation until something more lucrative came along. To characterize all in this manner, however, unfairly pictures those dedicated people, both men and women, who devoted their whole lives to the challenge, providing very competent and, at times, outstanding instruction. Particularly in the smaller settlements, the teacher served in a multitude of capacities, including janitor and carpenter, in order to keep the school in operation, for funds did not exist to hire other help.

The major drawback to securing qualified personnel was the salary, which did not measure up to the scale being offered for other jobs in the community, and at times hardly met the cost of living. The frequently poor financial condition of the school treasury failed to provide added security. For a teacher's pay to be several months in arrears was not an unknown occurrence. Without the advantage of room and board, often included in the contract, the teacher's plight might have forced the closing of the school. No specific statement can be made concerning salary levels during the period of this study, but the government census of 1880 reported that the average monthly amount paid in the United States was $36.39. In the eight states and territories under discussion, the salaries ranged from $30.67 in New Mexico to $76.58 in neighboring Arizona. Six of the eight averaged above the national mean. Many factors which did not pertain to mining communities were involved in arriving at these figures, yet they serve as an indication of prevailing wages. When it is considered that a miner in a good week could make $20 to $30, and a store clerk at least $50 a month without the duties and responsibilities of teaching, a better perspective is acquired. Men received a higher salary in Butte, Montana, for example, which in 1878 paid them $78.50 per month, as opposed to $65 for the women.[11] Such a disparity between sexes was not unusual for the era.

As public servants, teachers found themselves under continual scrutiny and the objects of public censure. Incompetence and inadequate preparation were sources of great criticism, while individual faults reflected on the community indirectly. Primitive conditions, isolation, low salaries, insecure financial arrangements, and the distance from training centers did not induce qualified applicants to come, and the camps could not or would not arouse themselves to do much about it. As a correspondent wrote in the White Oaks, *New Mexico Interpreter,* April 12, 1889, "severe pedagogic tact and skillfulness are needed nowhere more than among young denizens of the frontier." The schoolmarm most easily solved the problem. Without a great deal of training but in need of work, a single or unattached woman found the camp a good place to hunt for a husband. This added attraction hindered the completion of more than one contract once the matrimonial knot was tied. More than the rest of the community's populace, she was susceptible to criticism by stepping beyond the accepted norms of the day. One irate taxpayer was shocked to discover that the teacher had fallen into the dangerous custom of reading dime novels. He wanted it stopped posthaste and the lady in question removed.[12]

A good catch for any young woman was the eligible mining man. The mine owner, engineer, superintendent, and even foreman stood above the ordinary miner in the social hierarchy and community leadership. The bonanza kings, the mining millionaires, controlled the camps from behind the scenes. Their mines and money, more than anything else, supported the local economy. Next to them in the power structure stood the less wealthy owner and the superintendents of the large mines. Socially, these people were the accepted class; their influence was felt in areas other than social and mining economics. Money and influence carried weight in politics. Newspapers, even if not at least partially owned by mining money, were sensitive to their views and pressures. These men branched out to become silent or open partners in various enterprises. There probably was not one person in the camp whose life was not in some way affected by this group.

For many of the *nouveau riche* the isolated, urban existence of the camp became too confining. They deserted the place where their fortunes had been made for the big city. San Francisco and Denver had their millionaires' sections, where mansions lavishly reflected their owners' wealth. Society, politics, and business all took on new meanings for them. The East Coast and Europe beckoned others to broaden their horizons and break into the accepted social set. As they grew out of touch with their previous existence, their influence did not necessarily wane. In their place came corporation managers and superintendents who did their employers' bidding. Replacing the personal touch came impersonal industrialization and capitalist-labor relationships. Here were sowed the seeds which led to open conflict in some camps by the end of the century.

Uncle Sam also appeared in the mining camp. From securing town and mineral patents to providing mail service, he was involved in community life. The Federal official in the form of the marshal, assayer, surveyor, soldier, and judge helped bring order and stability. Alternately damned and praised, they represented the Federal government's interests and rights.

The news lines from the outside world—represented by the post office—most clearly touched everyone's life. Complaints about the mails, first heard with the rush of 1859, were still being aired at the close of the 1880s. It meant a great deal to these people, away from home and friends, to receive their mail. The formation of long waiting lines (in which places were sometimes sold) at mail time aptly testified to this, as does the comment of a fifty-niner: "Write *at least* once a month, for [I] assure you my interest in home matters can never be abated, let the distance between us be ever so great." [13] It remained impossible for the postal service to be omniscient in following the wanderings of the prospector and miner. It often was hard enough just to provide service to the established camps. All communities, big and small, wanted mail delivery. After petitioning Washington and what seemed interminable waiting, the camp received but one or two deliveries per week. This was not enough to satisfy the residents and petitioning would start all over again for something better—if possible, daily service. "Red tape formalities" by the bureaucracy in Washington angered these urban frontiersmen, for nothing but the best was good enough. The future, bright with expectancy, should not be hampered by the United States government's failure to provide service.

The problems faced by the post office department, especially until late 1867, when the Union Pacific tracks from the east reached the Rocky Mountain region, were staggering. Vast distances of unsettled land, Indians, and weather presented obstacles which were further complicated by vague addresses, mushrooming camps, and mobile inhabitants. The whole system had to be built from scratch to meet the instantaneous needs of an urban frontier. From the very start, it was a continual struggle to catch up, while simultaneously trying to keep up. In the 1860s the provoking irregularity of mails was somewhat accepted; not so in the following two decades. Frustration was answered with sarcasm.

> And with it only once a week to know that mail sometimes never gets through and at other times is long enough in reaching its destination to have made a trip round the world does not help the situation in the least.[14]

> This is, we believe, a Star Route, but from the erratic nature of its course it would seem to be more properly classed amongst the comet family.[15]

Protest meetings would be held, more petitions and letters fired to Washington concerning real or imaginary post office sins. To meet demands, mail was carried by snowshoe, pack mule, stage, and train, but the impatient public was not to be pacified until the day that regular, on-time deliveries were inaugurated.[16] This might never happen, certainly not until the country became settled, and by then many of the camps had become relics of the past.

The post office was a community gathering place, especially near the hour of the mail's arrival. To the lucky merchants nearby, it offered an excellent opportunity to increase business; therefore, the location of this government edifice was of prime importance. A so-called post office war might ensue, with different merchants trying to have it situated near their establishment. Free rent or land did not seem too big a price to pay. This was Uncle Sam's great symbol in the mining community. The source of profit for a few, agitation for others, it provided the majority with a source of expectation.

Some mention should be made of the women who came to the mining camps. They did not differ from other pioneering women of the nineteenth century who helped change the whole character of the frontier. Dissatisfied with the primitive conditions, rawness, and abject materialism which characterized the uninhibited masculine world of the mining community, they went to work to improve it. Before they finished, the old way of life had been swept out of existence. In its place came their version of Victorian America. They struggled to establish the social and cultural values once known in former homes, and even in little matters, such as painted cabins, shaving, and changing shirts more often, they made their influence felt.

Nothing outstanding in their character separated them from other women. They possessed the same fears, desires, dreams, and ideals of any age. But because they were fewer in number, they evoked greater distinction and homage. As a result, at least partially, of this, women received respect and even privileges not given their Eastern sisters. Mrs. Esther M. Morris of South Pass City, Wyoming, for example, became America's first woman justice of the peace in 1870. A great deal of respect came from their willingness to share the frontier life of their husbands. They worked beside the men, if needed, sparing the time from the never ending tasks of a frontier housewife and mother. One fifty-niner wrote in later years about her experiences:

> Really the women did more in the early days than the men. There was so much for them to do, the sick to take care of. I have had so many unfortunate men shot by accident, brought to my cabin to take care of. There were so many men who could not cook and did not like men's cooking and would insist upon boarding where there was a woman and they would board there all they could.[17]

To make what they did look glamorous and romantic would be an injustice. Toil, loneliness, and privation played a major role in their lives. Sadness was theirs, too, as they watched husbands and sons die in the mines, or children succumb to the epidemics which ravaged the camps. Youth and beauty faded early before such an onslaught. The English poet, James Thomson, who lived in Central City, Colorado, for seven months in 1872, drew a word portrait of the women he saw:

> They seem very respectable as far as I have observed. As a rule they are slender, dress lightly, with hats and bright scarves, so that they all look girlish till you get close to them.
>
> They are more French than English in taste, I fancy, and some of them would be very graceful if the absurd boots did not make

them hobble broken-backed with their Dolly Varden bunches behind. They incline to leanness, which one fears must grow somewhat scraggy with age, just as our fine women grow rather cor-
pulent.[18]

To the generation of women who lived in the mining communities a great debt is owed. In little ways, but with significant strides,
they improved the conditions for those who followed. Without all
of them, both proper and "frail sisters," where would the camp have
traveled? Their courage, persistence, endurance, adaptability, cheer-
fulness, and femininity sparked the whole community, moved it
beyond the mundane.

In their own way, the fraternal lodges promoted law, civil government, and the betterment of the community. Not only did they
provide a forum for men to meet and discuss local affairs, but a
vehicle for civic action and for individual improvement. The lodges
had come West with the first rush to the gold fields, and individual
members came from all over the country. Before long, a few brothers became acquainted and met together to establish ties with the
national organization and open their own chapter. While many
different lodges appeared in the camps, the most popular were the
Masons, Odd Fellows, Ancient Order of United Workmen, and
Knights of Pythias. At least one of these four would be organized
in the community, and probably members of all these and others
were scattered throughout the district.

The motives for organizing and the functions served varied considerably. They certainly provided a continuity and a sense of belonging for the members, as they drifted throughout the mining
West from camp to camp and year to year. Each lodge provided
social activities for its members, such as dances, parties, and dinners.
They offered association with men of similar cultural backgrounds
and perhaps political affiliations—a key to an unknown community.
More than this, they were benevolent and even beneficiary organizations, aiding less fortunate members and their families. Lodge
cemeteries were organized and maintained for the brotherhood to

find a last resting place. Special life insurance policies for members were another inducement to join. In the Ancient Order of United Workmen, for example, each man upon joining received a beneficiary policy of $2,000, which cost on the average $16 per year.[19] The dangerous work engaged in by a large proportion of the population made it almost mandatory for the family man to provide some aid for his wife and children in case an accident should befall him. In that day of fly-by-night insurance companies and high rates by respectable firms, the fraternal society provided a good substitute. Here one could count on his brothers to fulfill the obligations of the association, not some unknown stranger. Where else could the miner and merchant secure social and benevolent benefits for so little money?

In addition to these activities, the lodges made a contribution in the cultural field by sponsoring lectures and shows open to all. The importance of fraternal organizations in the community cannot be understressed. They provided charitable work (rivaling the church in this respect), represented an element of cohesion, permanence, and social control, and influenced social, political, and cultural development. The private and semiexclusive nature of the clubs even aggrandized the social aspirations of society. With all considered, the lodges had a comparatively greater impact on the community and were more popular than they have been since.

Similar to the fraternal organizations was another group of social-fraternal clubs which existed in the camps, a varied assortment with no common bonds. One club found frequently throughout the West, the Good Templars, humorously referred to as "water tanks," served the cause of temperance. Both men and women of good standing could join. Where foreign groups concentrated, they quite likely had their own clubs, for example, the German Turnverein societies and the Irish Fenians. The original rebellious purpose of the Fenians, to aid the Irish in overthrowing British control of Ireland, was satisfied in the camps by bombastic speeches and supplanted by social activities. The Grand Army of the Republic marched into the camps in the 1870s with posts, parades, and ceremonies. GAR motives were many—social, benevolent, political, and memorial, with its charitable activities eventually coming to equal, if not surpass, any other organization's. As a political pressure group, the veterans could not be outdone, although the camps had only a small voice in the national movement.

Each of these organizations had a stake in the mining camp, and each endeavored to improve the community. They worked not only internally, but externally. The camp itself was not initially a thing of beauty, unless naturally so. With the passage of time, however, an awareness of the need for civic improvement developed; the camp's outward appearance might not have mattered to a majority, but to a minority it was important. Attempts were made to improve it, to make it seem more like a settled town anywhere in the United States. Trees were conspicuously missing, either because they had been cut down for lumber, or because they did not grow in the area. Nothing would more quickly beautify the surroundings than to plant trees, along with shrubbery and perhaps grass. These were outward signs of civilized development, yet useful, and a source of pleasure.[20] Suggestions appeared in the newspapers relating to the construction of stone buildings for permanence and appearance. Removal of litter further enhanced the impression the visitor received when he or she arrived. Commendable as were these attempts for civic improvement, they did not always prove successful. Community-wide cooperation—vital to the program—seldom measured up to the task. Lack of money, as usual, hampered the program, and some camps made a start only to falter when mining declined. Certainly those people who based their future on the camp's continued existence desired to improve its appearance. Individual efforts were made and it would seem to be too harsh a judgment to state that in the average mining town there was, by deliberate intent, almost nothing beautiful, comfortable, or convenient.[21]

The editor, businessman, minister, and others openly or subtly guided local affairs and acted as community leaders. Social, political, and economic power rested in their hands; the decisions they made influenced not only the daily existence, but the future of the camp as well.

Twelve

Life Was Never Easy

Young America had come to the mining camp with high expectations, but realization of these dreams was often thwarted by circumstances unforeseen in the haste to gain these goals. Such mundane factors as the high cost of living, unhealthy living conditions, and lack of work depleted financial reserves and endangered physical well-being. Arriving in all the vigor of youth, many left within a few years, broken in spirit and body; one price was exacted on the people who came to the mining frontier. Few outside this group comprehended the toll or understood the personal sacrifices involved.

In the preceding chapters, a sketch has been drawn of the physical appearance of the mining camp—not a pretty picture despite attempts by the residents to improve it. Sanitation and public health, though recognized as issues of extreme importance in an urban environment, were not communally resolved. Natural drainage could not cope with the situation, and individuals were lax or negligent in self-regulation. Piles of offal, manure, and other filth accumulated in the alleys behind the business district. Trash of all descriptions was liberally scattered around the camp. The housewife, no more considerate, threw the garbage out in the backyard and allowed it to rot. Privies with shallow cess pools and vaults ranked perhaps as the greatest menace of all. In this disease-fermenting atmosphere, health was seriously threatened. The combination of putrid, rotten, decaying material and refuse produced a stench which hung over the camp and which would have been extremely offensive to later generations of Americans who were not accustomed to such conditions.

In the summer and fall, dust from the streets, mills, and mines added to the general discomfort. In the winter and spring, mud contributed its share. The summer months were the worst, for the warm sun brought into full strength all the odors which the cold of winter had helped to mask. With trees and natural shrubbery having been appropriated for other uses, erosion took place, so that a sudden shower might cascade mud, sand, and rocks into the camp. To be sure, the water washed away some of the filth but it was soon replaced.

Not a pretty picture, this camp scene, and the reader might be justified in declaring it too grim for any one camp. What cannot be denied is that all suffered to some extent, and in general, the larger the settlement, the more unfavorable the health conditions. Dysentery and diarrhea resulted from contaminated water, and even worse, typhoid, which swept through communities in epidemic proportions. Diphtheria, smallpox, scarlet fever, and other illnesses threatened both young and old. Before transportation improved, scurvy continued to be a menace in the winter-isolated camps. The common cold and sore throat were potentially dangerous, for even a mild cold weakened resistance and could lead to something far worse. Pneumonia, a dreaded killer at high altitudes, often resulted. These frontiersmen were not weak, unhealthy specimens susceptible to every illness, but in the crowded and unsanitary environment a host of diseases could emerge. Only the cautious and lucky citizen survived in this natural breeding ground of sickness.

The grim evidence supporting these statements can be found in any camp's cemetery. Walk through one and notice how many children are there, and if possible, compare death dates to see how many succumbed during an epidemic. Observe the number of adults who died in the relative prime of life. Old newspapers furnish further evidence of outbreaks, in the warnings which they gave concerning an illness then particularly prevalent.[1] Obituaries and short death notices provide further insights. That little was done to prevent the fundamental causes reflected a characteristic not only of the camps, but of American urban communities in general. The camps, while not behind the times, were not paragons of progress either.

Considering the period as a whole, one finds the medical profession well represented on the mining frontier. Most camps had their own doctors and even if they didn't, they usually had access to medical help from a nearby settlement. In a few of the smaller communities, in order to keep a physician, a retainer was voluntarily subscribed by the public or mine owners to supplement the regular income. Hospitals, though, were few and far between. The major problems in establishing them, as in so many other matters, were the lack of funds and the uncertain future of the district. During an epidemic such as smallpox, in which a danger of contagion existed, a temporary isolation ward was established and someone was hired to look after the patients. This was not the best medical method certainly, but the most economical and practical expedient in the circumstances. In those camps blessed with a hospital, a continual struggle was carried on to raise the necessary funds and to staff it with qualified people.

Dentists less frequently took up practice in the camps, not because aching teeth did not plague residents and a need for dental skills did not exist, but because a better practice could be built in the larger towns. Traveling dentists, appearing in the community for a specified period, filling cavities, pulling teeth, and providing other dental services, provided a substitute. To visit either the dentist or the doctor could be a harrowing experience, but the dentist seemed to be most vexing. Dental equipment and techniques still had a long way to go before minimizing inconveniences and solving the problems (intensified by the high altitudes) of pain-relieving drugs and anesthetics. The sufferer was left with the alternative of either submitting to the dentist or enduring a nagging toothache. The following poetic verses, entitled "My Dentist," while not meant to criticize the profession adversely, show what the patient had to endure.

> Who seats me in his easy chair,
> and hurts me more than I can bear,
> and pulls my tooth and doesn't care?
> My Dentist.
> Who lacerates my gums with files
> of different shapes and different styles,
> and coolly takes them out and smiles?
> My Dentist.
> Who twists his steel deep in my tooth,
> which makes me howl, and then, forsooth,
> Tells me 'the nerve's exposed,' in truth?
> My Dentist.[2]

The dentist, doctor, and other members of the medical profession who served the mining communities deserve a great deal of credit. Working under what were often primitive conditions, using whatever medicines and equipment were available, they made the lives of the people healthier and considerably more comfortable. In contrast, the gullible public too often turned in another direction. Medical quacks and traveling medicine shows made their spurious pitches. These men and their medicines promised to cure any and all illnesses, no matter how far advanced, to restore lost youth, and improve the general health of those willing to spend just a few pennies. Their total contribution was more harmful than beneficial.

The high cost of living in the camps aroused more comments and seemed to the participants more threatening than any possible health menace. Visitors and residents complained about the price of food, rooms, and merchandise. A visitor to Central City, Colorado, in 1866, thought it was the most outrageously expensive place to live in the state. He felt that you paid more and got less for your money than in any other part of the world.[3] Six years later an Englishman, decidedly less emotional about the matter, wrote that the well-stocked stores carried nearly everything at a very dear price, with the exception of, as he stated it, the mere necessities of life, which were almost as cheap as in England.[4] Reports from other communities soberly presented similar facts. The reasons for this fall into three categories: isolation, economic dependence, and transportation costs. While the coming of the railroad and increased local agricultural production helped somewhat to decrease the cost of living, the average still remained higher than in the East.

Examination of figures in the following charts indicates several trends. Living expenses in the new camps, in relation to the established ones, were proportionately higher throughout the period, although both declined from the 1860 levels. The effect of increased agricultural production is clearly reflected, for example, in the cost of flour and eggs in Central City. The coming of the railroad and the corresponding connection to older agrarian areas naturally reduced some prices, as indicated by the 1873 price lists for the same community. Unfortunately, the reporter from Elizabethtown, New Mexico, failed to list most of the market prices, but flour at ten dollars indicates that food prices in that already agriculturally established territory were lower than in its neighbors to the north. Silver Reef, located in Mormon farming country, shows the same result. Comparing these lists with those of Homer, New York, and Leavenworth, Kansas, one finds a marked difference. Even Denver, Colorado, while not a camp but the product of the mining frontier, had lower prices than the surrounding mining communities, although the difference was not so great. The camps occasionally undersold Denver, as is shown when comparing it to Leadville.

Room and board were correspondingly high, but the reasons should not be hard to see—demand and the expense of food. The cost of room and board per week at a boarding house in Silver City, Idaho, in 1865 was reported to be $18 per week; fourteen years later in Globe, Arizona, it was $11. Meals in boarding houses cost from 50¢ to $1 each.[5] These should be considered only as examples and not as standards for the entire frontier.

Despite the stories of fabulous discoveries, the mining frontier

COST OF LIVING

	Potatoes (lb)	Butter (lb)	Eggs (doz)	Dried Apples (lb)	Flour (cwt)	
Camps less than two years old						
Virginia City, Montana	20¢	85¢	—	46¢	$24-26.50	Sept., 1864*
South Pass, Wyoming	25¢	$1	$2	50¢	$30	March, 1868
Elizabethtown, New Mexico	—	—	—	—	$10	April, 1868
Leadville, Colorado	1-1¼¢	25-40¢	18-35¢	7¢	$6	April, 1879
Tombstone, Arizona	4½¢	—	—	18¢	$6	July, 1880
Camps two years old or more						
Idaho City, Idaho	15¢	$1.25	$2	37¢	$30	Feb., 1865
Helena, Montana	—	$.75-1.25	—	30¢	$9-15	Nov., 1866*
Butte, Montana	4¢	50¢	40¢	—	$5	April, 1878
Deadwood, South Dakota	1½¢	35¢	35¢	17¢	$5.75-6.25	Aug., 1879
Pinal, Arizona	4½-6¢	50-60¢	50-65¢	—	$4.40-5.50	July, 1881
Silver Reef, Utah	2½-3¢	35-40¢	35¢	—	—	April, 1882
Non-mining communities						
Homer, New York	50¢ (bushel)	33¢	18¢	—	—	1870
Leavenworth, Kansas	—	25¢	25¢	10-12½¢	$2.50-3.75	June, 1870
Denver, Colorado	2½-2¾¢	20-35¢	18-25¢	—	$3.25-3.50	March, 1880*

* Wholesale prices.

Variation in cost of living within one camp: Central City, Colorado

	1863 (Oct.)	1865 (Aug.)	1867 (Dec.)	1873 (Nov.)
Flour (cwt)	$8-10	$22	$12-15	$4.50
Eggs (doz)	$.65-1.00	$2	$1	40¢
Dried apples (lb)	16-20¢	30¢	30¢	15¢
Butter (lb)	35-50¢	50¢	—	40¢
Potatoes (lb)	6¢	50¢	6¢	1½¢

The higher prices for goods in 1865 reflect the Indian war which had started in late 1864, cutting off supplies and decreasing agricultural production in 1865. Food costs jumped throughout the territory.

was primarily a wage earner's settlement. The number of men who became owners of paying mines was probably less than one percent of the total. The owners of businesses, individual tradesmen, and others who were self-employed accounted for another quarter or better, excluding prospectors and miners working their own claims. The percentage of self-employed at mining is unknown, for the census returns make no differentiation between them and the employed miners. The vast majority, then, were hired labor, whether as clerks, engineers, or in some other capacity. The opportunity to start on one's own, while decreasing, never disappeared, however. With increased settlement, though, it became more expensive, and promised less immediate return and greater competition than in the earlier years.

Wages, on the whole, tended to decrease as a region became more settled. For example, this chart gives the average scales per day in Colorado at two different periods:

	1864-65	*1879*
Miners	$4-5	$2.-2.50
Laborers	$5-7	$3.-3.50
Carpenters	$5-6	$3.50-3.75[6]

The decline is noticeable, despite the fact that new camps were opening throughout these years. As the state developed, the desperate need for, and the scarcity of, capable men diminished, allowing wages to come down. The laborer's market of earlier years had gone, and the employer now had some selection in hiring. In contrast, wages in a new camp, no matter what year, were always better than in an older settlement or even later in the same camp's history. For example, 1879 was the year of Leadville's first great boom; wages offered miners ranged from $2.50 to $4 per day for the best, and carpenters received $4, both of which topped the previously listed Colorado figures.[7] The government census in 1880 reported that in this region the average salary of miners working in mines deeper than 300 feet and producing more than 100 tons of ore ran from $2.75 in New Mexico to $4 per day in Idaho and Arizona.[8] This left out the men who worked in the numerous smaller mines. Had they been included, the average would probably have gone down. In the report, Colorado's average was $3, while the figures of the previous year as stated ran from 50¢ to a dollar lower. The work day for these miners lasted anywhere from eight to twelve hours, depending on the area, and working conditions in the mines were not regulated as they are at the present time.

Some comment has already been made concerning the wages of other occupations. A brief summation will complete the picture. Once again the reader is reminded that the following serve only as indications of salaries, not as absolute figures. Common laborers received a varied pay scale, from $2 to $4 per day. In the Southern camps a form of discrimination was practiced against Spanish-Americans; they were paid from 50¢ to a dollar less per day for the same work as their white co-workers.[9] James Miller, in Virginia City, noted in his diary that he received $175 plus board for clerking, but other reports say clerks were paid as low as $50 per month. Bookkeepers received a high of $200 to $300 per month in newer camps, but less in others. Blacksmiths working for a mining company got from $3 to $5 per day, bricklayers a similar scale. Bartenders were higher paid, from $100 to $200 per month plus free drinks. Teamsters rested near the bottom of the scale, some being paid as low as $35 per month plus board. Considering the high cost of living, especially for a family man, these wages did not provide much extra to be set aside for emergencies or savings. It remained imperative that the man of the house work the full week all year; this was not always possible, particularly in the mines.

In light of this, the claim that the mining camp was a haven for the poor must be reevaluated. Perhaps because of the seemingly unlimited economic opportunities and the rags-to-riches stories of a few lucky people, the story gained some credence in the East during the three decades under discussion. The basic problems facing the would-be miner appear clearly in this letter written in 1859:

> . . . we have no means to purchase paying claims and no facilities for finding them, while hundreds of others are in the same conditions and worse, which makes it all the harder for us, as no employment can be obtained. . . . A few men are making fortunes rapidly, others amassing it slowly but regularly, some merely making a living while by far the greater portion are like bees in a broken comb rushing about unsettled, flying to whereever [sic] excitement, appearing not to know what the matter is, or where to settle.[10]

If this were true in 1859 with relatively simple mining methods, when the shafts went deeper and the ores became more complex, the little man found himself even farther on the outside. The ordinary individual had little opportunity to succeed under these circumstances; therefore, he looked for other jobs and came into competition with all those in the same predicament. James Chisholm, during his sojourn in South Pass, Wyoming, candidly wrote in his diary, "Nor is the life of hardship and privation very often compensated by the acquisition of riches. In 999 cases out of 1,000 the men who pursue the varied avocation of Western life, do not even acquire a decent competence." [11] He concluded that they remained partly from habit, partly because they were reluctant to return to their friends in a state of poverty, and partly because there was always a hope for the big strike.

The skilled person could usually find work, for his talents were at a premium. The men who came West without any knowledge of mining and related occupations or training in the skills needed in the frontier communities became the unemployed. Each settlement had a certain group who remained without employment either by choice or from lack of work, but in the larger and better known camps the problem became chronic. Though they found it worrisome, the town fathers made no great effort to solve the situation. About the only corrective measure devised was to have the local paper warn the unskilled and moneyless to stay away. This did little to stem the tide, for few heeded or believed that they would be the unfortunate ones.

Despite the long hours, low wages, high living expenses, poor working conditions, and uncertain prospects, the laboring class did not seem to turn to unions for redress. Not until after 1890 did real and violent labor difficulties break out in the Rocky Mountain mining states. Historians have speculated on this situation, and have presented possible causes. The miners and mine owners, in the early days, were hardly distinguishable, and to move from the ranks of one into the other was always possible. Labor could not count on popular support, nor did it have a strong and sound leadership. The general concern of the public logically would be directed toward the threat that a strike or unrest would pose to the business prosperity. Wages in new camps were always better, and the discontented could move on to seek better opportunities. Technological changes and introduction of new machines, which varied the job situation and working conditions, came in the 1880s and 1890s.[12] To these should be added the surplus of labor for unskilled jobs and the possibility of using these unemployed as strike breakers at even lower wages. The Eastern states suffered through a period of labor strife in the 1870s, but there were no major repercussions in the Rocky Mountain area. The trouble which developed in the Pennsylvania coal fields paralleled later strikes in the West, but at this time the Western mining industry was still too young, too expanding for widespread unrest to develop.

Unions made their first tentative appearances in the immediate postwar decade. The most widespread was the miners' union, although it was not a monolithic organization. In the seventies and eighties such deep rock camps as Butte, Montana; Lead, South Dakota; Globe, Arizona; and Leadville and Aspen, Colorado led in union organization. All were larger communities, and in each, corporation mining had come to the forefront. Labor-management conflicts heightened the tension, and the miners naturally turned to unions as a way to resolve differences. Wages and working conditions ranked as the primary considerations, although social activities were an important part of union life. The appeal was greater and the bonds tighter if the whole family became involved rather than just the wage earners. Suspect by many people who attributed to them radical, un-American tendencies, the unions faced an ever steepening uphill struggle to gain acceptance in the mining camps.

To illustrate why unions had so much trouble, one example will suffice. Leadville, one of the most unionized towns during the period of this study, had not only a miners' union but reportedly a barbers', bricklayers', printers', carpenters', and even a newsboys' union. Many of these groups, though, organized to protect themselves from price-cutting newcomers rather than from exploitation by management. Little evidence of wanting to strike or push demands, beyond keeping newcomers out, developed among them. The miners, however, had complaints about wages and hours. The only major strike attempted before 1890 occurred in June, 1880. The men struck for higher pay—$4 per day—and a standard eight hour shift. The owners united to resist the demand, and public support, markedly lacking at first, virtually disappeared after the threat of violence. The miners found themselves isolated. The strike was crushed and unionism received a setback. Rather than blaming all the men or believing their grievances to be widespread, the Leadvillites neatly chose to blame it on the work of a few agitators. The fear of violence, public apathy, and distrust combined with strong management to undermine the movement before anything constructive could be accomplished.[13]

Life in the camps was made harder by the climate. Located throughout a wide geographic area, the camps suffered through almost all the troublesome manifestations of nature, from earthquakes to sandstorms. Of them all, winter played the most havoc. A few inhabitants took almost sardonic pride in their winters, but most only adjusted to them, endured them, and waited for the spring. The persistent wind, a prevailing condition in many camps, whistled through the community, stirring up dust, sand, and drifting snow. For the housewife, it must have been discouraging to go to bed at night with a clean house, only to arise the next morning and have to sweep out the accumulation of snow or dirt which drifted in through the poorly constructed frame houses. For both men and women, the harsh weather brought moments of discouragement and doubt.

The often depressing and physically taxing environment of the camps, and the mining frontier in general, adversely affected some of the participants. Others succumbed to a lesser extent, but all ages were subjected to its stresses. Although newspapers as a rule reported few detailed circumstances surrounding suicides, enough occurred to warrant the assumption that for a few the pressures and ultimate discouragement was too great. Alcoholism, or at least an attraction to strong drink, could be a symptom of the same problem or a means to escape reality. Here, however, only a study of individual cases could conclusively provide the answer. To be sure, newspaper accounts represented extreme examples, since most people were able to make a suitable adjustment. Without a doubt, the environment helped convince some that the mining life was not for them, and they consequently sought their fortunes elsewhere.

These adverse factors of life in the camp also contributed to the mobility of the mining population. The reality of an older camp, balanced against the potential of a new one, tipped the scales in favor of the latter. Why stay where claims were taken, wages declining, and cost of living still high when the next discovery promised so much? By the 1870s, the desire to make a fortune and return to the states had subsided. Caught in the sweep of the frontier, people moved from habit as well as necessity, but the West would be their home. The editor of the *Silver Reef Miner,* April 12, 1879, wrote:

> There seems to be something inherent in the nature of the American miner which impels him to stampede wherever opportunity offers. No sooner is the discovery of ore reported in any locality

than a general struggle takes place to see who shall be first on the scene of the excitement. The more remote is the new Eldorado and the less the stampede know about it the more intense is their desire to go, and the impulse becomes quite irresistible as soon as their cash resources are exhausted. . . . In our opinion this complaint is fatal to the prosperity and financial condition of nine out of ten of what may be termed the floating population of a mining camp. . . .

Economic wanderlust, then, helped lead to mining stampedes to regions which had small mineral resources and kept the miners moving for over fifty years from Mexico to Alaska.

In another way the same tendencies were shown. Miners from more isolated locations often spent the winter in the nearest camp, and people went to the larger cities or even back East during colder months. To counteract this inclination, newspapers published editorials and articles stressing the advantages of year-round work and the difficulties faced by those who worked only during the summer. The problem was greater in the placer mining districts, but even with quartz mining, the tendency still concerned residents who wanted to stabilize their community.

No matter how many words were written on behalf of permanence and development, the mining frontier was nourished on expectancy and recurrent stampedes. Hope and optimism counterbalanced the grim realities. In time they would be unable to furnish support. As for the frontier, by then it had disappeared, dying with the advance of settlement which it had promoted and encouraged. When the next valley no longer held out the promise of untold wealth, and the ordinary individual could not realistically dream of the fortune he would soon find, the mining frontier had lost the essence which had given the period vibrancy and meaning.

Thirteen

A Time for Relaxation

To open the wilderness, mine the earth, and build a camp took time and work, long, hard work; it was a season of trial, of testing for the people and their community. It was not all work and no play, however. Money begets ways to spend it, and on the heels of the miners came the basic masculine entertainments. Other recreational activities soon appeared, until, when the camp reached maturity, numerous possibilities for the community, the group, and the individual presented themselves. Each offered an escape from the routine existence of work and worry. One should never paint too somber a picture, for gaiety and laughter entered even the most flaccid life. Social activities sparked the camps. Little of a lasting nature or of significance was here, but for the people themselves, diversions helped make their work bearable, their lives richer.

The small size and isolation of most mining camps produced among the people a strong community spirit and fellowship. Urban living and working continually brought them together to share their respective joys and sorrows. A bond developed which helped ameliorate the hardships and sharpen the pleasures. Wealth, growth, and social pretension weakened but did not entirely break this bond. A camp's decline brought it back as never before.

Two of the major holidays, July Fourth and Christmas-New Year, were celebrated on a large scale by the community, collectively and individually. To the people of the nineteenth century, July Fourth held special significance. The country was young and highly nationalistic. By the 1860s the revolutionary era was several generations removed, but the Civil War rejuvenated lagging sentiments. Then came the national centennial to revive memories further. July Fourth symbolized an occasion to renew and express patriotic feeling, to honor the founding fathers, and to take pride in the country's accomplishments.

The day's activities focused on the traditional flowery patriotic oration, preceded by the reading of the Declaration of Independence. Long before this, however, residents had been awakened by blasting powder, firecrackers, or small arms. Throughout the day these noisemakers kept the populace on its toes and small animals scurrying for cover. Main street decorations of evergreens, flags, and bunting testified to a committee's hard work. If possible, a parade with floats, carriages bedecked in holiday attire, horseback riders, just plain marchers, the fire company, and the brass band preceded the oratory, an imposing sight for all spectators. Sports, from baseball to horse racing, took up the afternoon. Somewhere a community picnic was sandwiched in, and the celebration was capped by a grand ball.[1]

Perchance a band concert enlivened the affair. It was a work day for few, although some merchants remained open to tap the stream of potential buyers. A full day of vigorous activity from dawn to dark or on into the early hours of the morning left the participants exhausted and, no doubt, weighed heavily on those who returned to work bright and early on July the fifth. Not all Independence Days, of course, passed with such outbursts of community patriotism. Family picnics, dinners, and perhaps some sporting events were substituted for the more tempestuous activities. Probably few celebrations passed without the familiar fireworks, firewater, and fights, however, with emphasis on the fireworks.

July Fourth came at the height of the working season, while the Christmas-New Year holiday came during the winter slack season. As a result, celebrations were concentrated on one day on the Fourth, while Christmas-New Years' was enjoyed for a week or more with activities spread over the entire period. The Fourth had the same general meaning for all residents, natives, and immigrants, but the same may not be said for Christmas. Traditionally, it was a religious holiday. To the merchant it represented increased trade during a dull business period. To many it meant a time for general celebration without any special connotations, while Christmas in children's eyes was a time bright with gifts and parties. If the year had been poor for the mines and camp, disappointment dampened the expectations of the young and occasioned a correspondingly sad time for their parents.

Assuming that such had not been the case, a flurry of activity highlighted the season. For the young it called for vacation from school, presentation of a program, and the exchange of gifts; stores had all manner of toys and treats to tempt them for weeks and sharpen their suspense. Their celebration of Christmas was crowned by the community or church party with the decorated tree and, if fortunate, the appearance of Santa Claus with presents for all. Often adults found gifts under the tree from their practical-joke-minded friends, much to the amusement of everyone and their own discomfort. The religious nature of the occasion was not forgotten. Special church services commemorated the sacred season and, especially in camps where the Cornish had settled, carolers went through the town singing the Christmas message.

The rest of the time was turned over to Dickens' "Spirit of Christmas Present," that jolly giant of myth and merriment. Parties, balls, sleigh rides, and dinners crowded the entire week. Saloons, dance halls, and hotels put on holiday attire, and fraternal organizations provided special festivities for their members and guests. Fireworks again added a noisy touch and their unexpected performance disrupted more stately occasions. In southern camps horse racing and athletic events were diversions denied those in the colder north. The holiday week came to a conclusion with a round of New Year balls and suppers. The church might have a year-end watch and prayer meeting to usher in the new year. The traditional January first custom of open house and calling on one's friends, common in the early years, gradually fell into disuse.[2] For most, the celebration the night before limited their enjoyment of such activities the following day.

Thus ended the holiday festivities.

> Our Christmas has come and gone.... There was nothing on the surface to distinguish it from a reign of dullness back in a rural village during harvest time. This condition of things doesn't argue well for a mining metropolis. It is a sure indication of the poverty which has overtaken the 'boys and the girls.'[3]

The prosperous mining camp knew how to celebrate Christmas, or at least thought it did. Any variation appeared like a dark cloud and was not to be tolerated.

The holiday calendar of the mining camps beyond these two festive occasions was spotty. Family gatherings replaced communal ones. Thanksgiving, observed with church services and perhaps a dance, came nearest in activity to the other two holidays. It had not yet developed into the traditional day of modern experience with turkey and all the trimmings, but even so the family dinner prevailed over community activities. For the patriotic and the Masons, George Washington's birthday ranked second only to July Fourth in importance. A grand ball and occasionally a civic celebration honored the day and the man. As the years passed, this holiday gradually receded into the background and observances became less frequent, almost going out of style by the late 1880s. Memorial Day, which had more meaning and significance for the postwar generation, also took its place. The community memorial service led by the Civil War veterans to honor their fallen comrades held a personal meaning for most Americans. Easter retained its strictly religious meaning, but Lent was seldom observed, except in New Mexico, where the Catholic church predominated. The various European nationalities scattered throughout the mining frontier celebrated their own holidays. St. Patrick's Day particularly caught the public's favor, no doubt because of the large sprinkling of Irishmen in the United States. Pranksters furnished their own amusement on April first, and caught many an unwilling or unsuspecting victim.

These were the days which the people chose to celebrate. Although community festivities highlighted many of them, it really was left to the individual to select and furnish his own amusements. Some worked, others loafed, and many did all their celebrating in private. Holidays did present the opportunity to enter into the spirit of hilarity. Probably because opportunities such as these were so infrequent, when they did come along everyone took full advantage of them.

Woven in and out of the holiday festivities were dances. From the polka, waltz, quadrille, redowa, and schottische to the "whoop 'er up" hoedown, the dancers paired for an evening's enjoyment. They danced the old year out and the new one in. Almost without ceasing, the St. Patrick's Day flings, calico hops, masquerade balls, grand opening dances, Masonic and Odd Fellows balls, and just ordinary get togethers followed one another. Leap Year specials and anniversary dances interposed on special occasions. Almost any excuse justified a dance. Women, of course, were in great demand at such times and almost continually called upon as dancing partners. Few had a chance to catch their breath before being swept back onto the floor. In dire situations it was not unknown for men to fill out a set when the ladies were unavailable.[4]

Probably the most painless and popular way to raise money for school, church, fire department, or any worthy cause was by sponsoring a dance. For two to five dollars per couple, the purchasers were provided a midnight supper laden with tempting food and a full evening of dancing, which often carried far into the early morning hours. The young people enjoyed these occasions immensely, for they eased the problem of a boy meeting a girl and escorting her to a respectable social activity where courting could be carried on without complete adult supervision. When the weary dancers finally turned homeward after the ball, they generally carried with them many a pleasant memory.

Although some dances sponsored by the social elite were highlights of the season, the majority were informal gatherings, in the sense that everyone was invited if they had the inclination and money. Great effort was put forth to decorate the hall and provide the repast. The ladies voluntarily brought the food and decorations, or organized themselves into committees to solicit donations. Despite such careful preparations, unfortunate incidents did occasionally occur. It is to be hoped that these only temporarily marred the evening's enjoyment. One such incident had the ladies decamping in numbers after being affronted by the presence of females deemed not quite acceptable. As the *Helena Herald,* November 15, 1866, described it: "The cause of the stampede, and consequent derangement and final break-up of the party, is said to have been the surreptitious introduction in the ball-room of two pretty, young milliners of town, against whom certain suspicions existed of their fair name and respectable standing in the community."

For those unfortunates who were unable to merrily waltz away the evening, but who could not bear to be left out, dancing schools provided the answer. They usually heralded the opening of the winter social season with advertisements in the paper for all who desired to learn the art of social dancing. Musical accompaniment was needed, too, and local musicians who furnished it found themselves in great demand for parties and dances. For those communities without this advantage, a violin, or whatever instrument could be found, served the purpose.

The location of many camps provided an ideal setting for picnics in the surrounding mountains and valleys; in the spring and summer they replaced the dance as a favorite activity for mixed company. Individuals and families, churches and fraternal groups, spent a day relaxing over good food and conversation. Weddings provided a time of merriment and celebration, particularly surrounding the custom of giving a charivari. This mock serenade, consisting of all types of racket, continued until the harassed bridegroom furnished refreshments for all assembled. Box suppers, candy pulls, and ice cream socials filled other evenings with courting opportunities for the young and relaxation for their elders.

These events should not be considered weekly happenings; with the exception of dances, they provided only occasional social outings. More typically, an evening was spent at home or visiting with one's neighbors. For the single man this included playing cards, chess, checkers, or if fortune smiled, a pleasant few hours with some of the camp's young ladies. The young blade could also spend a night on the town having a carousing time and perhaps, as James Miller called it, going "over the bay." For women, any opportunity to visit must have been a welcome distraction from the continual demands of housework. Considering all available forms of entertainment and social activities, one finds the majority to be reserved for men or oriented toward masculine tastes. Though this was natural, considering the proportion of men to women, it left the respectable lady limited to the social outlets of the church, community functions, and private parties.[5]

Besides the fraternal lodge, the men had access to another socializing organization, the private club. To be sure, this was exclusive, open only to those who passed the membership requirements and had the money to pay dues. One black ball could keep an applicant out of the more exclusive ones, but many had more liberal policies concerning membership. The purposes varied. Some simulated Eastern and European clubs, with private dining, reading, and game rooms. The mining man wanted the same refinements that his wealth and position would have given him access to in the older communities. Bachelors, too, formed clubs to help pass the time away with social, intellectual, and perhaps athletic recreation. The volunteer fire company was a social club in the truest sense of the word, as well as a community servant. The Harrison Hook and Ladder Company of Leadville, Colorado, for example, elected its members by ballot, established rules and regulations concerning conduct, and gave dinners and dances.[6] Once a month official meetings and frequent informal gatherings were held at the firehouse, the club house for members. A ladies' auxiliary on rare occasions provided the women with a chance to support the fire fighters and have another social outlet.

For the children and even the adults of the mining community nothing could quite measure up to the excitement and attraction of the circus. Here, in one performance, the wonders of the world were presented; who could resist the temptation? Early acts featured performing dogs and ponies, acrobats, bareback riders, monkeys, and, once transportation improved, a few of the now familiar circus animals such as elephants and lions. Tent shows traveled from camp to camp, appearing in Montana and Idaho as early as 1865. At least one show combined the circus with a dramatic company to provide further entertainment.[7] Perhaps not as wonderful, but certainly as exciting, were balloon ascensions. These occurred rarely, but those who saw one had a tale to tell for years to come.

Athletic endeavors, the grand American pastime whether one participated or watched, held an important place in the social-recreational-gambling life of the community. Although primarily masculine in both intent and purpose, they never totally excluded women, who could always come to cheer the locals on to victory.

The men of the mining camps displayed a catholic interest in sports. All types gained some amount of popularity, as both European immigrants and Americans played their traditional games. No doubt the majority of the active participants were younger men, but the physical endurance required of a miner produced a breed of men who were hardened to such rigors and enjoyed vigorous recreation. Contests of all sorts were immensely popular, for both their sporting aspect and their gambling possibilities. Rivalry between towns and districts frequently reached heated proportions when the local nines played, or the fire companies raced against each other. Not only community pride but individual money rested on the outcome.

The mining camps give support to baseball's claim of being the national pastime, for no sport became more popular or more generally played. As early as the mid-1860s, newspapers reported scores and descriptions of the most recent game. Some of the scores reached astronomical heights. A Helena, Montana, team outslugged a rival 85 to 19 in a game called after five innings, but primitive equipment and playing fields handicapped the players. Town teams, private clubs, and sandlot nines participated in regularly scheduled games and in spontaneous sessions after work and on Sundays.

The Silver Plume, Colorado baseball team in 1889. Despite primitive conditions, baseball was popular in mining communities. *Denver Public Library Western Collection.*

Baseball's popularity rested upon its broad-based appeal, where anyone could join in and have a good time. As the years went by the skill of the players improved, if the scores serve as an indication. By the late seventies and eighties, in nine inning games, the better teams scored less than ten runs in winning. Larger scores were still commonplace in the ordinary contest, but the winning totals dropped into the teens and twenties.[8]

Few July Fourths passed without the traditional baseball game. Important matches like these were frequently followed by a dinner or party, sponsored by the home team, with appropriate toasts and ceremonies. Less graciously, perhaps, the losing bettors paid the price for their overconfidence. In the Rocky Mountains, the camps were the earliest centers of baseball interest, and the game became well entrenched, easily surviving the decline of mining to move into the twentieth century far ahead of any rivals for the public's attention.

To be able to handle firearms was taken almost for granted by the frontiersman. In the urban mining community not everyone could claim this skill, but hunting was popular. For a few it meant a way of life, although to most it was a sport or a means to provide extra food. Fishing had its enthusiastic advocates, and catches were often outstanding. The people who lived in the West during the years of this study found themselves in a hunting and fishing paradise which, doomed by their coming, declined rapidly. Before long the warning was issued, but far too few heard or cared to pay attention. As early as 1877 the interested citizens of Helena, Montana, formed a rod and gun club to enforce all territorial laws and ordinances for the protection of game birds, animals, and fish. The *Butte Miner*, August 7, 1877, commented, "The genuine sportsman looks upon the taking of game out of season as the meanest and most unmanly of crimes, but unfortunately there is a race of pot hunters who render the vigilant care of our game a necessity." The problem was immense and the worried were too few to curb such excesses. As a direct result of the number and use of guns, shooting matches were extremely popular. A community pitted its best against a rival team or held matches open to all challengers, with the winner receiving a prize.

Professional boxing came West early; indeed, after reading about some of the saloon brawls, one could surmise there were a great many amateur practitioners as well. Prize fights and exhibitions took place throughout the entire period, though they were never completely acceptable to all classes of the community. Some of the best-known fighters of the day appeared in the larger camps, lured by the larger purses. One of the most popular and earliest, Con

Orem, fought in Colorado in 1859 and during 1864-66 in Montana against both Eastern and local opponents. Amateur fights, in the ring, also generated a good deal of enthusiasm among the fans. The excitement, the man-to-man physical conflict of the encounter appealed to the mining camp crowd. Wrestling, too, received support, although not so much as boxing. Football, a novelty, certainly, because it never reached the stature of a popular sport, made its appearance in the 1880s. The game seems to have been the exclusive property of the school boys. During these thirty years hard rock drilling contests, later to come into vogue, were not commonly held as public exhibitions.

One sport, track, recognized now solely for its amateur status, bordered on being strictly professional, and was a gambling event in the camps. Track meets as such were not held, but foot racing was, especially over short distances. Local races produced the fastest man in camp, who met the best of the other communities. Frequently a professional runner was entered as a ringer backed by those on the inside. For the winner a prize, usually money, was offered. Bets were placed, for few cared to watch this solely as a test of speed. Civic pride virtually dictated that the local man be backed, and unless he was exceptionally fast, many of the sporting crowd were apt to be sadder but wiser at the conclusion of the race. Not all running had such serious overtones. Some races were held for the pure enjoyment of participants and spectators. The *Black Hills Times*, June 28, 1879, announced a 100-yard dash open to none but men less than five feet ten and over 180 pounds, the prize being a keg of beer. Walking contests were even more of an exhibition. Professionals toured the country, taking on all comers for a purse and percentage of the gate. Such shows went on for several days with breaks only for meals and sleeping. Although the sport was dominated by men, celebrated pedestriennes displayed their talents to appreciative male audiences.

Horse racing became exceedingly popular on the mining frontier. In fact, a great many more camps than might be imagined had a track or were close to one. Nothing like the sport of kings seemed to bring out the sporting blood and gambling instinct among the men. Though few camps went so far as to have a regular racing season, most were limited only by the availability of good horses and by the weather. The races were run almost any day, but particularly on Sunday, when the populace had the free time to participate. The course might be staked out on a flat stretch of ground or could possibly involve more elaborate facilities, including grandstands and a bar. Usually the race matched two horses for a specified purse, and in the course of the day several were run. Some tracks required entrance fees, but most were opened freely to all. Betting, carried on individually and in pools, could result in spirited interest in the outcome, and substantial sums changing hands. Trotting was never so popular, but had its followers where money was available to purchase the horses and needed equipment. Novelty races, such as between mules or around two specified points, whetted the betting urge and offered something different for the spectators. More than a love of the sport or admiration for fast horses made racing popular; wagering on the outcome stimulated interest and maintained it.

Almost anything on which a bet could be placed or which might be termed unusual aroused excitement among certain segments of the community. Cockfighting achieved a measure of notoriety for both of these reasons. Searching for the unusual left the customer open to swindles. A purported bullfight staged in Montana in 1864 drew this comment from one who was taken, "No fight in the bulls, being some old stags, who have hauled goods over the plains, but the getters up got their $2.00 a head from a large crowd of fools." [9] So it was in 1864; it had not changed noticeably by 1874 or 1884. Gullible Americans, P. T. Barnum's lifeblood, paid their money and took their chances, whether at the bullfight or in worthless mining stock.

Winter did not chill the sporting blood; activity merely shifted indoors. Saloons offered such means of recreation-gambling as bil-

liards, bowling, and shuffleboard. Billiard halls and bowling alleys
provided the same attractions, but in a slightly different atmosphere.
Billiards, particularly, drew enthusiastic players and crowds for
matches between the best players and professionals. Even such a
sedate game as chess took on a different air when the local cham-
pion offered to play anyone in the district, the winner to take all,
which might mean anything from prize money to champagne.
Poker, cribbage, and other card games furnished further entertainment and possible profit for the gambler.

When other out-of-doors activity was curtailed by winter weather,
sledding was popular. Coasting down hills and through the streets
of the camp was not limited to the younger set; all ages participated. Sleigh riding in a cutter replaced picnicking for those of
courting age and the young at heart. Without much inciting, snow-
ball fights broke out, some with bruising results. A newspaper, part

Irwin, Colorado, 1883. Some mining camp residents avidly took
to the slopes long before skiing became an important recreational business. *State Historical Society of Colorado.*

in jest, part in seriousness, reported that half the town had been engaged in snowballing the day before. The result had been broken windows, black eyes, swollen noses, bad colds, and the police ending numerous fisticuffs.[10]

For the women to indulge in these vigorous activities was considered unbecoming. The woman's place was in the home; to wander far from it left her open to serious questions about her character. Milder forms of recreation suited the feminine image much better. Croquet or, as it was called, "Presbyterian billiards," was thought to be a most innocent and healthy game for the young and the ladies. It passed through periods of great popularity.

Younger girls, excepted from the dictum, were permitted to participate in more energetic exercise, like horseback riding and even coasting in the winter. It should not be inferred by the reader that the ladies did not enter into the spirit of recreation or perhaps participate in the activities. They did, and some with great relish. As the camps became more settled, however, the feminine behavior codes became more restrictive, and in line with those of the East. Eventually, it became daring to bend or break them, but not at this time.

Probably the most vigorous sport open to all was roller skating. Although seldom a permanent feature in a camp, skating at times drew an exuberant following. Women were encouraged to participate by such devices as free ladies' nights, and the more enthusiastic of both sexes organized skating clubs for increased enjoyment. But even in the skating rink, gambling made its appearance, with wagering on the outcome of endurance and stake races. When this happened, the Victorian lady probably lost a great deal of her interest in appearing at the rink along with that other crowd. Almost anything was used for a rink, few being built for this specific purpose; the temporary nature of the business weighed heavily against any great outlay of money. Skating, new and different to most of the residents, caught their fancy. As advertised, "Exhilarating—good for the body, soul and the mind," [11] who could resist the temptation to put on a pair of skates and try the new wonder?

Although the question of keeping physically fit did not loom so large or important to people in the mining camps as it does to their sedentary descendants, it still had its advocates in the earlier period. Athletic clubs, formed with the avowed purpose of providing exercise and training facilities, attempted also to produce the well-rounded individual by providing social activities as well. The businessmen, the camp's young bloods, and others of similar interests patronized the clubs. Boxing and vigorous exercise were stressed by some members, while more genteel sports appealed to others. Whether these great plans were carried out for more than one season may be doubted, for the distractions were many, and the goals required concentration and hard work. For the less committed, the clubs offered social contacts primarily and physical fitness secondarily, if at all.

The social and athletic activities of the mining communities resembled those found elsewhere on the frontier or in the East. Hamlin Garland's *A Son of the Middle Border* and Everett Dick's *Sodhouse Frontier* describe similar developments in the agrarian Great Plains and Mississippi Valley. The main difference, one of timing and emphasis, resulted from the urban nature of the mining frontier. While the farmer still concentrated on improving his homestead, the miner was surrounded by a community, with its variety of possibilities and attractions. That these recreational and social activities were needed is self-evident. Without them, life in the mining camp would have passed through an endless cycle of routine and work. No more justification for them need be given than that life was more pleasant for their existence.

Fourteen

The Tiger Is Found

THE Bank Exchange Saloon of Silver City, New Mexico, ran the following advertisement in the local paper: "The belligerent portion of the community can find a particularly rampant specimen of the Feline species, usually denominated the 'Tiger' ready to engage them at all times."[1] This tiger, the bank in faro, openly stalked its pleasure-seeking victims, although this was only one of the hedonic activities in which the men could take part. Almost all the male members of the community at one time or another took their pleasure in the saloons, gambling houses, or brothels, which were as much a part of the community as the store or church. For a price, here could be found many and varied diversions to break the routine existence of mining life. The miner, freighter, clerk, and businessman mingled as equals in this atmosphere, where the only factor to limit enjoyment was the size of one's purse. Visitors were amazed, titillated, and scandalized by what they observed. The New Englander, Charles Francis Adams, Jr., wrote in his diary, in 1886, "In the evening we saw Leadville by gaslight—an awful spectacle of low vice."[2] By then the great boom had passed, and he had seen the camp after its rowdy peak. This licentiousness, like no other feature, created over the years the glittering, sinful facade which stood for so long as the essence of the mining camp. The heyday of vice, a brief time, coincided with the period of greatest prosperity. In these fleeting moments, however, it created a flurry never to be forgotten by visitor and resident.

The gamblers and saloonkeepers arrived almost with the first miners, and soon after came the girls. No matter how short the camp's life span, they all lingered on the scene, especially the saloon. The primary entertainment section included not only these establishments, but also variety theaters, dance halls, billiard parlors,

Gambling in a Leadville, Colorado saloon. *Denver Public Library Western Collection.*

bowling alleys, and occasionally an opium den. Often one building housed several of these amusements. Not all of these, certainly, can be characterized as disreputable vice, but when the respectable ladies started reforming the camp, a guilt-by-association rule predestined a common fate, perhaps because virtually all offered temptations to the wavering husband.

That apex of masculine society and the epitome of its culture, the saloon, appeared in every camp. There the working man relaxed and Dad headed on his night out. Amid the companionship of his friends a man could relax, play cards, have a drink, sample from the free lunch counter, conduct business, or do well-nigh anything within reason that he desired. This stronghold of masculinity was seldom breached by the opposite sex, although a limited number of establishments had a stage and offered female companionship. In decorations and design they adapted themselves strictly to masculine tastes. Each had its own distinctive name, some denoting the owner or town, others having no special connotation; The Mint, Hunts, Miners' Home, Palace, Centennial, Butte, Union, and Last Chance are a few of the thousands to be found. A small number had special mixed drinks for which they became famed, but all served the basic beverages, beer and whiskey. This advertisement, which appeared in the *Tombstone Nugget*, Oct. 20, 1880, reflected a common hope: "Call Frequently, Drink Moderately, Pay on Delivery, Take your Departure Quietly."

The men of the mining frontier must have had an amazing capacity for drink. Liquor represented a large percentage of the goods shipped into the camps and was one of the most sought after items. A dearth of it was considered by some almost as serious as a shortage of food. Many communities supported their own breweries and took great pride in the local product. An indication of the district's prosperity could be seen in the number of saloons operating, for this more than any other business served as a gauge of the number of miners. Consider, for example, that a business census conducted by the *Daily Chronicle*, Leadville, Colorado, in June 1879, reported 10 dry goods stores, 4 banks, 31 restaurants, and 4 churches. In contrast, it uncovered 120 saloons, 19 beer halls, and 118 gambling houses and private club rooms.[3] No other camp could approach the totals of the Queen, but these figures indicate the economic impact of the saloon on the mining community. Few more lucrative occupations could be undertaken than operating a saloon.

Naturally, competition was intense among rival grog shops. Some distinction developed between the bit and two-bit saloons and their clientele, but this was only a minor distinction in most camps, as the patrons chose freely the establishment they preferred. In order to attract customers, the owner resorted to various lures. Bands provided music and perhaps, in conjunction with the saloon, a concert-dance hall with female companionship opened. "Pretty-waiter girls" were employed to corral customers and loose change. Price wars between competitors developed, to the delight of the patrons. In and around some of the saloons the prostitutes plied their trade. Yet all of these were frills which detracted from the basic masculine atmosphere and in most cases were not permanent additions.[4]

The saloonkeeper or bartender reigned as the uncrowned but unchallenged king of this domain. He stood in a class by himself in mining camp society. This was predominantly a man's occupation, for only occasionally did a woman own and tend her own bar. Mark Twain, from firsthand experience, described this community fixture thus:

> The cheapest and easiest way to become an influential man and be looked up to by the community at large, was to stand behind a bar, wear a cluster-diamond pin, and sell whisky. I am not sure but that the saloon-keeper held a shade higher rank than any other member of society. His opinion had weight. . . . No great movement could succeed without the countenance and direction of the saloon-keeper. . . . Youthful ambition hardly aspired so much to the honors of the law, or the army and navy as to the dignity of proprietorship in a saloon.[5]

Liquid refreshments, an extremely popular attraction, were rivaled by the gambling opportunities offered by the saloon. In previous chapters, repeated mention has been made of the way in which gambling permeated all aspects of life on the mining frontier. Even in their leisure hours, miners seemed to prefer it to the more sedate activities. The why of this has been speculated on since the nineteenth century. Perhaps the solution was no more complicated than the fact that it represented excitement and recreation, a change of pace from conventional daily work. Certainly the philosophy that tomorrow would bring an opportunity to recoup all losses served to rationalize some gamblers' wastefulness; here was epitomized the basic tenet of the mining frontier, twisted only slightly to justify yet another aspect of life. Whatever the causes, the gambling urge certainly was satisfied to a degree probably unmatched in American history. Gambling was more prevalent in the early years of a camp, and, as a general tendency, tapered off as the boom passed. This is both interesting and understandable. Easy money or the expectation of it was conducive to squandering; when conditions stabilized, the speculative, transitory period passed and contracted the availability of currency. The very nature of the early settlement, then, had a great deal to do with the gambling fever which seemed to affect the populace.

The gambling hall could be one of the fanciest structures in the community. Granville Stuart, who went from California to Montana, described one he had visited in the former state during the 1850s. Magnificently decorated with plate glass mirrors and brilliantly lighted chandeliers, it contained at one end a balcony where a string band performed. Situated on the floor were numerous gaming tables and a bar.[6] All manner of games were provided, but faro, roulette, and poker remained the favorite standbys. Professionals, amateurs, and the curious mingled together, wagering large and small sums on the whims of lady luck. How honestly the games were run is a matter of conjecture. Seth Bullock, marshal and long-time resident of the mining frontier, commented about Deadwood, "That rare avis, the square gambler, and his associate, the law-abiding saloon keeper, were not much in evidence in any of the town. . . ."[7] The odds always favored the house and were, no doubt, occasionally increased by manipulation. For those caught in the act of cheating, a punishment was found to fit the crime and might be short and to the point.

Occasionally, a local editor spoke out against the corrupting influence of gambling. According to a story published in the *Butte Miner,* December 4, 1877, a husband became irate at his wife and caused a scene because she admonished him for his regularity in visiting the tables. Concluded the paper, "What sensible man wants a wife if she refuses to support him, and even goes so far as to discourage his little recreations, such as faro, poker, etc." The *Silver Reef Miner,* March 27, 1882, warned that draw poker, while fascinating, was a deceiving game in which you eventually find a player better than yourself. This results in the loss of money and some conceit, and "You will never think as much of yourself after it is over as you did before, but you will be worth more to society."

The gamblers, the knights of the pictured pasteboards, have become some of the most romantically portrayed individuals on the frontier. From the tinhorn to the dedicated professional, they mined the miners with varying success. Legendarily tall, slim, well-dressed, and with iron nerve, they nevertheless were not cut from such an heroic mold. Drifting from camp to camp, seldom far ahead of the game or seldom doing an honest day's work, they fit easily into the transitory, exploitative life around them. The career of one Charles Storms, revealed in his obituary following his untimely demise in a Tombstone gunfight, illustrates typical characteristics. Storms, born in New Orleans, came West with the California rush, only to return East with a large amount of money which rapidly disappeared after a season of riotous living. Drifting back to the frontier, he appeared subsequently in the Black Hills, Leadville, Denver, and finally Arizona. Reportedly, at the time of his death, he left behind a family in San Francisco and a "wife" in Leadville. On the side Storms did a little prospecting but always returned to his first love, gambling. Never making a permanent fortune, Storms continued to drift through the mining bonanzas of the mid-nineteenth century.[8] Nor was this solely a man's profession; a few women dealers dealt the cards as ruthlessly as their male co-workers and when the occasion demanded could be equally tough.

For the unwary, the bunko and confidence artists laid their traps in and around the saloons and gambling houses. These individuals operated all manner of rackets to fleece their victims. The fake mining stock, the gold brick scheme, the mock lottery, the completely crooked card game, and other tricks, limited only by imagination and ability, enticed enough victims to make the risk profitable. Knockout drops and even physical force separated the customer from his money, if regular procedures failed to produce the desired results. The bigger camps which had achieved a degree of national fame readily attracted these con men. In Tombstone or Butte it was much easier to bilk somebody than in the smaller camp, where daily incidents quickly became common gossip and the stranger was conspicuous.

The gambler has had many critics, for indeed very little of a constructive nature came from the activities associated with his life. But as individuals they have defenders. Many were generous, especially among their own crowd, and their contributions in behalf of the church have already been noted. They grubstaked prospectors and became silent partners in other mining ventures.[9] Thus did the money taken from the miners complete the cycle, as it was spent searching for still more wealth. They and their games were craved by the mining community. It might be said that they were the incarnation of the camp, for gamblers made their living from those who gambled on the fortunes of mining. Nowhere else was this phenomenon developed with such finesse.

From the gambling house and saloon to the red-light district was not a far walk, perhaps only out the door. Prostitution flourished in the camp's live-and-let-live atmosphere. In this masculine world of few women and easy money the environment was favorable, and naturally the girls, the "soiled doves," appeared. Until the respectable women and their allies finally forced reform upon the reluctant males, prostitutes remained one of the traditional appurtenances to all young mining communities. The following verse well describes the situation:

> First came the miners to work in the mine,
> Then came the ladies who lived on the line.[10]

The girls in the houses and cribs were known by many titles designed to appease Victorian sensibilities: "fair but frail," "fallen angels," and "erring sisters." Isolated in their own districts, the Belles, Minnies, Julies, and Mollies lived out their existence beyond the pale of respectability, pariahs to the other members of their sex. In the early years, when their numbers were extremely few, these women held a somewhat less degraded position, and the fortunate ones left their work to become the wives of miners or other residents. By the mid-1870s, however, their social standing had regressed with the changing times and the appearance of respectable Victorian ladies. One of the latter, who signed herself "mother," wrote concerning the threatened expansion of the red-light district:

> Hitherto, . . . we have at least been allowed certain limits for a retired house, where little children could run and play without danger of such contamination. This, it seems, is now to be denied us, and the owners of real estate are to be defenseless against the incursions of the vilest element of the community. It is possible there are not righteous men left to save the city. . . . May we not at least petition this august body [city council] to define certain limits to restrict the respectable, if they are so sadly in the minority? [11]

While the good lady was, no doubt, sincerely worried about the problem, it took care of itself. Tacitly or legally, the demimondaine was restricted to her own section of town. Her time was brief, spanning the heyday of mining and then disappearing. If her departure was not swift enough, an added push from the campaigning reformers speeded it. This type of item was newsworthy, especially if the editor happened to be crusading, or interested in seamy stories for the sake of increased publication. "Disturbance in Red Light District" headlined one article. The "boys and girls" at one of the "immoral factories" had a special little matinee which resulted in the breaking up of furniture. Not content to stop here, the "wicked young men inverted the boss of the house compelling her by force to stand on her head several minutes, and afterwards corded her and the balance of the female actors up in a corner, using the portly body of the madame for the bottom. . . ." [12]

The girls worked either as individuals or in small groups, perhaps in the house of a madam. The latter establishment, often lavishly furnished and decorated, generally reserved its favors for a more select clientele. Here amid costly furniture, tapestries, velvet carpets, rich Oriental hangings and all accessories of luxurious elegance, the customers found their pleasure for a price compensatory to the surroundings. At the other extreme, in the cribs, the single individual plied the same trade without the lush trimmings. Within this economic framework the prostitutes had their own caste system. The women in the elaborate seraglio scorned their sisters who found male companionship in the dance halls and theaters. The latter, in turn, viewed with derision the dregs of vice represented by the low-class dens and cribs. On the lowest level were found Chinese, Negro, and Spanish-American harlots, although the latter appeared in the higher echelons as well.

All types of women became prostitutes. Both native and foreign-born entered the profession and they ranged in age from the early teens into the fifties. The following cases are illustrative. A girl known only as Red Stockings appeared in Colorado in 1860. Reportedly born into a wealthy Boston family, she had been seduced in the wicked city of Paris and, humiliated, left home for the West. Her real name, unknown or forgotten, does not matter; the nickname came from her continual habit of wearing stockings of that bright color. Remembered as a beauty of the fairest and most bewitching type, she left the territory in 1861 with several thousand dollars. According to a friend, that departure marked the date of Red Stockings' reformation and she later married respectably. The second woman, known as Mollie May, reached the top of her profession by becoming a madam in one of Leadville's best-known houses. Mollie, like Red Stockings, had been wooed early by a lustful suitor, surrendering "the legacy that nature bestows but once upon its children." Having begun her wayward career, she left for the frontier, appearing in the 1870s in Cheyenne, the Black Hills, and finally, in 1878, in Leadville. Here Mollie remained until her death, becoming both a well-known and, to a degree, a respected figure. Many turned out for her fancy funeral and a poem was published in her honor in the local paper. The following stanza indicates somewhat why Mollie gained this respect.

> Talk if you will of her
> But speak no ill of her—
> The sins of the living are not of the dead.

> Remember her charity,
> Forget all disparity;
> Let her judges be they whom she sheltered and fed.[13]

The careers of Red Stockings and Mollie exemplify several points. Prostitutes, like gamblers, were members of the drifting crowd, attracted wherever money flowed freely, then moving on with the end of plush times. Real names were a rarity, although Mollie used hers, Melinda May Bryant. Victorian moralism had to have the young girl wronged before turning from the virtuous path; though such was often the case, there were those who did so by choice. As both of these stories testify, the frontier served as one possible safety valve for those who had morally transgressed and did not care to face the ostracism of their neighbors. A certain amount of charity to these women is noticeable in the newspaper accounts, which reflect an attitude on the part of the men, at least, to regard personal characteristics as more important than one's occupation.

A young girl who lived in both Colorado and Montana during the early 1860s remembered clearly her impression of the "fancy ladies."

> [They] were easily recognizable by their painted cheeks and the flaunting of their gaudy clothes on the streets. They were always to be seen either walking up and down or clattering along on horseback or in hacks. Sometimes one was glimpsed through a window, lounging in a dressing-gown and puffing on a cigarette. These women were so in evidence that I felt no curiosity about them. I knew that besides being so much upon the streets, they went to hurdy-gurdy houses and to saloons and that they were not 'good women,' why, I did not analyze.[14]

Writing some years later, a woman who had grown up in Dead-wood described how briefly the prostitutes' span of glory lasted. She recalled seeing them, after only two or three years, slipping furtively down alleys in quest of the price of a drink or a shot of dope, then in a pathetically short while disappearing from town. The reaction of a mature woman was even less sympathetic to the gaudily attired, paint-bedaubed creatures, boldly parading up and down. Men, too, viewed the occupation in a somewhat less than favorable light. George Parsons wrote in his diary that some of the prostitutes he saw were the most depraved women—entirely and apparently totally—ever known.[15]

In spite of some elegant trappings, reflected in the clothes and living quarters, and a seemingly tinsel-covered existence of easy hours and gaiety, the life of the prostitute was drab and ugly. Whether working in a house or as just the "wife of a single man," the women were trapped on a treadmill to oblivion. Only a few left the past behind and managed to start a new life. For the rest, little real future existed. They testified to this themselves in the frequent reports of those who attempted or succeeded in suicide. Alcohol and narcotics eased reality only briefly, and failed to provide an escape. Nor is there anything admirable in the fact that girls not over fourteen and some reportedly as young as twelve worked in the houses. A still more lurid aspect of prostitution, but one not mentioned in the respectable society of the day, was abortions. In the larger communities these became quite a business, although always performed illicitly. In the red-light district a healthy percentage of the camp's crime occurred, for it attracted all types of criminals. Even within the establishments, disturbances broke out as two would-be suitors fought for the affections of one of the inmates, or the girls themselves got into a tussle over a client. This, then, was the environment in which the women resided, the life which they led. Isolated from much of the rest of the community and a normal life, they quickly lost any ideas of glamor or even riches connected with prostitution.

The end, when it came, left no illusions. In the October 1, 1880 issue of the Central City, Colorado, *Weekly Register-Call* the pathetic career and death of a woman identified only as Viola was recounted, with appropriate admonishments against her way of life. She once had a husband and family but had in an "evil hour consented to follow the fortunes of her deceiver . . . ; he soon tired of his toy; and satiated with his lust, he cast her off as he would a worn-out garment, and left her a dishonored wife, a false mother, overcome with shame, to battle with a world that knows no pity for a fallen woman." Eventually, she arrived in Central City, where, despite an ill-fated attempt to reform, Viola died at the age of 33 and was "deposited in a narrow grave in Potter's Field, in the bleak mountains of Gilpin County."

Although newspapers initially took little real notice of the evils of prostitution beyond a few short comments, many eventually were caught in the mounting pressure against the institution. Usually by the time a camp reached its second decade, attempts were being made to end the abomination. Comments like this appeared: "The reckless manner in which the soiled doves settle around in various portions of our once moral village should at least suggest a herd law. Let the evil be concentrated or bounced." Under such circumstances the local paper generally championed the movement. The social evil, according to one editor, could be eradicated by a higher and better system of mental, moral, and physical education supported by religious worship. He felt that the men should be blamed as much as the women themselves. "The taint of pollution on the character of woman lasts forever, but the taint of pollution on the character of man is forgotten or varnished over by an indulgent— too often by anxious mamas—under the innocent and harmless name of 'sowing wild oats.' " [16] Thus went the argument, with each camp adding its own personal touch as to why reform was needed. In the end the reformers won out, with vice first being curtailed, then forced to retreat from the main thoroughfares, and finally perhaps driven entirely from the community. The victory achieved was not so much one of refined morals and attitudes, but rather of changing economic and social conditions which no longer supported the vices of the boom days.

Prostitution gained a foothold and flourished because it was needed and accepted as part of the mining frontier. The feeling existed that the soiled doves comprised a normal part of the community, the sign of a real camp which had arrived. Then, too, the settlers tolerated almost any means of livelihood as long as it did not threaten the safety of the community. Even if enforcement of regulations against prostitution had been wanted, public apathy and the weakness of the police force would have made it difficult to accomplish successfully. It took years to generate the support needed to abolish the institution.

The open, devil-may-care attitude which affected those who resided in and visited the camps helps explain further why the red-light district flourished. The following comment, in all its Victorian moralism, directly concerns this consequence as it related to the "erring damsels" and their gentlemen:

> Men of decent appearance seen elsewhere, as soon as they reached Leadville jibed, sang low songs, walked openly with the painted courtesans with whom the town teems, and generally gave themselves up to what they term 'a time' each one promising the other one not to 'give him away'. Secure in the fact that their boon companions would not 'give them away,' that their women folks were safe and snug in their distant homes, that their children, prayers said, were tucked in their little beds, these whilom gentlemen announced that they were going 'the whole hog or none.' [17]

The fact remains that prostitution fulfilled certain functions—social, sexual, and recreational—for which particularly the young camp provided no other outlet. The universality of the institution provided mute testimony to its importance. Newspapers throughout the period make references to it, and the census returns, whether disguising it in such terms as "boarding-school girls," keeping house, or openly listing occupations such as courtesan or prostitute, provide supporting evidence. The miner, no matter where he might have been and if he were so inclined, could find some of the girls.

Prostitutes made several contributions to the mining frontier. A certain element of refinement came to the camps with their fashionable clothes and their fancy houses. Some enforced a code of behavior which, for at least a short span of time, nearly made gentlemen out of the miners. Their places of business, whether in an elegant parlor or a hurdy-gurdy, offered a combination club, amusement center, and confessional for the lonely males of the community.[18] From their earnings they grubstaked miners and invested in other pursuits. It cannot be denied that prostitution was degrading for the participants, the source of much demoralized pleasure-seeking and disturbance, and that the effect of a lowered moral standard was more harmful than beneficial. However, it was accepted as part of the frontier environment. If one judges by the standards of the period, it is possible to conclude that the institution had a definite place and served at least partially to fill a need of the community.

Another profligacy associated with the red-light district was the hurdy-gurdy houses. Strictly speaking, these served as dance halls, not as centers for prostitution, although a fine line often separated the two. Their popularity reached a peak in the 1860s in Colorado, Idaho, and Montana. In some camps they maintained an honest reputation for entertainment and dancing; a miner could engage a partner for a dance at a nominal fee, plus the cost of drinks. In the hall adjoining the dance floor, a bar and usually a gambling area operated for the amusement of the patrons, but the strong attraction remained the presence of "ye gals that do so much towards making nights lively." The name apparently originated with the dancers, in these earlier years usually Germans, who were called hurdy-gurdies.[19]

A good stepper could make a fair wage, but the job of dancing for hours on end physically taxed the girls. They dressed to suit their individual tastes and, although many were reportedly unattractive, they certainly offered a pleasant diversion for an evening. Even in the more respectable days of the sixties, opinion concerning the girls and their craft varied. According to some men who knew them, the girls danced because they needed the money and looked upon the occupation as a legitimate livelihood. Others felt they were but a shady and dangerous substitute for more legitimate associations. Alexander McClure had a revealing experience with a hurdy when he visited a Virginia City, Montana, establishment. According to him he was invited by one "not fair, but fat and forty" to dance, but modestly declined saying that he had never done it. Whereupon the lady replied with the "bewitching air" of the sex, "Damn it, don't tell me you don't, I've saw [sic] you dance forty times." [20]

It was not long before the hurdy-gurdies declined in public estimation. Trouble involving some damaged the reputation of all, for it occurred quite openly for everyone to observe. Rowdiness, excessive drinking, and periodic fights aroused the wrath of the more sedate citizenry. As early as January, 1865, the *Montana Post* editorially criticized them as a useless waste of hard-earned money and a source of much local mischief.[21] Other papers followed suit and the hurdies soon found themselves the object of much discussion. As criticism mounted, attendance slumped. Soon, in order to attract patrons, the hurdy-gurdies became quasi-brothels frequented by the demimonde. Thus the worst fears of their opponents were realized, and before long they were not tolerated in the community. Even before the crusade against prostitution got seriously started, the hurdies had moved on, the victims of public censorship and declining profits.

By the 1870s the hurdy-gurdy establishments were openly part of the red-light district, where the name, if not the service, dropped into disuse. The revulsion of the residents of Butte, Montana, to the mere opening of an establishment was typical. The *Butte Miner,* February 12, 1878, noted that the hurdies would not molest anyone who remained away from them, but it was a sad commentary that

Hurdy-gurdy girls as they appeared in *Harper's Monthly,*
June, 1865. *Denver Public Library Western Collection.*

men would not seek a higher, more elevating kind of amusement.
In the months that followed, the paper closely followed what
chanced to ensue in the establishment, reporting with alacrity all
rowdiness. Finally enough pressure was brought to bear so that the
city fathers enforced an ordinance prohibiting such establishments
and closed it. The editor, while happy to see the hurdy gone, worried about the fundamental reason for its existence. "The dancing
saloon nuisance has abated but the moral miasma in which it germinated and flourished still exists. No sophistical plea of necessity,
or selfish interest should be permitted to excuse the indecent or-
gies. . . ." [22] The point was well taken, for the hurdy-gurdy was
but an effect of an underlying cause, the same attitude which permitted the red-light district to flourish unregulated.

The dance halls which became popular in the 1870s were closely
akin to the hurdy-gurdy, the moral climate being no better than it
had been formerly. Similar in all respects, with a bar and dance
floor, they might also include a small stage and shows for the fur-

ther enjoyment of the miners. The girls employed as dancers usually were as much a part of the red-light district as their sisters in the houses. The prostitute, in fact, utilized the halls for displaying her wares. Dance halls, while generally prosperous for the owner and enjoyable for the patrons, disgusted the respectable residents of the community. Summing it up neatly, the editor of the *Leadville Daily Chronicle* wrote on October 10, 1879, "Men are fools and women devils in disguise. That's the reason the dance halls clear from one to two hundred dollars per night."

Entertainment, drinking, and women, all combined in one show, created for the miners a rowdy good time at the variety theater. A poor relation of the legitimate theater, this forerunner of vaudeville made no pretense concerning drama. All types of acts appeared, including comedians, acrobats, Indian rubbermen, and singers. The program, planned primarily for that portion of the populace accustomed to fewer constraints, offered unrestrained entertainment. According to Eddie Foy, who played in numerous camps, the audience expressed its approval or disapproval rather vociferously but never became violent except for a few irresponsible drunks. Between acts the actresses and painted darlings of the chorus enticed the customers to purchase refreshments.[23] There was little or nothing cultural here, for the men had come to see feminine performers and would have had it no other way.

To add to the pleasure, some variety theaters had their own gambling houses to divorce the patrons from their money more freely. Almost anything happened in this house of pleasure. The last show of the evening apparently took the honors for being the wildest. Many of the girls, of course, were prostitutes and this performance served as little more than a come-on. After visiting a variety theater, one reporter gave a description of what he had observed. Purchasing an upstairs seat for $1, he found out later that it cost only 50¢ on the main floor. The 100 percent markup in price resulted from the fact that the upstairs price entitled the bearer to hug the girls who came around periodically to sell liquid refreshments. At one time or another from ten to twenty "stuffed angels," dressed in "the airy drapery of Venus," appeared on the stage, seldom more than one or two at a time. The rest occupied their off-stage moments in the private boxes entertaining the patrons. Though they were called actresses, very few fit the term, and the same could be said of the waiter-girls: "in fact the term waiter is an assumed title, their true vocation is something else, and this is a good place to advertise it." Continuing with his comments, he wrote,

> A few of them are even pretty (when the paint is on), in fact they are well adapted for just the work the proprietors have intended of the actresses to be employed; they first asked about qualifications, 'Is she a good wine-room girl?' Talent is a secondary consideration.

Concluding his expose, the writer stated, "One institution of this kind has wrought the ruin of more young men than all the grog shops in the city." [24] Not all camps had this type of theater nor were all variety theaters of this class. In the larger and wealthier settlements, one at least would open its doors. Nowhere else could so many enticements be found for an evening's revelry. It is little wonder, then, that they retained popularity despite widespread disapproval.

It may be inferred that the more refined residents avoided such performances rather than risk their social reputations. Perhaps the better shows attracted the more curious, but the loyal patron remained the miner and his peers. The variety theater definitely emphasized a cleavage in society and was the miner's answer to the more sophisticated legitimate drama and literary societies. In many ways the essence of the rough, materialistic life of the young camp was exemplified by it; for this reason, the variety theater could not hope to retain popularity when stability and permanency were brought about. While good times held out, it prospered, but when the glory days passed, this was one of the first to go. In an attempt to keep pace, shows might be modified, but eventually the doors of the variety theater closed permanently.

The use of narcotics was one of the most lurid aspects of the red-light district. Opium dens housed this debased habit, and, though blamed on the Chinese, the traffic was not limited to these people. Public reaction against the obvious dens developed more quickly than to any other shady activity, and suppression soon followed.[25] To close the known establishments suppressed only part of the traffic; dope continued to pass clandestinely, and opium was smoked in shabby, secret dens. The problem seems to have been concentrated in those areas of dense population or where the Chinese settled in large numbers, which left the majority of the camps with few, if any, addicts. No real answer for the prevention of the use of narcotics was found; rather as the situation stabilized or declined, the problem itself lessened and could be forgotten or conveniently hidden from view.

The red-light district had a great deal to do with shaping the image of the mining camp for the American generation of that day and since. Much of this reputation rests upon the skillful pen of Eastern writers who visited the West and amused readers with their lusty accounts. In particular, three communities, Deadwood, Leadville, and Tombstone, synonymous with the wild West, depicted the popular image of a mining camp. These three became prominent in the short period from 1876 to 1882. Each had a roaring red-light district and a high crime rate. Factors conducive to such developments appeared almost at once in each—large, transitory populations, boom conditions, and easy wealth. Deadwood mushroomed first in 1876, followed by Leadville in 1878, and two years later by Tombstone. By the time one was tamed, another boomed, and a quasi-crime, pleasure circuit developed. Truthfully, this might be characterized as the last stand of a passing frontier.

Of the three, Deadwood probably least deserved the fate. Its reputation, however, was established the day James Butler (Wild Bill) Hickok drew the last card in the now famous dead man's hand. The center of the Black Hills, Deadwood acquired more than the usual number of frontier characters, saloons, gambling dens, and prostitutes. While it cannot be denied that a certain amount of lawlessness took place, the testimony of residents and local newspapers contradict the wild, weird stories about the camp.[26]

Tombstone's descriptive name reflects the reputation of the town. George Parsons, the shrewd observer of the turbulent early years, testified in his diary to the frequent occurrence of violence. A brief examination of the *Epitaph* or *Nugget* corroborates his testimony. The entire blame for this situation did not rest with the mining frontier. Cochise County, a favorite rendezvous for cattle rustlers and border bandits, deserved as much credit as Tombstone. The Earp-Clanton feud, culminating in the classic gunfight at the OK Corral, reflects this multiple causation. As a mining center, Tombstone was of secondary importance. However, it owed its existence to mining; therefore, its reputation reflected on the entire frontier.

Leadville offers no similar rationalization. Born of a mining excitement, it became the wealthiest, biggest, and wildest mining community of the era. City government, the police, and local citizenry seemed unable to master the situation. Leadville, in turn, gained a national reputation for its wickedness. Literally flowing with money, the camp acted as a magnet for a steadily increasing lawless element. For a while it almost appeared that the problem could not be solved, but eventually order triumphed and the town was tamed.

Of them all, Leadville was the only camp which seemed to take real pride in its depravity and enjoyed the reputation it thus acquired. In no other locality did the newspaper carry so many items concerning the red-light district nor appear more to relish the sordid details. In a way, it never died, for Leadville, as the Queen, became a yardstick by which to measure other camps. What happened there and elsewhere was the legend of the frontier, so affecting the study of mining camps that some writers feel that without violence and vice a community failed to live up to its promise.

The fame of these three, and easier transportation to the West, produced a virtual flood of visitors and reporters who naturally recounted and frequently embellished what they saw. The accounts that emerged strengthened the exotic at the expense of the real. The wild West, consequently, became a living legend in its own time.

Now that we have examined the camp's seamy side, as displayed in the red-light district and its immediate environs, the obvious contrasts within the communities become apparent. Education, culture, and religion, for example, flourished in the same environment as vice and gambling. Approximately side by side the residents built their schools and maintained the cribs. Municipal governments in some camps relied heavily on fines based upon illegal, yet open, operation of the red-light district, while at the same time local residents prided themselves upon the law and order they had achieved. Women were respected for their virtue, although men did not consider prostitutes contemptible for their lack of morals. This list could be continued, but is sufficient to demonstrate the double standards accepted as part of life.

Probably no other aspect of the mining camp had such a transitory existence, yet had such an impact on the community. Basically, the effect was negative, tempered somewhat by the realization that this type of entertainment and social life was desired by many men. To judge them too harshly, however, would be to do so by standards other than their own, which is hardly fair. For the services rendered, they should be adjudged no more severely than the society which condoned and heartily indulged in their pleasures.

Fifteen

The Promised Land

THE promised land—to the men and women of the mining frontier it meant a new home, a fresh start, wealth, adventure, the chance to be part of the frontier movement, or any of a multitude of aspirations. They came by the thousands, some to find the answer to their searching, many to partake of, but not fulfill, the dream. Their experiences became the saga of the settlement of the Rocky Mountain West. Individually, few have been recorded in historical accounts, the names now forgotten with the passage of time. They came, endured, and died, but the story belongs to them. It is the story of the West, for they were the builders.

Within one generation these people conquered and settled a land which, until then, had been considered of little worth except as a desert and mountainous habitation for the Indian and nomadic fur trapper. A man in his early twenties who had gone to Colorado in 1859, but who in 1890 would have been in his fifties, might have witnessed much of the history of the mining West, had he had a wanderlust. Having spent his lifetime in that spacious and sometimes strikingly beautiful country, he probably had grown to love it and the life he led, although both were demanding and sometimes brutal.

As this fifty-niner no doubt observed, the frontier changed over the decades. The years of his youth had long since disappeared and now reappeared in folklore and legend. Perhaps wistfully, he would have liked to return to the day before the coming of the railroad, electricity, telephones, and corporation mining. The new West might have seemed alien to him; perhaps he felt shunted aside, unappreciated by the younger generation. Yet he did not love the old, or he would not have turned from it to move to a virgin land; so conceivably he was happy with the fruits of his labor. No doubt his life, like that of so many of his contemporaries, had originally emphasized personal gain and temporary residence, but then a change had come over him, with an increasing sense of public responsibility and the potential possibility for lasting settlement. Growing out of this sentiment came the great changes of the period. He had arrived with a dream of a better life with bountiful blessings. Without doubt he failed to achieve all of his goals, yet optimism and hope had propelled him on, for certainly somewhere in this land of plenty, rich with gold and silver, would be found his personal Eldorado.

Our miner spent many of his years living in the camps, carousing with his friends. Probably by 1890 several camps in which he resided had become mere skeletons and had possibly been abandoned. Much that he had witnessed and in which he had participated was gone.

The mining camp, the cutting edge of the frontier, the island of permanent settlement, the base for continued growth and transformation, symbolized a development new to the expansion of America, the urban frontier. Nowhere else did the frontier become so widespread and universally urbanized. Richard Wade, in his *Urban Frontier*, wrote of the Mississippi Valley settlement: "The towns were the spearheads of the frontier . . . their establishment . . . preceded the breaking of soil in the transmontane West." [1] His point is valid, yet only a scattered few had been started before the coming of general settlement. Geographical considerations played an important role in founding Pittsburgh and Louisville, two of the five towns he examined; both were located on important stations on the Ohio River route into the valley. The general influx of towns came after the initial agrarian settlement, not as an integral part of it.

Not so in the Rocky Mountains, for here the camps preceded and helped bring about general settlement. Per capita, the ratio of urban dwellers was greater in the early mining years than since. The number of settlements also was correspondingly higher when compared to the general population in this area.

The individual frontiersman did not vanish to become part of the communal whole. Individuality in all its forms remained in the camps, yet the importance of society increased at the expense of each member's personal freedom of choice. For the community to survive, all had to work together to provide at least a fundamental economic and social order. Nor could the miner hope to emulate the farmer, who with his family cleared the land and became relatively self-sufficient. To work a mine profitably took capital, knowledge, machinery, and a skilled laboring crew. For these the miner needed outside assistance; he had to depend upon others to furnish the essentials he lacked.

Despite the frequently overdrawn picture of the rugged individualist pitting himself against the forces of nature and man, the miner relied upon his government for aid and succor. He cried for mail service, lenient federal policies toward mining and land, military protection, and territorial government. Aroused protests greeted any dereliction of responsibility or failure to meet expectations. Up to a point Uncle Sam was welcome, but the miner and townsman did not want the government to interfere too much. Quite definitely Federal regulation or close supervision was not desired. This ambiguous attraction and repulsion typify the Western attitude toward government.

As the urban center of an urbanized frontier, the camp reflected clearly the change in the frontier pattern. Primarily, the process was accelerated. Businessmen, tradesmen, and other typical inhabitants of established settlement appeared almost simultaneously with the miners. Closely on their heels came schools, churches, theaters, and other refinements. The self-sufficient stage of pioneering was readily bypassed, for little existed here which could be called self-sufficient. Food, clothing, equipment, and working capital came from external sources. The miner might possess knowledge of minerals and mining, but even in these matters, time and time again the trained engineer and geologist came to the rescue.

As a consequence of this urban environment, developments occurred which have influenced the Rocky Mountain region to the present day. Immediate emphasis was placed on transportation, not merely the most rudimentary, but safe, fast, and cheap methods. Being dependent on others for food germinated encouragement for the expansion of farming into a region which had long been described as the "Great American Desert." In a similar manner such other industries as manufacturing, lumbering, and freighting grew to satisfy the demands of the camps. As urban centers, the communities attracted and nurtured cultural activities more swiftly than had been known previously on the frontier. The camp was a nucleus that attracted, encouraged, and transmitted intellectual, social, economic, and political foundations from which a rich harvest has been reaped.

Because this was an urban frontier, the settlers encountered unique problems, or familiar problems with a changed emphasis. Concentration of population brought to the wilderness the complexities of the city: sanitation, municipal government, finances, fire protection, and maintenance of streets. The criminal element and its followers, attracted by the possibilities of the booming camps, drifted in to practice their trades. Not only did they need to be controlled, but a framework of ordinances had to be devised to protect both individual and community rights within society. Though none of these problems were unknown in American history, the necessity for finding immediate solutions was unusual. The frontier specialty of governmental organization was displayed at every level. The Colorado fifty-niners organized the extralegal territory of Jefferson when the Federal government failed to act quickly or decisively enough to suit the settlers. In other regions, requests for territorial government appeared soon after the initial mining rush. On the local scene the situation demanded instantaneous action with the rapid influx of population. The immediate response, the miners' meeting and court, set the groundwork for the eventual growth of an enduring governing body.

A novel type of pioneer emerged—the urban dweller, a frontier individualist restrained by the compact social world in which he lived. As only a part of a communal whole, he either obeyed the dictates of the community or found himself suffering the penalties for nonconformance. Within this society the inhabitant was subject to the anxieties and tensions typical of any settlement but compounded by the frontier environment. His world was largely impersonal; outside of a few acquaintances, the populace took very little notice of his presence. Transitory by the nature of his work and often by choice, he followed the ever moving mining frontier until circumstances warranted his settling down or abandoning the chase. Much more quickly than in previous decades the refinements of civilization, along with all the problems and temptations, enticed him to spend his hard-won gold or silver. The cosmopolitan nature of the community brought the individual into contact with varied cultures, some of which he assimilated, while he rejected others. The man who emerged was not the fifty-niner or sixty-niner warmed over, but a Westerner whose mining camp environment and experience had helped create an outlook and characteristics different from other areas of the country.

Both the community and its residents displayed contradictions in thought and deed. One of the most obvious resulted from the interplay of one on the other. The people wanted their camp to resemble the image of the older Eastern cities. Architecture, social institutions, and government were patterned after the familiar home town. While desiring these improvements, the Westerner seemed unwilling or unable to provide needed monetary support. Partially as a consequence of this, the emerging settlement differed in appearance and substance from the Eastern model.

Conversely, the availability of money dictated much of what went on within the camp. Most residents, to be sure, did not have a great amount of ready cash, but the frontier as a whole had the resources. As a result, much was overdone—a stately opera house would be built in a soon-to-be-abandoned community, while a public water system might suffer because tax funds were not available to build or maintain it. Money passed into the hands of the gamblers and prostitutes but not into the hands of teachers or the school budget. Another contradiction appears; though these miners wanted permanence almost fanatically, their philosophy of "easy come, easy go, to be found again tomorrow" pulled them in the opposite direction.

Only by stretching the imagination could one call the mining camp a safety valve for the discontented. The poor of the Eastern cities found no haven here, for it was much too distant and called for skills they did not possess. For the Midwesterners it might more reasonably do so, but these people were of pioneering stock and accustomed to moving West. They came, but did not necessarily find themselves better off financially. Some turned back early, others became wanderers, while a portion returned to their older trades, where they found a measure of wealth and security. The indigent, unskilled person, no matter from which part of the country or the world, found this to be a cold, hostile environment. Additional research on individual camps, however, will indicate, I believe, that they served as safety valves for each other.

Although the Easterner looked upon his Western brother as being something of a political radical, such a case was rare. The liberal-democratic attitudes of the early years gave way to a juxtaposition of conservative-progressive tendencies. In a progressive manner the camps accepted such innovations as the telephone. In contrast, having made their personal fortunes, the Westerners assumed a protective attitude of "I've made mine and do not intend to lose it," which became political conservatism. Even the election of 1896, which found the West aligned with William Jennings Bryan and silver, illustrates the fight to protect an already-gained plateau from the encroachment of the government and the Eastern establishment. The attitude toward women's rights reflected the same tendency. The men were quite willing to give women unheard-of privileges and a great amount of respect but hesitated to give them the vote.[2] Yet by the turn of the century three Rocky Mountain states—Wyoming, Colorado, and Utah—had granted women suffrage to put them in the vanguard of the movement. More correctly, the Westerner could be called a maverick rather than a radical.

An urban society evolved before the rural one. It came to dominate the region for a decade or better, depending on the locality. Then with the decline of mining in the 1890s, but even before that with the increasing number of farmers in the postwar years, the pendulum started to swing toward a rural-dominated legislature and society. The urbanity of the mining frontier faded except for isolated pockets. The region became rurally oriented and not until the mid-twentieth century would it again assume such importance in politics, economy and regional activities. The mining camps, then, might be said to have failed to produce a permanent urban civilization. More justifiably, one may note that the urban tradition was passed on to cities like Denver and Helena, where it remained in the mainstream of Western progress. Its taproots have gone deep into Western experience.

To imagine that settlement and growth would not have come without mining would be absurd. Certainly railroads, schools, farming, roads, and towns would have appeared eventually, but the tempo, direction, influence, and significance were changed by the mining frontier and its camps. This is true not only for the immediate region, but to a lesser degree, for the surrounding states as well.

With some validity, historians have accused the mining frontier of wastefulness, exploitation, and transitoriness. One needs only to look at the mine dumps, which scar so many valleys and hillsides, or the places where a dredge has done its work along a stream, to understand why this assertion has merit. The wealth has been taken out, it cannot be replaced. Walk over the abandoned site of a camp and consider the amount of labor, money, and materials which went into building the settlement and the reason for the argument becomes apparent. On the surface, no doubt, the frontier was these things, but much which was the essence of the era has been ignored by such a cursory examination. Thorough study supports the conclusion that this period of transition, whether intentional or not, was but the means to an end—the enduring settlement and growth of the West.

In the history of the mining era the camp played an integral role. Much of the lasting significance, as well as the intensity, vitality, urgency, and vigor of the frontier springs primarily from this source. A curious blending of the new and the familiar, of innovation and imitation, the camp became home for many divergent groups— Americans, Europeans, and Orientals. In a short span of time they created the social, political, and economic institutions needed to provide and insure permanence. In each camp the pattern started over again with the impatient crowd of prospectors, merchants, miners, gamblers, and others who swarmed to the discovery site. America has never, before or since, seen on such a scale the type of life they took for granted. Because it was picturesque, however, did not necessarily make it romantic or even pleasant. In time most of the camps declined and the people moved, leaving behind the waste and litter of civilization. This cycle might extend for a generation or only over a few years, but relentlessly it claimed its victims.

When the miners abandoned a district to drift to other more promising areas, they left behind a residue of economic development which withstood the decline of mining. The farmer had come, and with him small agrarian villages. Although hurt by the subsequent deterioration of the camp market, the agricultural economy was firmly enough established to remain and guarantee continued expansion. Commercial and industrial interests which had been attracted to the camps did not die with the frontier; they found different markets and continued business. Capital, which was needed so desperately to develop the West, had come from the mines, much of it to go into the pockets of individuals and corporations outside the region. Some of it remained, however, or returned to help develop the states.

The transcontinental railroad, dreamed of years before the 1849 gold rush, came to fruition partly because of the Western mining regions and their prospective markets. The railroad network in the Rocky Mountains reached its height just as the period under discussion came to a close. Not only did it aid mining but it brought in settlers and opened new markets. To serve the needs of the camps, trading, smelter, and transportation towns were established in and around the districts. Long before the mining frontier had disappeared, then, the basic institutional framework for the regional economy had evolved, so that with only a minimum of delay and recession the demise of mining could be overcome.

A more intangible contribution of the camps was toward what has become one of the most significant industries of the West—tourism. Having become one of the primary attractions for visitors, whether as ghost towns or refurbished replicas, such as Central City, Colorado, and Virginia City, Montana, the camps still have an impact on Western economy. Earlier though, when mining flourished, tourists were encouraged to visit and enjoy the wonders to be seen. The editor of the *Yankee Fork Herald* praised Idaho as the "resort of the seeker," with scenery the "grandest and most picturesque imaginable."[3] Even the invalid should travel here to regain health and find relaxation. Ouray, Colorado, which has become a Mecca for tourists, advertised itself without exaggeration in 1883 as a "most desirable place for all who can appreciate the beauties of nature," with romantic drives, hot springs, and fish and game.[4] Such advertising helped lure people to come, and those who did went back to tell others of the scenic grandeur of the West. A start had been made.

In other areas, the mining camp made tangible and intangible contributions. It acted as a transmitter for social and esthetic institutions, and as a magnet not only for merchants, bankers, and miners, but also for musicians, artists, and actors. Where else on the frontier, within months after the initial settlement, could the pioneer hope to enjoy Shakespeare or the opera? Along with these advances came the school, literary society, church, lodge, and other trappings of a maturing culture. At the same time, the inhabitants were being freed from the typical frontier hardships; especially did this appear rapid when compared to agrarian frontiers where a decade or more elapsed before similar advances could be contemplated. Not only did this improve the life of the townspeople, but by example and direct participation it encouraged like endeavors throughout the West.

A critic of the mining camps wrote in 1932 that they contributed little to what was thought to be Americanism, "but in its own bizarre way something after the manner of warped mirrors that intrigue children and some adults in our amusement parks, the mining camp reflected much." [5] Americanism was an interesting term to use, for what constitutes Americanism? If it is our cultural, political, economic, and social heritage, then the camps made a contribution, both as transmitters and originators, in the trans-Mississippi West. If the historian and hobbyist examined only the glitter and tinsel of the camps, which unfortunately far too often has been viewed as the essential part, such an assumption might be valid. Charles Shinn, one of the first students of the camp, stated as early as 1884 that if the rush, excitement, freedom, and splendor of the period have any value to the American historian, that value exists entirely independently of the price set upon them by writers of tales and upholders of state pride. [6] Shinn maintained the success of the frontier was the development and maintenance of government. His conclusions are still valid, although government is only one facet of the significance. As Shinn pointed out, the image of the mining frontier has too often suffered because of the failure to probe deeply enough into the less glamorous but more important aspects of the camp.

Pathos permeates the story of the mining frontier. The camps spent their hour upon the stage and disappeared, hardly mourned by the former resident or the newer generation. A description of Elizabethtown, New Mexico, written in 1882, only slightly more than a decade after its boom, comments:

> It makes one lonesome to walk the streets of Elizabethtown. Although not an old place, it is deserted, and instead of the crowded streets, or crowded houses, rum shops, gambling saloons, and hourly knock downs of a few years ago, a sort of grave yard stillness, deserted buildings, . . . a good deal of broken glass, and other fragments of former prosperity left, but the pith, the vitality of the village life had departed. . . .[7]

For everything, as it has been written, "there is a season, a time to be born, and a time to die."

Were the mining camp residents, whose story has been told in the preceding chapters, to return to view again their promised land they probably would be pleased with the change which has come over it. The age that they knew has gone beyond redemption. Their children, grandchildren, and great-grandchildren have built upon the heritage left to them, not always with wisdom but with much of the same boldness and faith that typified their ancestors. The land itself has not changed markedly, but this land has an epic name today, and to these pioneers must go the credit for winning the name and laying the cornerstone for future achievement.

Bibliographical Essay
Works Cited
Notes
Index

BIBLIOGRAPHICAL ESSAY

Unlike other aspects of the history of the trans-Mississippi West, the mining frontier has failed to capture the pens of authors. This has been particularly true in the realm of fiction, but, until the last few years, even scholars have relatively ignored it. Bret Harte, who knew the era from firsthand experience, early portrayed the mining West in his short stories, such as "The Outcasts of Poker Flat." Harte, in fact, did his best work in this area but overromanticized and overdramatized the setting.

The inequality of production clearly appears when one compares the myriad of fictional short stories and books written about the cattlemen or the fur traders to the handful of those written about miners. If television and motion pictures are an indication of the appeal which the West holds for the general public, this failure can even more clearly be shown. The mining frontier in these media receives little attention, indicating a failure to capture popular taste.

It is interesting to note that in the realm of opera the mining era has been more successful. Verdi's "Girl of the Golden West" has a California semimining setting and Douglas Moore and John LaTouche's "The Ballad of Baby Doe" tells the story of Tabor and his second wife against the background of the rise and fall of Colorado silver mining. The latter is by far the better in depicting the frontier, and, although music critics might disagree, in its musical score. The melodrama, popular in the camps and still played today, has used the setting extensively. Numerous legends, folktales, and ballads, handed down from the days of the forty-niners and fifty-niners, give in their own way excellent insights into the era and have occasionally emerged in twentieth-century musical adaptations to capture passing popular fancy. Nevertheless, the mining West still remains in the shadow of its contemporaries.

Why this should be cannot be pinpointed accurately. Drama, excitement, danger were as much a part of mining as of the cattle or Indian frontiers. If the public taste runs to stories of the tinsel facade of gamblers and prostitutes, Leadville can match Dodge City with ease and surpass it in volume and time span. Probably the answer lies partially in the concept of the urban frontier. The classic Western story of the individual pitting himself against nature and man does not readily fit into the mining mold. The prospector remains the outstanding symbol of individuality but lacks the versatility of setting and adventure of the cowboy or the mountain man.

Nor does the mining frontier present as kaleidoscopic a cast to play the drama. The Indian, gunfighter, and outlaw (gunsmoke and gallop variety), the soldier, or such conflicts as the farmer vs. the rancher—all traditional trappings in Westerns—were generally absent or incidental to the mining story, as mentioned in Chapter Six. It apparently has been hard to sustain great interest in the contest of capitalistic corporations over control of a mineral deposit with these elements missing. The six-gun, too, has little significance in individual lives or the community. Still, there would seem to be a great potential here which has remained untapped, for each camp's history contains a wealth of human interest and other stories.

For those concerned with pursuing further an examination of mining camps, the only general study to date is Charles Shinn's *Mining Camps, A Study in American Frontier Government* (reissued as Harper Torchbook, 1965). This volume, originally published in 1885, has become the classic in the field, although Shinn's knowledge was limited largely to the Pacific coast region. Despite being somewhat dated, if read carefully and critically it remains an excellent introduction. The mining frontier in general has received only a little more attention until the past decade. Rodman Paul, who edited the recent edition of Shinn's book, has written the outstanding interpretative examination, *Mining Frontiers of the Far West 1848-1880* (1963). His essay on bibliography should be a first guide for all students of this field. In the same year, 1963, William Greever's *The Bonanza West* appeared. Written more for the general reader, it is a chronological survey-summary of the mining frontiers from California to Alaska. Both of these works have weaknesses: Paul tends to stress the California-Nevada experience and Greever totally ignores the Southwest and relies exclusively on secondary sources. Despite these defects, both volumes provide the necessary framework and background which has so long been lacking. Earlier general works include Glenn Quiett, *Pay Dirt* (1936) and T. A. Rickard, *A History of American Mining* (1932).

The scholarly examination of an individual mining camp and district has been bypassed in favor of the more glamorous accounts of well-known people and events. It is to be hoped that a new era dawned with the publication of W. Turrentine Jackson's *Treasure Hill* (1963), which I recommend highly. More popularly written is Larry Barsness' *Gold Camp* (1962), an account of Virginia City, Montana. Don and Jean Griswold's *The Carbonate Camp Called Leadville* (1951) is also worth the reader's time. Unfortunately, a good many of the other so-called history books on the market claiming to discuss camps and districts are not worth the effort.

Hubert H. Bancroft's multivolume histories contain much useful information, if the reader is willing to spend the time looking for it. Numerous state histories are also valuable for references to individual communities, but one must be on guard against provincialism. Scattered throughout the Western universities are theses and dissertations written on camps and mining districts, an outstanding example being Eugene Irey's "A Social History of Leadville, Colorado" (Ph.D. dissertation, University of Minnesota, 1951). State historical journals and magazines also serve as a valuable depository for primary and secondary sources. Varying considerably in worth, depending on the amount of mining carried on within the area, they cover each one of the Rocky Mountain states. Of particular importance are the *Colorado Magazine* and *Montana, The Magazine of Western History*.

Another category of mining camp literature, the pictorial history, which in recent years has been gaining in quantity if not quality, has attracted many readers. In this field the three volumes by Muriel Wolle, *Stampede to Timberline, The Bonanza Trail,* and *Montana Pay Dirt,* rank as unequaled achievements.

While secondary sources serve as a good sample and survey, in order to really savor life in the mining camps one needs to go to the original records and material. Doing research on the communities is similar to mining, for a high percentage of waste has to be sorted to uncover the ore. The rewards are great, however, for the persistent and the lucky.

There exists a multitude of contemporary sources, some of which have been published; many more may be found in library and historical society collections. To approach any, the student must have a critical, questioning eye, but an insight can be gathered from each. Especially noteworthy are James Miller's diary (Andrew Rolle, editor), George Parson's journal, the Matthew Dale letters and Seth Bullock's account of Deadwood (Harry Anderson, editor). The books of Thomas Dimsdale and Nathaniel Langford provide examinations of specific areas and a general discussion as well. Agnes Spring's edition of Richard Hughes's *Pioneer Years in the Black Hills* gives an excellent account by a newspaperman. For a slightly different aspect see *The Golden Frontier* (edited by Doyce Nunis), which sets forth the recollections of Herman Reinhart, a freighter over much of the mining West. The Easterner, too, visited the West and left many and varied accounts. Two among them are Bayard Taylor's *Colorado: A Summer Trip* and Grace Greenwood (Sara J. Lippincott), *New Life in New Lands*.

A book which should not be missed by any student or general reader is Mark Twain's *Roughing It*. This account relates Twain's adventures and misadventures in and around the Comstock and Virginia City, Nevada. Well-written and humorous, it is recommended reading, although a warning needs to be issued concerning its complete reliability.

Government documents provide further information, especially the original census reports. These returns furnish a gold mine of statistics relating to the residents and their family lives. Essential to the study of local government are the few ordinance books and town records still in existence. Pictures found in many historical society and museum collections also are invaluable to anyone studying the camps. It is hard to overestimate them as a correlating and supplementary record.

The principal and best sources of information concerning the camps, however, are the newspaper files which are found in almost every Western state. These contain a wealth of material on every conceivable topic. Once again the researcher must be careful to ascertain any bias of the editor and where possible verify or cross-check with other sources. The editors were not above slanting the news, overstressing local events, and, on occasion, fabricating a story for the enjoyment of their readers. The papers vary in quality and in coverage. Some are extremely valuable for local items, but others will prove frustrating in this respect. Nor should the researcher expect the quality of an individual paper to remain standard. They reflected the condition of the camp and often declined after the boom days passed. Among the better papers examined were the *Butte Miner*; *The Idaho World* (Idaho City—declines sharply after 1865); *Leadville Weekly Herald*; *The Montana Post* (Virginia City); *The Park Record* (Park City, Utah); *Silver World* (Lake City, Colorado); and the *Yankee Fork Herald* (Bonanza City, Idaho).

The bibliography included on the subsequent pages is limited to material which has been cited in the text. It is not, nor was it meant to be, all-inclusive. It should, however, give the reader a sampling of the type and quantity of records available for the study of a mining camp.

WORKS CITED

I. LETTERS, DIARIES, REMINISCENCES,
AND AUTOBIOGRAPHIES

Anderson, Harry H., ed. "An Account of Deadwood and the Northern Black Hills." *South Dakota Department of History Collections,* 31 (1962), pp. 287-364.

Ashley, James H. "Message of Governor Ashley." *Contributions to the Historical Society of Montana,* 6 (1907), pp. 252-89.

Athearn, Robert. See Dale, Matthew.

Barney, Libeus. *Letters of the Pike's Peak Gold Rush.* San Jose: Talisman Press, 1959.

Barrows, John R. *Ubet.* Caldwell: Caxton Printers, 1936.

Beardsley, Isaac. *Echoes From Peak and Plain.* Cincinnati: Curts & Jennings, 1898.

Bennett, Estelline. *Old Deadwood Days.* New York: J. H. Sears, 1928.

Bristol, Sherlock. *The Pioneer Preacher: An Autobiography.* New York: F. H. Revell, c.1887.

Bryan, Jerry. *An Illinois Gold Hunter in the Black Hills.* Springfield: State Historical Society, 1960.

Clark, Charles M. *A Trip to Pike's Peak.* San Jose: Talisman Press, 1958.

Clum, John. "It All Happened in Tombstone." *Arizona Historical Review,* 2 (Oct., 1929), pp. 46-72.

Dale, Matthew. "Life in the Pike's Peak Region," ed. Robert G. Athearn. *Colorado Magazine,* 32 (Apr., 1955), pp. 81-104.

Darley, George M. *Pioneering in the San Juan.* Chicago: F. H. Revell, 1899.

Davis, Carlyle C. *Olden Times in Colorado.* Los Angeles: Phillips Publishing Co., 1916.

Dickson, Arthur J., ed. *Covered Wagon Days.* Cleveland: Clark, 1929.

Dimsdale, Thomas J. *The Vigilantes of Montana or Popular Justice in the Rocky Mountains.* Helena: State Publishing Co., n.d. (4th ed.).

Dyer, John L. *The Snow-Shoe Itinerant.* Cincinnati: Cranston & Stowe, 1890.

Edgar, Henry. "Journal of Henry Edgar." *Contributions to the Historical Society of Montana*, 3 (1900), pp. 124-42.

Ellis, Anne. *Life of an Ordinary Woman*. Boston: Houghton, 1929.

Fergus, James. "A Leaf from the Diary of James Fergus." *Contributions to the Historical Society of Montana*, 2 (1896), pp. 252-54.

Foy, Eddie, and Alvin Harlow. *Clowning Through Life*. New York: E. P. Dutton, 1928.

Goulder, W. A. *Reminiscences of a Pioneer*. Boise: Timothy Regan, 1909.

Greeley, Horace. *An Overland Journey from New York to San Francisco in the Summer of 1859*. New York: C. M. Saxon, Barker, 1860.

Hafen, LeRoy R., ed. *Colorado Gold Rush, Contemporary Letters and Reports, 1858-1859*. Glendale: Arthur H. Clark, 1941.

Homsher, Lola M., ed. *South Pass, 1868, James Chisholm's Journal of the Wyoming Gold Rush*. Lincoln: University of Nebraska Press, 1960.

Howbert, Irving. *Memories of a Lifetime in the Pike's Peak Region*. New York: G. P. Putnam, 1925.

Hughes, Dan de Lara. *South from Tombstone*. London: Methuen, 1938.

Langford, Nathaniel P. *Vigilante Days and Ways*. Chicago: A. L. Burt, 1890.

Larsen, Arthur J., ed. "The Black Hills Gold Rush." *North Dakota Historical Quarterly*, 6 (July, 1932), pp. 302-18.

Lockwood, Frank. *Pioneer Days in Arizona*. New York: Macmillan, 1932.

McLemore, Clyde, ed. "Bannack and Gallatin City in 1862-63: A Letter by Mrs. Emily R. Meredith." *Sources of Northwest History*, No. 24, pp. 5-6.

Mills, James H. "Reminiscences of an Editor." *Contributions to the Historical Society of Montana*, 5 (1904), pp. 273-88.

Nunis, Doyce B. See Reinhart, Herman Francis.

Parsons, George W. *The Private Journal of George Whitwell Parsons*. Phoenix: Arizona Statewide Archival and Records Project, 1939.

Pendleton, Mark A. "Memories of Silver Reef." *Utah Historical Quarterly*, 3 (Oct., 1930), pp. 99-118.

Pierce, A. E. "Reminiscences of a Pioneer." *Sons of Colorado*, 2 (Nov., 1907), pp. 3-8.

Reinhart, Herman Francis. *The Golden Frontier: The Recollections of Herman Francis Reinhart 1851-1869*, ed. Doyce B. Nunis. Austin: University of Texas Press, 1962.

Rolle, Andrew F., ed. *The Road to Virginia City: The Diary of James Knox Polk Miller*. Norman: University of Oklahoma Press, 1960.

Spring, Agnes W., ed. *Pioneer Years in the Black Hills*. Glendale: Arthur H. Clark, 1957.

Stanton, Irving W. *Sixty Years in Colorado*. Denver: n.p., 1922.

Steiner, Bernard C., ed. "The South Atlantic States in 1833, as seen by a New Englander." *Maryland Historical Magazine*, 13 (Dec., 1918), pp. 295-385.

Stuart, Granville. *Forty Years on the Frontier*. 2 vols. Cleveland: Arthur H. Clark, 1925.

Talbot, Ethelbert. *My People of the Plains*. New York: Harper, 1906.

Thom, William B. "In Pioneer Days." *The Trail*, 19 (Oct., 1929), pp. 9-15.

Toponce, Alexander. *Reminiscences of Alexander Toponce, Pioneer*. Ogden: Century Printing Co., 1923.

Tuttle, Daniel. *Reminiscences of a Missionary Bishop*. New York: Thomas Whittaker, 1906.

Twain, Mark [Samuel Clemens]. *Roughing It*. Hartford: American Publishing Co., 1872.

Weaver, David B. "Early Days in Emigrant Gulch." *Contributions to the Historical Society of Montana*, 7 (1910), pp. 73-96.

Young, Francis C. *Echoes from Arcadia*. Denver: Lanning Bros., 1903.

II. UNPUBLISHED MATERIAL

Bancroft Scraps. "Arizona Miscellany." Bancroft Library.

———. "Colorado Miscellany." Bancroft Library.

———. "Idaho Miscellany." Bancroft Library.

———. "New Mexico Miscellany." Bancroft Library.

———. "Utah Miscellany." Bancroft Library.

Dale, Matthew. "Letters." Western Historical Collection, University of Colorado.

Donald, William. "Dictation." Bancroft Library.

Fraser, Duncan. "Letters written by Robert Carswell for Duncan Fraser, 1864." Montana Historical Society.

Hawley, H. J. "Diary of H. J. Hawley, 1860-61." Typed copy, Colorado State Historical Society.

Hill, Clifford C. "Wagon Roads in Colorado, 1858-1876." Master's thesis, University of Colorado, 1950.

Hough, Charles M. "Leadville, Colorado, 1878-1898. A Study in Unionism." Master's thesis, University of Colorado, 1958.

Irey, Eugene. "A Social History of Leadville, Colorado, During the Boom Days, 1877-1881." Dissertation, University of Minnesota, 1951.

Jensen, Billie Barnes. "The Woman Suffrage Movement in Colorado." Master's thesis, University of Colorado, 1959.

Leach, Samuel. "Excerpts from the Autobiography of Samuel Leach, 1837-1911." Montana Historical Society.

Liftchild, Charles. Typewritten manuscript,. Arizona Pioneer's Historical Society.

Locke, George Adams. "Letters." Bancroft Library.

Louder, James. "Autobiography." Bancroft Library.

Love, Alice E. "The History of Tombstone to 1887." Master's thesis, University of Arizona, 1933.

Minnick, Nelle F. "A Cultural History of Central City, Colorado, from 1859-1880, in Terms of Books and Libraries." Master's thesis, University of Chicago, 1946.

Morley, James H. "Diary of James Henry Morley in Montana, 1862-1865." Montana Historical Society.

Nickerson, H. G. "Scrapbook of the South Pass Area." Wyoming Archives.

Perrigo, Lynn I. "Life in Central City, Colorado, as Revealed by the *Register*: 1862-1872." Master's thesis, University of Colorado, 1934.

————. "Social History of Central City, Colorado, 1859-1900." Dissertation, University of Colorado, 1936.

Rogers, Fred. "Adam Aulback Interview 1931." Bancroft Library.

Rogers, Isaac W. "Diary January-December, 1865." Montana Historical Society.

Ronan, Margaret. "Memoirs of a Frontier's Woman, Mary C. Ronan." Master's thesis, State University of Montana, 1932.

Tabor, Augusta. "Cabin Life in Colorado." Bancroft Library.

Tabor, H. A. W. "Early Days." Bancroft Library.

————. "Life of H. A. W. Tabor." Bancroft Library.

Thompson, Thomas G. "The Social and Cultural History of Lake City, Colorado, 1876-1900." Master's thesis, University of Oklahoma, 1961.

Young, Arch B. "A Social History of Early Globe, Gila County, Arizona." Master's thesis, University of Colorado, 1939.

III. DOCUMENTARY SOURCES

The Charter and Ordinances of the City of Central. Central City: Collier & Hall, 1871.

Constitution and By-laws of the Harrison Hook and Ladder Co., No. One of Leadville, Colorado. Denver: Daily Times Printing House & Book Co., 1879.

The General Ordinances of the City of Aspen. Aspen: Aspen Times Print, 1886.

Mineral Resources of the States and Territories West of the Rocky Mountains, 1867-1875. Washington: Government Printing Office, 1868-1876.

Ordinances of the City of Virginia, Territory of Montana. Davenport: Egbert, Fidlar & Chambers, 1879.

Report on the Agencies of Transportation in the United States. Washington: Government Printing Office, 1883.

Report on the Statistics of Wages in Manufacturing Industries. Washington: Government Printing Office, 1886.

Report of W. T. Sherman. *House Ex. Doc.* No. 1 (Serial 1285), 1866.

Statistics and Technology of the Precious Metals. Washington: Government Printing Office, 1885.

United States Bureau of the Census. 8th, 9th, 10th, 11th, and 12th Reports.

IV. NEWSPAPERS

Arizona Silver Belt (Globe, Arizona). May, 1878-June, 1880; Feb.-Apr., 1888.

The Aspen Times (Aspen, Colorado). Jan., 1885-Apr., 1886.

Beaver Head News (Virginia City, Montana). Mar. 26, 1867.

Black Hills Daily Pioneer (Deadwood, South Dakota). Feb.-Mar., 1879.

The Black Hills Daily Times (Deadwood, South Dakota). Aug., 1877; July, Nov., 1878.

The Black Hills Pioneer (weekly; Deadwood, South Dakota). July. 1876-July, 1877; Oct.-Nov., 1879.

Black Hills Weekly Times (Deadwood, South Dakota). Sept., 1877-May, 1878; May-Aug., 1879.

Boulder Camera (Boulder, Colorado). Mar. 17, 1899.

Boulder County News (Boulder, Colorado). Scattered issues 1870s.

Boulder News and Courier (Boulder, Colorado). July 25, 1879; July 1, 1881.

The Butte City Union (Butte, Montana). Nov., 1883-Feb., 1884.

Butte Miner (Butte, Montana). Aug., 1876-May, 1878.

Caribou Post (Caribou, Colorado). July, 1871-Aug., 1872.

Colorado Banner (Boulder, Colorado). Scattered issues 1870s.

The Cottonwood Observer (Alta, Utah). July, 1873.

Daily Central City Register (Central City, Colorado). Scattered issues 1868-1872.

Daily Chronicle (Leadville, Colorado). Scattered issues Jan.-Oct., 1879; Sept. 22, 1883.

Daily Denver Times (Denver, Colorado), Feb. 2, 1879.

The Daily Miners' Register (Central City, Colorado). Oct., 1863-June, 1864; scattered issues 1864-1867.

Daily Nugget (Tombstone, Arizona). Nov. 20, 1880.

Denver Daily Tribune (Denver, Colorado). Sept. 21, 1878; scattered issues Jan.-Mar. 1879.

The Frontier Index (Laramie and elsewhere in Wyoming). Mar.-June, 1868.

Georgetown Daily Miner (Georgetown, Colorado). Jan. 27, 1873.

The Grant County Herald (became *The Herald,* Apr., 1875; Silver City, New Mexico). Mar., 1875-Apr., 1875.

Harper's Weekly (New York, New York). Feb. 2, 1878.

The Helena Herald (Helena, Montana). Nov., 1866-Jan., 1868; May, 1869.

The Herald (Silver City, New Mexico), Apr., 1875-Jan., 1878.

The Idaho World (Idaho City, Idaho). Feb., 1865-Sept., 1866; May-Aug., 1867.

Inter-Mountains Freeman (Butte, Montana). Apr.-Sept., 1881.

Las Vegas Daily Gazette (Las Vegas, New Mexico). July 16-27, 1881.

Leadville Democrat (Leadville, Colorado). Scattered issues Jan.-Feb., July-Sept., 1880.

Leadville Daily Herald (Leadville, Colorado). March 2, 1881.

Leadville Weekly Herald (Leadville, Colorado). Nov., 1879-Jan., 1880.

The Montana Post (Virginia City, Montana). Aug., 1864-Aug., 1867.

The Montana Radiator (Helena, Montana). Jan.-Oct., 1866.

The New Mexican (Santa Fe, New Mexico). Feb. 1868-Aug., 1869.

New Mexico Interpreter (White Oaks, New Mexico). May-July, 1887; Sept.-Oct., 1888; Mar., 1889-Oct., 1890.

New York Times (New York, New York). Sept. 28, 1876.

Niles Register (Baltimore). May 16, 1835.

Ouray Times (Ouray, Colorado). June, 1877-Feb., 1880.

The Owyhee Avalanche (Ruby City and Silver City, Idaho). Aug., 1865-Dec., 1867.

The Park Record (Park City, Utah). June-Aug., 1880; July, 1881-Oct., 1883.

The Pinal Drill (Pinal City, Arizona). Sept., 1880-Dec., 1881.

Rocky Mountain News (Denver, Colorado). Apr.-Oct., 1859.

Rocky Mountain Sun (Aspen, Colorado). July, 1881-Jan., 1882.

San Francisco Chronicle (San Francisco, California). Sept. 15, 1880.

Santa Fe Daily New Mexican (Santa Fe, New Mexico). Scattered issues 1881-86.

Santa Fe New Mexican Review (Santa Fe, New Mexico). Jan. 3, June 8, 17, 18, July 11, 1884.

Santa Fe Weekly Gazette (Santa Fe, New Mexico). Jan., 1868-Sept., 1869.

Semi-Weekly Inter-Ocean Times (Chicago, Illinois). Mar. 13, 1879.

The Silver Cliff Miner (Silver Cliff, Colorado). Scattered issues 1879-1880.

The Silver Reef Miner (Silver Reef, Utah). Apr., 1879-Feb., 1883.

Silver World (Lake City, Colorado). June, 1875-June, 1877.

The Solid Muldoon (Ouray, Colorado). Sept., 1879-Feb., 1880; Dec., 1882-Dec., 1883.

The South Pass News (South Pass, Wyoming). Oct. 27, 1869.

Southwest Sentinel (Silver City, New Mexico). May 19, 1883; Jan., 1886; Nov., 1887.

The Sweetwater Mines (Ft. Bridger, South Pass, Bryan City, Wyoming). Mar., 1868-June, 1869; July 14, 1869.

Tombstone Daily Nugget (Tombstone, Arizona). Oct.-Dec., 1880; Oct., 1881; Jan., 1882.

Tombstone Epitaph (Tombstone, Arizona). Daily—July-Aug., 1880. Weekly—May, 1880-Jan., 1881; Dec., 1881-Mar. 1882.

Tri-Weekly Capital Times (Virginia City, Montana). 1870.

The Union-Freeman (Butte, Montana). Apr., 1883-June, 1883.

Weekly New Mexican (Santa Fe, New Mexico). Scattered issues 1870-75; 1877.

Yankee Fork Herald (Bonanza City, Idaho). July, 1879-Aug., 1880.

v. BOOKS

Arizona, The Grand Canyon State. New York: Hastings House, 1940.

Arrington, Leonard. *Great Basin Kingdom: An Economic History of the Latter-day Saints, 1830-1900*. Cambridge: Harvard University Press, 1958.

Athearn, Robert G. *Rebel of the Rockies*. New Haven: Yale University Press, 1962.

————. *Westward the Briton*. New York: Charles Scribner, 1953.

Bancroft, Hubert H. *History of Washington, Idaho and Montana*. San Francisco: History, 1890.

————. *Popular Tribunals*. 2 vols. San Francisco: History, 1887.

Barsness, Larry. *Gold Camp*. New York: Hastings House, 1962.

Bishop, William. *Old Mexico and Her Lost Provinces*. New York: Harper, 1883.

Black Hills Illustrated. 1904.

Bowles, Samuel. *Across the Continent*. Springfield: Samuel Bowles, 1866.

Brayer, Herbert O. *William Blackmore: the Spanish-Mexican Land Grants of New Mexico and Colorado 1863-1878*. Denver: Bradford-Robinson, 1949.

Brown, Jesse, and A. M. Willard. *The Black Hills Trails*. Rapid City: Rapid City Journal Co., 1924.

Burlingame, Merrill G., and K. Ross Toole. *A History of Montana*. 3 vols. New York: Lewis Historical Publishing Co., 1957.

————. *The Montana Frontier*. Helena: Montana State Publishing Co., 1942.

Caughey, John W. *Their Majesties the Mob*. Chicago: University of Chicago Press, 1960.

Chittenden, Hiram M. *History of Early Steamboat Navigation on the Missouri River*. 2 vols. New York: Francis P. Harper, 1903.

Cook, David J. *Hands Up: or Thirty-Five Years of Detective Work in the Mountains and Plains*. Norman: University of Oklahoma Press, 1958 (reprint 1882 edition).

Countant, C. G. *The History of Wyoming*. Laramie: Chaplin, Spafford & Mathison, 1899.

Crane, Walter R. *Gold and Silver*. New York: J. Wiley & Sons, 1908.

Crofutt, George A. *Crofutt's Grip Sack Guide of Colorado*. Omaha: Overland Publishing Co., 1881.

De Voto, Bernard. *Mark Twain's America*. Boston: Little, Brown, 1932.

Douglas, William A. *A History of Dentistry in Colorado 1859-1959*. Boulder: Johnson Publishing Co., 1959.

Dresher, George B. *A Description of Colorado, Leadville and the Sovereign Consolidated Silver Mines*. Philadelphia: G. W. Arms, 1881.

Dunraven, Earl of [Windham, Thomas Wyndham-Quin]. *Hunting in the Yellowstone*. New York: Macmillan, 1925.

Farmer, Elihu J. *The Resources of the Rocky Mountains*. Cleveland: Leader Printing Co., 1883.

Fielder, Mildred, ed. *Lawrence County for the Dakota Territory Centennial*. Lead: Seaton Printing Co., 1960.

Fossett, Frank. *Colorado: A Historical, Descriptive and Statistical Work*. Denver: Daily Tribune Steam Printing House, 1876.

———. *Colorado Its Gold and Silver Mines*. New York: C. G. Crawford, 1879.

Frink, Maurice, W. Turrentine Jackson, and Agnes W. Spring. *When Grass was King*. Boulder: University of Colorado Press, 1956.

Fulton, Maurice G., and Paul Horgan. *New Mexico's Own Chronicle*. Dallas: Banks, Upshaw, 1937.

Gandy, Lewis Cass. *The Tabors: A Footnote of Western History*. New York: The Press of the Pioneers, 1934.

Goodykoontz, Colin B. *Home Missions on the American Frontier*. Caldwell: Caxton Printers, 1939.

Greenwood, Grace [Sara J. Lippincott]. *New Life in New Lands*. New York: J. B. Ford, 1873.

Greever, William S. *The Bonanza West*. Norman: University of Oklahoma Press, 1963.

Griswold, Don and Jean. *The Carbonate Camp Called Leadville*. Denver: University of Denver Press, 1951.

Hailey, John. *The History of Idaho*. Boise: Syms-York, 1910.

Hale, Horace. *Education in Colorado 1861-1885*. Denver: News Printing Co., 1885.

Hamilton, Patrick. *Resources of Arizona*. San Francisco: Bancroft, 1884.

Hill, James M. *Mining Districts of the Western United States*. Washington: Government Printing Office, 1912.

History of Arizona Territory. San Francisco: W. Elliott, 1884.

History of the Arkansas Valley, Colorado. Chicago: O. L. Baskin, 1881.

Howlett, W. J. *Life of the Right Reverend Joseph P. Machebeuf*. Denver: Register College of Journalism, 1954 (reprint 1908 edition).

Illinois a Descriptive and Historical Guide. Chicago: A. C. McClurg, 1947.

Ingersoll, Ernest. *Knocking Around the Rockies*. New York: Harper, 1883.

Ingham, George T. *Digging Gold Among the Rockies*. Philadelphia: Hubbard Bros., 1888.

Jackson, W. Turrentine. *Treasure Hill*. Tucson: University of Arizona Press, 1963.

Jensen, Vernon H. *Heritage of Conflict: Labor Relations in the Nonferrous Metals Industry*. Ithaca: Cornell University Press, 1950.

Keeler, Bronson C. *Leadville and Its Silver Mines*. Chicago: E. L. Ayer, 1879.

Kent, Lewis A. *Leadville in Your Pocket*. Denver: Daily Times Steam Printing House, 1880.

Lass, William E. *A History of Steamboating on the Upper Missouri River*. Lincoln: University of Nebraska Press, 1962.

Marshall, Thomas M. *Early Records of Gilpin County, Colorado, 1859-61*. Boulder: University of Colorado Press, 1920.

Martin, Douglas D., ed. *Tombstone's Epitaph*. Albuquerque: University of New Mexico, 1958 (originally published 1951).

McClure, A. K. *Three Thousand Miles Through the Rocky Mountains*. Philadelphia: Lippincott, 1869.

McConnell, William J. *Early History of Idaho*. Caldwell: Caxton Printers, 1913.

Morrell, William P. *Gold Rushes*. New York: Macmillan, 1941.

Morris, Maurice. *Rambles in the Rocky Mountains*. London: Smith, Elder, 1864.

Old, R. C. *Colorado . . . Its Mineral & Other Resources*. London: British & Colorado Mining Bureau, 1872.

Paul, Rodman W. *California Gold: The Beginning of Mining in the Far West*. Cambridge: Harvard University Press, 1947.

———. *Mining Frontiers of the Far West 1848-1880*. New York: Holt, Rinehart & Winston, 1963.

Paxson, Frederic. *The Last American Frontier*. New York: Macmillan, 1910.

Pearson, Jim Berry. *The Maxwell Land Grant*. Norman: University of Oklahoma Press, 1961.

Quiett, Glenn C. *Pay Dirt*. New York: Appleton-Century, 1936.

Randall, George M. *First Report of Bishop Randall of Colorado*. New York: Sanford, Harroun, 1866.

Richardson, Albert D. *Beyond the Mississippi: From the Great River to the Great Ocean*. Hartford: American Publishing Co., 1867.

Salt, H. S. *The Life of James Thomson*. London: Reeves & Turner, 1889.

Schoberlin, Melvin. *From Candles to Footlights: A Biography of the Pike's Peak Theatre, 1859-76*. Denver: Old West Publishing Co., 1941.

Shinn, Charles H. *Mining Camps: A Study in American Frontier Government*. New York: Knopf, 1948 (reissue 1885 edition).

Silversparre, Axel. *Appendix to New Map of Colorado.* Chicago: J. M. Jones Stationery & Printing Co., 1882.

Sonnichsen, C. L. *Billy King's Tombstone: The Private Life of an Arizona Boom Town.* Caldwell: Caxton Printers, 1951.

Sprague, Marshall. *Massacre, the Tragedy at White River.* Boston: Little, Brown, 1957.

Sprague, William F. *Women and the West: A Short Social History.* Boston: Christopher Publishing House, 1940.

Spring, Agnes W. *The Cheyenne and Black Hills Stage and Express Routes.* Glendale: Arthur H. Clark, 1949.

Steinel, Alvin T. *History of Agriculture in Colorado.* Ft. Collins: State Agricultural College, 1926.

Stewart, Edgar I. *Custer's Luck.* Norman: University of Oklahoma Press, 1955.

Strahorn, Carrie A. *Fifteen Thousand Miles by Stage.* New York: G. P. Putnam, 1915.

Strahorn, Robert E. *To the Rockies and Beyond.* Omaha: New West Publishing Co., 1879.

Sweet, Willis. *Carbonate Camps, Leadville and Ten-Mile of Colorado.* Kansas City: Ramsey, Millett & Hudson, 1879.

Tallent, Annie D. *The Black Hills: or, The Last Hunting Ground of the Dakotahs.* St. Louis: Nixon-Jones Printing Co., 1899.

Taylor, Bayard. *Colorado: A Summer Trip.* New York: G. P. Putnam, 1867.

Tice, J. H. *Over the Plains and on the Mountains.* St. Louis: Industrial Age Printing Co., 1872.

Toole, K. Ross. *Montana: An Uncommon Land.* Norman: University of Oklahoma Press, 1959.

Trimble, William. *The Mining Advance into the Inland Empire.* University of Wisconsin History Series, Vol. III, No. 2, Madison, 1914.

Vaughn, Robert. *Then and Now or Thirty-Six Years in the Rockies.* Minneapolis: Tribune Publishing Co., 1900.

Wade, Richard C. *The Urban Frontier.* Chicago: University of Chicago Press, 1964.

Willson, Clair E. *Mimes and Miners: A Historical Study of the Theater in Tombstone.* Tucson: University of Arizona, 1935.

W. P. A. Writer's Program. *Cooper Camp.* New York: Hastings House, 1943.

———. *Wyoming: A Guide to its History, Highways and People.* New York: Oxford University Press, 1941.

VI. ARTICLES

Anderson, W. W. "Gold Camp Tubers." *Montana, the Magazine of Western History,* 3 (Autumn, 1953), pp. 46-9.

Arrington, Leonard. "Abundance from the Earth." *Utah Historical Quarterly,* 31 (Summer, 1963), pp. 192-219.

Atherton, Lewis, ed. "Fire on the Comstock." *The American West,* II (Winter, 1965), pp. 24-33.

Blake, Henry N. "The First Newspaper of Montana." *Contributions to the Historical Society of Montana,* 5 (1904), pp. 253-64.

Bonner, I. "Leadville." *Lippincott's Magazine* (Nov., 1879), pp. 604-15.

Burkhart, J. A. "The Frontier Merchant and Social History." *The Montana Magazine of History,* 2 (Oct., 1952), pp. 5-15.

Coon, S. J. "Influence of the Gold Camps on the Economic Development of Western Montana." *Journal of Political Economy,* 38 (Oct., 1930), pp. 580-99.

Dakis, Mike. "Bogus Gold." *Idaho Yesterdays,* 5 (1961), pp. 2-7.

"David K. Wall." *Sons of Colorado,* 1 (May, 1907), pp. 14-20.

Derig, Betty. "The Chinese of Silver City." *Idaho Yesterdays,* 2 (Winter, 1958-59), pp. 2-5.

Edwards, George. "Presbyterian Church History." *Contributions to the Historical Society of Montana,* 6 (1907), pp. 290-445.

Green, Fletcher M. "Georgia's Forgotten Industry: Gold Mining." *The Georgia Historical Quarterly,* 19 (June-Sept., 1935), pp. 93-111, 210-28.

————. "Gold Mining: A Forgotten Industry of Ante-Bellum North Carolina." *The North Carolina Historical Review,* 14 (Jan.-Apr., 1937), pp. 1-19, 135-55.

H. H. [Helen H. Jackson]. "To Leadville." *Atlantic Monthly* (May, 1879), pp. 567-79.

Hayes, A. A. "Grub Stakes and Millions." *Harper's Monthly* (Feb., 1880), pp. 380-97.

Hill, Jim D. "The Early Mining Camp in American Life." *Pacific Historical Review,* 1 (1932), pp. 295-311.

Holter, A. M. "Pioneer Lumbering in Montana." *Contributions to the Historical Society of Montana,* 8 (1917), pp. 251-81.

Hunt's Merchants' Magazine and Commercial Review. July, 1848, pp. 112-13.

Ingersoll, Ernest. "The Camp of the Carbonates." *Scribner's Monthly* (Oct., 1879), pp. 801-24.

Jackson, William. "Railroad Conflicts in Colorado in the Eighties." *Colorado Magazine,* 23 (Jan., 1946), pp. 7-25.

Kuppens, Francis X. "Christmas Day in Virginia City, Montana." *Montana, the Magazine of Western History,* 3 (Autumn, 1953), pp. 12-16.

Larsen, Arthur J., ed. "The Black Hills Gold Rush." *North Dakota Historical Quarterly,* 6 (July, 1932), pp. 302-18.

Park, S. W. "The First School in Montana." *Contributions to the Historical Society of Montana,* 5 (1904), pp. 187-99.

Paul, Rodman W. "Colorado as a Pioneer of Science in the Mining West." *Mississippi Valley Historical Review,* 46 (June, 1960), pp. 34-50.

Richardson, Leander P. "A Trip to the Black Hills." *Scribner's Monthly* (Apr., 1877), pp. 748-56.

Shinn, Charles H. "California Mining Camps." *The Overland Monthly* (Aug., 1884), pp. 173-75.

"Silver Reef." *Utah Historical Quarterly,* 29 (July, 1961), pp. 281-87.

"Steamboat Arrivals at Ft. Benton, Montana." *Contributions of the Historical Society of Montana,* 1 (1876), pp. 280-87.

NOTES

Further bibliographical details are given in the bibliography.

1. THE URBAN FRONTIER

1. *Hunt's Merchants' Magazine and Commercial Review* (July, 1848), 112-13.
2. Bernard C. Steiner, ed., "The South Atlantic States in 1833, as seen by a New Englander," *Maryland Historical Magazine,* 13 (Dec., 1918), p. 346. The town in question was Dahlonega, Georgia.
3. For further information, see Rodman W. Paul, *California Gold*; Charles H. Shinn, *Mining Camps*; and William Trimble, *The Mining Advance into the Inland Empire.*
4. Horace Greeley, *An Overland Journey,* p. 121. The letters were originally written for the *New York Tribune.*
5. "Cherry Creek Emigrant's Song," *Rocky Mountain News,* June 18, 1859.

2. YOUNG AMERICA

1. George W. Parsons, *Journal,* p. 225.
2. See for example *Montana Post,* June 29, 1867; *Butte Miner,* June 5, 1877; *Silver World,* Apr. 8, 1876; *Yankee Fork Herald,* Aug. 7, 1877.
3. John Hailey, *The History of Idaho,* pp. 91-92, 107; Thomas J. Dimsdale, *The Vigilantes of Montana,* pp. 14-19; Irving W. Stanton, *Sixty Years in Colorado,* p. 50; Jess Brown and A. M. Willard, *The Black Hills Trails,* p. 422; Granville Stuart, *Forty Years on the Frontier,* p. 267; Francis G. Young, *Echoes from Arcadia,* p. 87; Horace Hale, *Education in Colorado,* pp. 13-14; Clyde McLemore, ed., "Bannack and Gallatin City in 1862-63," *Sources of Northwest History,* No. 24, p. 5; *Idaho World,* Sept. 2, 1865.
4. John L. Dyer, *The Snow-Shoe Itinerant,* p. 325.
5. George M. Darley, *Pioneering in the San Juan,* pp. 65, 69-70;

Daniel Tuttle, *Reminiscences of a Missionary Bishop*, pp. 172-77; Dyer, *Snow-Shoe Itinerant*, p. 144. See also Ethelbert Talbot, *My People of the Plains*.

6. *San Francisco Chronicle*, Sept. 15, 1880. Material for the preceding paragraphs is found in the following: George T. Ingham, *Digging Gold Among the Rockies*, p. 297; J. H. Tice, *Over the Plains and on the Mountains*, pp. 118-22; A. K. McClure, *Three Thousand Miles Through the Rocky Mountains*, p. 212; Ernest Ingersoll, "The Camp of the Carbonates," *Scribner's Monthly*, 5 (Oct., 1879), pp. 803, 821; Albert D. Richardson, *Beyond the Mississippi*, p. 500; Maurice Morris, *Rambles in the Rocky Mountains*, p. 164; Earl of Dunraven [Windham Thomas Wyndham-Quin], *Hunting in the Yellowstone*, pp. 63-64; Lola M. Homsher, ed., *South Pass, 1868*, pp. 89-91, 103, 111-12; H. H. (Helen H. Jackson), "To Leadville," *Atlantic Monthly* (May, 1879), p. 576; Ernest Ingersoll, *Knocking Around the Rockies*, pp. 83-84.

7. Charles M. Clark, *A Trip to Pike's Peak*, pp. 88-89; Leander P. Richardson, "A Trip to the Black Hills," *Scribner's Monthly*, 13 (Apr., 1877), pp. 748, 755-56; Hailey, *Idaho*, p. 107; McClure, *Three Thousand Miles*, p. 107. See also references in preceding footnote.

8. Parsons, *Journal*, p. 164; Homsher, *South Pass*, p. 105; Morris, *Rambles*, p. 134; *Santa Fe Weekly Gazette*, Feb. 1, 1868; H. J. Hawley, "Diary of H. J. Hawley," Colorado State Historical Society, p. 30; *Silver World*, July 3, 1876. See also Rodman W. Paul, *Mining Frontier of the Far West*, pp. 164-65.

9. Matthew Dale, "Letters," Mar. 12, 1861. For more on Dale, see Robert Athearn, ed., "Life in the Pike's Peak Region," *Colorado Magazine* (Apr., 1955).

10. *Montana Post*, May 6, 1865. See also Margaret Ronan, "Memoirs of a Frontier's Woman, Mary C. Ronan" (thesis, State Univ. of Mont., 1932), pp. 42-48, 61-69, 101; *Park Record*, Mar. 17, 1883; *Montana Radiator*, Feb. 24, 1869.

11. *New Mexican*, Nov. 3, 4, 24, 1868; Mar. 16, June 1, July 27, 1869.

12. *Daily Chronicle*, June 18, 1879.

13. The statistics for this paragraph and succeeding pages are from the census records of the following camps. Both a sampling process and utilization of the entire returns were used. Unfortunately, more than 99 percent of the 1890 census was destroyed by fire; none pertinent to this survey survived. 1860: Central City and Mountain City, Colorado. 1870: Atlantic City and South Pass, Wyoming; Virginia City, Diamond City, Beartown, and Bannack, Montana; Elizabethtown, New Mexico; Breck-

enridge and Oro City, Colorado; Silver City, Idaho. 1880: Bonanza, Custer, Silver City, Placerville, and Idaho City, Idaho; Caribou, Ouray, Georgetown, Silver Cliff, Leadville, Cornwall, Forest City, and Magnolia, Colorado; Pinal, Arizona; Deadwood, Gayville, and Galena, South Dakota; Silver City, New Mexico. All of these records are found in the National Archives. The Colorado census records are also available in the Denver Public Library and the Wyoming returns in the Wyoming State Archives (Cheyenne).

14. William Donald, "Dictation" (Bancroft Library).
15. Augusta Tabor, "Cabin Life" (Bancroft Library), p. 5.
16. Parsons, *Journal*, p. 230.
17. The ages 16 through 49 were selected arbitrarily. Those children 15 years and younger were not normally part of the working force. The people 50 or older represented a small percentage of the total until the 1880 census, even then seldom approaching 1/10 of the total. By that decade the rapid increase of children more than balanced the older group.

3. NOT ALL WERE WELCOME

1. Rodman W. Paul, *Mining Frontiers of the Far West*, p. 149.
2. *Montana Post*, Sept. 8, 1866.
3. *Park Record*, Mar. 11, Apr. 8, 1882.
4. *Tombstone Epitaph*, Feb. 13, 1882.
5. *Boulder County News*, Mar. 20, Apr. 8, May 1, 1874; *Tombstone Epitaph*, July 26, 29, 1880; *Daily Chronicle*, Feb. 10, Mar. 8, 1879; *Idaho World*, May 27, 1865; *Yankee Fork Herald*, Aug. 14, 1879; *Aspen Times*, Nov. 22, 1884.
6. *Ordinances of the City of Virginia, Territory of Montana*, p. 37. See also James H. Ashley, "Message of Governor Ashley," *Contributions of the Historical Society of Montana*, 6 (1907), p. 267; Hubert H. Bancroft, *History of Washington, Idaho and Montana*, p. 427.
7. *Owyhee Avalanche*, Sept. 14, 1867.
8. *Pinal Drill*, Aug. 27, 1881; *Butte Miner*, June 12, 1877; *Cottonwood Observer*, July 16, 1873; *Owyhee Avalanche*, Aug. 25, 1866; *Helena Herald*, Oct. 24, 1867; *Yankee Fork Herald*, Mar. 6, Apr. 17, 1880; Daniel Tuttle, *Reminiscences of a Missionary Bishop*, p. 132; Estelline Bennett, *Old Deadwood Days*, pp. 27-30; A. K. McClure, *Three Thousand Miles Through the Rocky Mountains*, pp. 273, 372. See particularly 1880 census for Placerville and Idaho City, Idaho.

9. *Montana Radiator,* Jan. 27, 1866; *New Mexico Interpreter,* June 24, 1887; *Pinal Drill,* Dec. 25, 1880. See also census records previously cited in this chapter. Betty Derig, "The Chinese of Silver," *Idaho Yesterdays,* II (Winter, 1958-59), pp. 2-5.

10. Tuttle, *Reminiscences,* p. 216; William Trimble, *The Mining Advance into the Inland Empire,* p. 279; Lynn I Perrigo, "Social History of Central City, Colorado, 1859-1900" (diss., Univ. of Colo., 1936), p. 353; Ethelbert Talbot, *My People of the Plains,* p. 162. See census records previously cited in this chapter.

11. *Park Record,* Mar. 18, 1882; Maurice Morris, *Rambles in the Rocky Mountains,* p. 100; *Daily Central City Register,* Jan. 15, 1869.

12. *Tombstone Epitaph,* July 26, 1880.

13. *Leadville Democrat,* Aug. 14, 1880; *Silver Reef Miner,* July 30, 1879, Mar. 15, 24, 1882; *Park Record,* Apr. 1, May 6, 1882. See also Paul, *Mining Frontiers,* pp. 150-51; Leonard Arrington, *Great Basin Kingdom,* pp. 204, 241-243; Leonard Arrington, "Abundance from the Earth," *Utah Historical Quarterly,* 31 (Summer, 1963), p. 194.

14. See *Ouray Times,* 1877-79, for a camp's reaction.

15. *Montana Post,* Aug. 10, 1867; *Arizona Silver Belt,* Feb. 14, 1879; *Pinal Drill,* Oct. 8, 1881; *Silver Reef Miner,* Feb. 4, 1882.

16. Bennett, *Old Deadwood Days,* pp. 247-55; Morris, *Rambles,* pp. 99-100; Bayard Taylor, *Colorado,* p. 58; Thomas J. Dimsdale, *The Vigilantes of Montana,* pp. 18-19; McClure, *Three Thousand Miles,* p. 390; Francis C. Young, *Echoes from Arcadia,* pp. 45, 94; Eugene Irey, "A Social History of Leadville, Colorado, During the Boom Days, 1877-1881" (diss., Univ. of Minn., 1951), pp. 159-61; Perrigo, "Social History of Central City," pp. 343-50, 357.

17. The editor of the *Owyhee Avalanche,* Oct. 14, 1865, wrote "In all new communities, what is termed 'society' does not appear till the people become convinced that the settlements in which they reside will be permanent."

4 . WHEN YOUNG AMERICA FINDS
   A GOOD GOLD GULCH

1. Diary of George V. Ayres, quoted by Agnes W. Spring, ed., *The Cheyenne and Black Hills Stage and Express Routes,* p. 363.

2. William McConnell, *Early History of Idaho,* p. 56; Horace Greeley, *An Overland Journey,* pp. 120-125; *Helena Herald,* Oct. 31, 1867;

San Francisco Chronicle, Sept. 15, 1880; Charles M. Clark, *A Trip to Pike's Peak,* p. 95.

3. A. K. McClure, *Three Thousand Miles,* p. 285. See also H. H. (Helen H. Jackson), "Leadville," *Atlantic Monthly* (May, 1879), p. 575; Nathaniel P. Langford, *Vigilante Days and Ways,* pp. 222-23; Clark, *Trip to Pike's Peak,* pp. 94-95; *Rocky Mountain News,* Aug. 27, 1859; George T. Ingham, *Digging Gold Among the Rockies,* pp. 292-93.

4. James H. Morley, "Diary of James Henry Morley in Montana, 1862-65," Montana Historical Society, Nov. 11, 1864; Ingham, *Digging Gold,* p. 292.

5. *Sweetwater Mines,* Mar. 25, 1868.

6. Henry Edgar, "Journal of Henry Edgar," *Contributions to the Historical Society of Montana,* 3 (1900), pp. 141-42. Edgar was a member of the original prospecting expedition.

7. Thomas M. Marshall, *Early Records of Gilpin County, Colorado, 1859-61,* pp. 10-33, 55, 70, 100-104, 233, 262-66, 281. These are just samplings of an entire book of district records. Merrill G. Burlingame, *The Montana Frontier,* pp. 95-97.

8. Marshall, *Early Records,* pp. 103, 191, 242, 257-58.

9. Grace Greenwood (Sara J. Lippincott), *New Life in New Lands,* pp. 76-77.

10. Earl of Dunraven (Windham Thomas Wyndham-Quin), *Hunting in the Yellowstone,* p. 63.

11. Morley, "Diary," May 22, 1864.

12. Jerry Bryan, *An Illinois Gold Hunter in the Black Hills,* p. 33; C. G. Countant, *The History of Wyoming,* pp. 651-53; *Weekly New Mexican,* Nov. 1, 1870; *Santa Fe New Mexican Review,* June 8, 1885; Rodman W. Paul, *Mining Frontiers,* pp. 143, 155.

13. Agnes W. Spring, ed., *Pioneer Years in the Black Hills,* pp. 69-70; *Butte Miner,* July 31-Aug. 28, 1877; *Helena Herald,* May 21, 1867; *New Mexican,* July 14, 1868.

14. *Weekly New Mexican,* Apr. 4, 1871. See also *Ouray Times,* Dec. 22, 1877; Clyde McLemore, ed., "Bannack and Gallatin City," *Sources of Northwest History,* No. 24, pp. 5-6.

15. See Edgar I. Stewart, *Custer's Luck,* pp. 71-72.

16. *Ouray Times,* Aug. 4, 1877. See also *Silver World,* Nov. 11, 1876, and *Pinal Drill,* Oct. 23, 1880.

17. Marshall, *Early Records,* pp. 82, 84, 143, 169, 189-90, 203-204, 223; *Butte Miner,* Jan. 8, 1878; *Ouray Times,* Sept. 29, 1877; *New*

Mexican, May 2, 1867; *Helena Herald,* May 2, 1867; *Boulder County News,* Apr. 4, 1872; Clifford C. Hill, "Wagon Roads in Colorado, 1858-1876" (thesis, Univ. of Colo., 1950), pp. 34, 53, 86-88.

18. Mark Twain, *Roughing It,* p. 142; Hill, "Wagon Roads," pp. 35-47; *Ouray Times,* Sept. 29, 1877; *Silver World,* Nov. 11, 1876; Marshall, *Early Records,* pp. 127, 154, 169, 189-90, 195-96, 208, 260-61.

19. *Owyhee Avalanche,* Apr. 14, 1866. See also *Montana Post,* Mar. 4, 1865.

20. William E. Lass, *A History of Steamboating on the Upper Missouri River,* pp. 32-37; "Steamboat Arrivals at Ft. Benton, Montana," *Contributions of the Historical Society of Montana,* 1 (1876), pp. 280-85; Hiram M. Chittenden, *History of Early Steamboat Navigation on the Missouri River,* vol. 2, pp. 273-76; John Hailey, *The History of Idaho,* p. 116.

21. *Montana Radiator,* June 16, 1866; Lass, *History of Steamboating,* p. 39.

22. K. Ross Toole, *Montana: An Uncommon Land,* pp. 81-82, has an interesting discussion on this topic.

23. Morley, "Diary," Nov. 11, 1864.

5. BOOM DAYS

1. Charles M. Clark, *A Trip to Pike's Peak,* p. 95.

2. *Owyhee Avalanche,* Sept. 30, 1865; *Arizona Silver Belt,* May 16, 1878; *Yankee Fork Herald,* July 24, 1879; *Silver Reef Miner,* Apr. 12, 1879; *The Herald,* July 18, 1875.

3. Augusta Tabor, "Cabin Life in Colorado" (Bancroft Library); H. A. W. Tabor, "Early Days" and "Life of H. A. W. Tabor" (Bancroft Library); Horace Hale, *Education in Colorado, 1861-1865,* p. 23; Lewis Gandy, *The Tabors,* pp. 95-96; 124-35, 148-52, 162-64, 180-83.

4. *History of the Arkansas Valley, Colorado,* pp. 379-80; Lewis A. Kent, *Leadville in Your Pocket,* pp. 167-68; George T. Ingham, *Digging Gold Among the Rockies,* p. 401.

5. Tabor, "Cabin Life." Augusta Tabor wrote, concerning the help she gave her husband: "He found I was a better hand at keeping the books than he was."

6. Daniel Tuttle, *Reminiscences of a Missionary Bishop,* pp. 129-32; *Daily Chronicle,* July 7, 1879; Ingham, *Digging Gold,* p. 290; Grace Greenwood (Sara J. Lippincott), *New Life in New Lands,* pp. 100-102; Carrie A. Strahorn, *Fifteen Thousand Miles by Stage,* pp. 114, 225-26.

7. A. K. McClure, *Three Thousand Miles,* p. 291; Jerry Bryan, *An Illinois Gold Hunter,* p. 34.

8. *Montana Post,* Aug. 27, 1864.

9. *Silver World,* June 19, 1875.

10. *Yankee Fork Herald,* July 24, 1879.

11. *New Mexico Interpreter,* Aug. 29, 1890.

12. Henry N. Blake, "The First Newspaper of Montana," *Contributions to the Historical Society of Montana,* 5 (1904), pp. 259-61; James Louder, "Autobiography" (Bancroft Library); *The Union-Freeman,* June 24, 1883.

13. Doyce B. Nunis, ed., *The Golden Frontier: The Recollections of Herman Francis Reinhart, 1850-69,* pp. 231-35, 277, 291-94, 305-306; John Hailey, *The History of Idaho,* pp. 91-92, 99, 127; Eugene Irey, "A Social History of Leadville, Colorado" (diss., Univ. of Minn., 1950), pp. 50-56; *History of the Arkansas Valley, Colorado,* p. 223.

14. *Pinal Drill,* Feb. 19, 1881; *Park Record,* Mar. 31, 1883; *Butte Miner,* Jan. 23, May 29, Dec. 25, 1877; *Leadville Weekly Herald,* Nov. 22, 1879; *Owyhee Avalanche,* Mar. 3, 1866; *Silver World,* July 15, 1876; George B. Dresher, *A Description of Colorado,* pp. 79-80.

15. *Rocky Mountain News,* Aug. 27, 1859; *Butte Miner,* June 5, Aug. 21, 1877; *New Mexican,* Apr. 21, 1868; *Aspen Times,* Feb. 7, 1885; Frank Fosset, *Colorado: Its Gold and Silver Mines,* p. 414; Lewis A. Kent, *Leadville in Your Pocket,* p. 137; *Helena Herald,* June 26, 1867.

16. Tuttle, *Reminiscences,* p. 132; George W. Parsons, *Journal,* p. 126; *Silver World,* Apr. 28, 1877; *Daily Chronicle,* Feb. 22, 1879.

17. Granville Stuart, *Forty Years on the Frontier,* pp. 257-58; Andrew F. Rolle, ed., *The Road to Virginia City: The Diary of James Knox Polk Miller,* p. 82.

18. *Helena Herald,* June 26, 1867. See also *Silver World,* Apr. 28, 1877.

19. *Owyhee Avalanche,* Oct. 13, 1866; *Weekly New Mexican,* Feb. 11, 1873; *Black Hills Weekly Times,* Mar. 3, 1878; *Yankee Fork Herald,* Sept. 25, 1879.

20. James H. Morley, "Diary," Montana Historical Society, Dec. 21, 1862-Jan. 10, 1863, Mar. 24, 1863; Arthur J. Larsen, ed., "The Black Hills Gold Rush," *North Dakota Historical Quarterly,* 6 (July, 1932), p. 309; *Ouray Times,* Aug. 3, 1878; *Helena Herald,* Apr. 11, Oct. 31, 1867; *Weekly New Mexican,* Feb. 11, 1873; *Tombstone Epitaph,* Oct. 25, Nov. 8, 1880.

21. *Cottonwood Observer,* July 19, 1873.

22. Agnes W. Spring, ed., *Pioneer Years*, pp. 108-109.

23. A good example of this is found in the *Silver World*, Oct. 23, 1875-Feb. 17, 1877.

24. Nathaniel P. Langford, *Vigilante Days and Ways*, p. 108; Robert G. Athearn, ed., "Letters from Pike's Peak," *Colorado Magazine*, 32 (Apr., 1955), p. 92.

6. GROWING PAINS

1. *Idaho World*, Feb. 4, Apr. 15, Oct. 28, 1865; *Montana Radiator*, Feb. 3, Sept. 1, 1866; *Black Hills Daily Times*, Nov. 18, 1879; *Butte Miner*, Feb. 5, 1878; *Yankee Fork Herald*, Aug. 28, Oct. 25, 1879; *Tombstone Epitaph*, Jan. 17, 1881; *Park Record*, Apr. 1, 1882; Lynn I. Perrigo, "Social History of Central City, Colorado" (diss., Univ. of Colo., 1936), pp. 251-58.

2. *Daily Chronicle*, May 22-July 7, 1879.

3. Clyde McLemore, ed., "Bannack and Gallatin City," *Sources of Northwest History*, No. 24, p. 5.

4. Robert G. Athearn, ed., "Life in the Pike's Peak Region," p. 96; James Fergus, "A Leaf from the Diary of James Fergus," *Contributions to the Historical Society of Montana*, 2 (1896); p. 254; Hubert H. Bancroft, *Popular Tribunals*, vol. 2, pp. 690-91; A. K. McClure, *Three Thousand Miles*, p. 227; William J. McConnell, *Early History of Idaho*, p. 253.

5. Thomas J. Dimsdale, *The Vigilantes of Montana*, p. 16.

6. *Montana Post*, Aug. 27, 1864, Jan. 5, 1867; *Arizona Silver Belt*, May 29, 1880; Bancroft, *Popular Tribunals*, vol. 2, pp. 655-712; William B. Thom, "In Pioneer Days," *The Trail*, 19 (Oct., 1929), p. 14; David Cook, *Hands Up*, pp. 216-221. See also Dimsdale, *The Vigilantes of Montana*.

7. *Silver Belt*, May 29, 1880.

8. George Adams Locke, "Letters" (Bancroft Library), Feb. 26, 1869.

9. *Idaho World*, Apr. 21, 1866. See also Sept. 2, 1865.

10. *Idaho World*, Apr. 14, 21, 1866. See also *Park Record*, Jan. 27, 1883.

11. Nathaniel P. Langford, *Vigilante Days*, xii-xiv; Dimsdale, *The Vigilantes of Montana*, pp. 192-94; Bancroft, *Popular Tribunals*, vol. 2, pp. 704, 749. See also Alexander Toponce, *Reminiscences of Alexander*

Toponce, *Pioneer*, pp. 171-72; *History of the Arkansas Valley*, pp. 247-50; K. Ross Toole, *Montana*, p. 78.

12. *New Mexican*, Apr. 21, 1868; *Daily New Mexican*, Oct. 13, 1870; Locke, "Letters," Apr. 2, 1869. Richard Hughes noted that it was a remarkable fact that a lynching never occurred in Deadwood despite the rampant crime. Agnes W. Spring, ed., *Pioneer Years*, p. 162.

13. Spring, ed., *Pioneer Years*, pp. 152-58.

14. Thomas M. Marshall, *Early Records of Gilpin County, Colorado*, pp. 24-30, 37-38, 55-64, 215-23, 228-29, 281-88; Langford, *Vigilante Days*, pp. 139-40; K. Ross Toole, *Montana*, pp. 76-77; Charles H. Shinn, *Mining Camps*, pp. 6-7.

15. Harry H. Anderson, ed., "An Account of Deadwood and the Northern Black Hills," *South Dakota Department of History Collections*, 31 (1962), p. 351; Spring, ed., *Pioneer Years*, pp. 166-67.

16. *Park Record*, Jan. 7, 1882.

17. Eugene Irey, "A Social History of Leadville, Colorado" (thesis, Univ. of Colo., 1950), pp. 10-12; Annie D. Tallent, *The Black Hills*, p. 375; *Daily Miners' Register*, Dec. 28, 1863; *Black Hills Pioneer*, Aug. 5, 1876, May 26, 1877.

18. An example of the effort put forth by a camp may be found in the *Park Record*, Jan.-Mar., 1882.

19. Anderson, ed., "Account of Deadwood," pp. 337-40; *Silver World*, Feb. 19, 1876; *Ouray Times*, Feb. 15, 1879; *Tombstone Epitaph*, Jan. 23, 1882; *Boulder County News*, Oct. 9, 1874; *Boulder Camera*, Mar. 17, 1899; Jim Berry Pearson, *The Maxwell Land Grant*, pp. 29-30; *Ordinances of the City of Virginia, Territory of Montana*, pp. 6-9.

20. *Helena Herald*, Dec. 12, 1867.

21. *Black Hills Pioneer*, July 22, 1876, May 5, 1877; *Helena Herald*, Jan. 16, 1868; *Owyhee Avalanche*, Sept. 8, 1866; *Idaho World*, June 17, 1865; *Ouray Times*, July 21, 1877; Lynn I. Perrigo, "Life in Central City, Colorado, as Revealed by the *Register*, 1862-1872" (thesis, Univ. of Colo., 1934), 117-19.

22. *Herald*, June 6, 1875; *Butte Miner*, Dec. 5, 19, 1876; *Cottonwood Observer; Owyhee Avalanche*, June 1, 1867; *Black Hills Times*, Aug. 9, 1879; *Montana Post*, Nov. 17, 1866.

23. *Leadville Democrat*, Jan. 15, 1880; Irey, "Social History," p. 260.

24. Letter from Gideon Anthony Hamilton to S. Frank Dexter, quoted in Lewis Atherton, ed., "Fire on the Comstock," *The American West*, II (Winter, 1965), pp. 27-28, 31.

25. Descriptions of fires can be found in *Black Hills Daily Times,* Aug. 18, 23, 1877; *Cottonwood Observer,* July 30, 1873; *New Mexico Interpreter,* Oct. 3, 1890; *Idaho World,* May 27, 1865; *Ouray Times,* Jan. 10, 1880; *Silver Reef Miner,* May 24, 31, 1879; *Santa Fe New Mexican Review,* July 11, 1884; *Helena Herald,* Feb. 18, 1869.

26. *Tombstone Epitaph,* May 27, 1882, quoted in Douglas Martin, ed., *Tombstone's Epitaph,* pp. 132-33. See also *Idaho World,* July 24, 1867; Spring, ed., *Pioneer Years,* p. 267; Tallent, *The Black Hills,* pp. 486-87.

7. MATURING IN SPITE OF ITSELF

1. *Pinal Drill,* Feb. 26, 1881; *The Herald,* July 18, 1875; *Owyhee Avalanche,* Sept. 30, 1865; *Butte Miner,* June 5, 1877. A great deal of information on the business district can be found in the advertisements of the newspapers. The above is but a sampling.

2. *Silver Reef Miner,* Apr. 12, 1879.

3. *Cottonwood Observer,* July 16, 1873.

4. George M. Randall, *The First Report of Bishop Randall of Colorado,* p. 21.

5. Lola M. Homsher, ed., *South Pass, 1868,* p. 112. See also Clyde McLemore, ed., "Bannack and Gallatin City in 1862-65," *Sources of Northwest History,* No. 24, p. 5.

6. John L. Dyer, *The Snow-Shoe Itinerant,* p. 135; George M. Darley, *Pioneering in the San Juan,* p. 37; *Owyhee Avalanche,* May 19, 1866; Isaac Beardsley, *Echoes from Peak and Plain,* pp. 226-28; Ernest Ingersoll, "Camp of the Carbonates," *Scribner's Monthly* (Oct., 1879), p. 823; Lynn I. Perrigo, "Social History of Central City, Colorado" (diss., Univ. of Colo., 1936), pp. 137-39, 144-46; Colin B. Goodykoontz, *Home Missions on the American Frontier,* pp. 306-27; George Edwards, "Presbyterian Church History," *Contributions to the Historical Society of Montana,* 6 (1907), pp. 295-99.

7. Randall, First Report, p. 19. See also Ethelbert Talbot, *My People of the Plains,* p. 117, and Beardsley, *Echoes,* pp. 466-67.

8. Daniel Tuttle, *Reminiscences of a Missionary Bishop,* p. 169.

9. Talbot, *My People,* pp. 55, 94-96; Darley, *Pioneering in the San Juan,* pp. 21-22, 67-68; Dyer, *Snow-Shoe Itinerant,* pp. 322-25, 334-35; W. J. Howlett, *Life of the Right Reverend Joseph P. Machebeuf,* pp. 294-96, 330-31; Irving Howbert, *Memories of a Lifetime in the Pike's Peak Region,* p. 31; *Butte Miner,* Nov. 28, 1876; A. K. McClure, *Three*

Thousand Miles, p. 386; Francis Kuppens, "Christmas Day in Virginia City, Montana," *Montana, the Magazine of Western History,* 3 (Autumn, 1953), p. 13; Tuttle, *Reminiscences,* p. 142-48.

10. George W. Parsons, *Journal,* p. 248; George Adams Locke, "Letter to Mother" (Bancroft Library), 1870.

11. Parsons, *Journal,* p. 100. Samples of attitudes of newspapers may be found in *Idaho World,* Sept. 9, 1865; *Owyhee Avalanche,* June 1, 1867; *Black Hills Daily Times,* July 11, 1878; *Arizona Silver Belt,* Jan. 24, 1880.

12. Maurice Morris, *Rambles in the Rocky Mountains,* p. 131; *Owyhee Avalanche,* Sept. 9, 1865; *Yankee Fork Herald,* Oct. 25, 1879; *Pinal Drill,* Sept. 11, 1880; Tuttle, *Reminiscences,* pp. 178-79; Talbot, *My People,* p. 160; Agnes W. Spring, ed., *Pioneer Years in the Black Hills,* pp. 235-36; Darley, *Pioneering in the San Juan,* pp. 17-18; Kuppens, "Christmas Day in Virginia City, Montana," pp. 13-15.

13. Albert D. Richardson, *Beyond the Mississippi,* p. 365.

14. *Rocky Mountain News,* Sept. 3, 22, 1859; *Silver World,* Jan. 8, 1876; *Montana Radiator,* Mar. 31, 1866; *Sweetwater Mines,* June 19, 1869; *Owyhee Avalanche,* Oct. 26, 1867; *Pinal Drill,* June 11, 1881; William Trimble, *The Mining Advance into the Inland Empire,* pp. 168-69.

15. The *Black Hills Daily Times,* Aug. 16, 1879; *Herald,* Apr. 18, Dec. 5, 1875; *Arizona Silver Belt,* Dec. 6, 1878; *Silver World,* Oct. 16, Nov. 27, 1875; Horace Hale, *Education in Colorado,* p. 14.

16. Quotes from the *Silver World,* Oct. 16, 1875, Sept. 30, 1876; *The Charter and Ordinances of the City of Central,* pp. 115-16; *Silver Reef Miner,* Aug. 13, 20, 1881; *Park Record,* May 27, 1881, July 23, 1883; Lynn I. Perrigo, "Life in Central City" (thesis, Univ. of Colo., 1934), pp. 59-60; *Black Hills Daily Times,* Aug. 12, 1877; *Ouray Times,* Feb. 28, 1880; *Idaho World,* Aug. 12, 1865; *Silver World,* Mar. 24, 1877; *Pinal Drill,* Oct. 29, Nov. 5, 1881; *Owyhee Avalanche,* Nov. 17, 1866; *New Mexico Interpreter,* Oct. 10, 1890.

17. S. W. Park, "The First School in Montana," *Contributions to the Historical Society of Montana,* 5 (1904), p. 191. For a description of a good mining camp school, see the *Butte Miner,* Mar. 5, Apr. 30, 1878.

18. Sources for the preceding section are found in: *Montana Post,* Apr. 7, 1866, Feb. 9, Apr. 13, 1867; *Butte Miner,* Sept. 25, Oct. 23, Dec. 18, 1877; *Daily Nugget,* Oct. 19, 1880; *Ouray Times,* Nov. 3, 1877; *Silver World,* Jan. 13, 1878; *New Mexico Interpreter,* Jan. 31,

Feb. 14, 1890; *Daily Miner's Register,* Oct. 19, 1863; *Weekly New Mexican,* Mar. 25, 1873; Park, "First School," p. 192; Margaret Ronan, "Memoirs of a Frontier's Woman, Mary C. Ronan" (thesis, State Univ. of Mont., 1932), pp. 52-55; Perrigo, "Life in Central City," pp. 52-53, 58.

19. *Montana Post,* Sept. 17, 1864; *Park Record,* Jan. 6, 27, 1883; *New Mexico Interpreter,* Mar. 8, 1889; *Owyhee Avalanche,* Dec. 22, 1866; *Leadville Democrat,* Jan. 22, 1880; *Daily Central City Register,* Nov. 3, 1869.

20. Matthew Dale, "Letters," Western Historical Collection, Nov. 27, 1859; Ernest Ingersoll, *Knocking Around the Rockies,* p. 31; Parsons, *Journal,* p. 234; Andrew Rolle, ed., *Road to Virginia City,* pp. 90, 96, 98; W. A. Goulder, *Reminiscences of a Pioneer,* pp. 221-22; *Yankee Fork Herald,* Aug. 28, 1879.

21. *Tombstone Epitaph,* July 21, 1880; *Idaho World,* Nov. 11, 1865; *Silver World,* Mar. 3, May 26, 1877; *Butte Miner,* Dec. 18, 1877; *Daily Chronicle,* Apr. 12, 1879; *Owyhee Avalanche,* Feb. 9, 1867; Estelline Bennett, *Old Deadwood Days,* p. 47; Merrill G. Burlingame and K. Ross Toole, *A History of Montana,* vol. 2, pp. 259-60; Francis C. Young, *Echoes from Arcadia,* pp. 38, 66-67; A. E. Pierce, "Reminiscences of a Pioneer," *Sons of Colorado,* 2 (Nov., 1907), p. 4; Nelle F. Minnick, "A Cultural History of Central City, Colorado, from 1859-1880, in terms of Books and Libraries" (thesis, Univ. of Chicago, 1946), pp. 82-83, 114.

22. Bennett, *Old Deadwood Days,* pp. 68-69. See also Agnes W. Spring, *Cheyenne and Black Hills Stage.*

23. Sources used for preceding paragraphs: Alexander Toponce, *Reminiscences of Alexander Toponce, Pioneer,* pp. 203-208; *Silver Reef Miner,* Oct. 22, 1881; *Boulder County News,* Jan. 26, 1877; *Daily Chronicle,* Aug. 8, 1879; *New Mexican,* Mar. 23, 1881; "David K. Wall," *Sons of Colorado,* 1 (May, 1907), pp. 17-18; McClure, *Three Thousand Miles,* pp. 428-35; Augusta Tabor, "Cabin Life" (Bancroft Library), p. 5.

24. *Daily Nugget,* Nov. 20, 1880; *Ouray Times,* July 14, 1877; *Helena Herald,* Apr. 18, Oct. 3, 10, 1867; *Yankee Fork Herald,* July 31, 1879; *Ordinances of the City of Virginia, Territory of Montana,* pp. 9-11; Harry H. Anderson, ed., "An Account of Deadwood," *South Dakota Department of History Collections,* 31 (1962), pp. 342-43; *The General Ordinances of the City of Aspen,* pp. 8, 11-16; Eugene Irey, "Social History of Leadville, Colorado" (diss., Univ. of Minn., 1951), pp. 229-

31; Perrigo, "Life in Central City," pp. 110-11; *History of the Arkansas Valley, Colorado*, p. 306.

8. MAGNET IN THE MOUNTAINS

1. W. T. Sherman, Annual Report of the Secretary of War, *House Exec. Doc.* No. 1 (1285), p. 20.

2. See Matthew Dale, "Letters," Mar. 2, 1861; Charles M. Clark, *Trip to Pike's Peak*, p. 123; Clyde McLemore, ed., "Bannack and Gallatin City," *Sources of Northwest History*, No. 24, pp. 5-6; William McConnell, *Early History of Idaho*, pp. 121-23; Robert Vaughn, *Then and Now*, p. 64; W. W. Anderson, "Gold Camp Tubers," *Montana Magazine of Western History*, 3 (Autumn, 1953), pp. 46-49; Sherlock Bristol, *The Pioneer Preacher, an Autobiography*, pp. 276-78, 282; J. H. Tice, *Over the Plains*, pp. 158-59.

3. McLemore, ed., "Bannack and Gallatin City," p. 5; McConnell, *Idaho*, pp. 121-23. See also Arthur J. Dickson, ed., *Covered Wagon Days*, pp. 174, 253.

4. *Montana Post*, Aug. 27, 1864.

5. Harry H. Anderson, ed., "Account of Deadwood," *South Dakota Department of History Collections*, 31 (1962), p. 349; *General Ordinances of Aspen*, p. 40; *Montana Post*, Sept. 3, 10, Nov. 26, 1864, Oct. 14, 1865; *Weekly New Mexican*, Mar. 25, May 20, 1873; *Helena Herald*, May 28, 1867; *Las Vegas Daily Gazette*, July 27, 1881; *Park Record*, Sept. 30, 1882, *Black Hills Daily Times*, July 11, 1878; *Yankee Fork Herald*, July 24, 1879; *Ouray Times*, Nov. 9, 1878; *Silver World*, July 31, Sept. 4, 1875, June 26, 1876; *Butte Miner*, May 15, Nov. 27, 1877.

6. Dale, "Letters," Mar. 2, 1861; "David K. Wall," *Sons of Colorado*, 1 (May, 1907), p. 16; *Rocky Mountain News*, July 23, 1859; Clark, *Trip to Pike's Peak*, p. 123.

7. Alvin T. Steinel, *History of Agriculture in Colorado*, pp. 50-61, 109-11, 180-81, 283, 311, 451-63; Bayard Taylor, *Colorado*, pp. 40-46; Frank Fossett, *Colorado*, pp. 164-73.

8. Merrill G. Burlingame and K. Ross Toole, *History of Montana*, vol. 1, pp. 311-17, vol. 2, pp. 123, 179; S. J. Coon, "Influence of the Gold Camps on the Economic Development of Western Montana," *Journal of Political Economy*, 38 (Oct., 1930), p. 592; Merrill G. Burlingame, *Montana Frontier*, pp. 334-38.

9. A. K. McClure, *Three Thousand Miles*, pp. 240, 263-69.

10. Tice, *Over the Plains*, pp. 158-59.

11. Robert E. Strahorn, *To the Rockies and Beyond*, pp. 24-26; Arch B. Young, "A Social History of Early Globe, Gila County, Arizona" (thesis, Univ. of Colo., 1939), p. 22; Burlingame and Toole, *History of Montana*, vol. 1, pp. 311-13; K. Ross Toole, *Montana*, pp. 140-41; Maurice Frink, W. Turrentine Jackson, and Agnes W. Spring, *When Grass was King*, pp. 345-50.

12. *Park Record*, May 6, 1882; Leonard Arrington, *Great Basin Kingdom*, p. 204; "Silver Reef," *Utah Historical Quarterly*, 14 (July, 1961), p. 283; Rodman W. Paul, *Mining Frontier*, p. 151.

13. *Daily Miner's Register*, June 30, 1866, Jan. 27, 1867; *Montana Post*, Sept. 8, 1866; *New Mexico Interpreter*, Oct. 5, 1888.

14. The following is just a sampling: *Boulder News and Courier*, Sept. 5, 1879; *Butte Miner*, Sept. 26, Oct. 17, Nov. 14, 1876, Jan. 23, Dec. 4, 1877; *Black Hills Pioneer*, June 22, 1877; *Daily New Mexican*, Dec. 22, 1881; *Silver World*, Oct. 9, 1875.

15. *Daily Central City Register*, Dec. 15, 1872. For the struggle to secure a railroad, see the same paper, 1869-72.

16. Quoted in Robert G. Athearn, *Rebel of the Rockies*, p. 16.

17. Athearn, *Rebel*, pp. 43, 52-55, 60-66, 100-109, 128, 356-60.

18. Estelline Bennet, *Old Deadwood Days*, p. 300.

19. *Black Hills Weekly Times*, May 4, 1878; *Leadville Democrat*, July 2-4, 1880; *Santa Fe Daily New Mexican*, May 17, 1883; *Butte City Union*, Feb. 24, 1884; Francis C. Young, *Echoes from Arcadia*, pp. 116-17; Fossett, *Colorado*, pp. 68, 74-76; Rodman W. Paul, "Colorado as a Pioneer of Science in the Mining West," *Mississippi Valley Historical Review*, XLVII (June, 1960), p. 44; William F. Sprague, *Women and the West; A Short Social History*, p. 131.

20. Paul, *Mining Frontiers*, p. 9. See also Burlingame, *Montana Frontier*, p. 147; Agnes W. Spring, *Cheyenne and Black Hills Stage*, p. 309.

21. Quote from *Leavenworth Conservative*, May, 1867, found in Bancroft Scraps, "Colorado Miscellany," p. 26; *San Francisco Alta*, Mar. 17, 1868; Bancroft Scraps, "Colorado Miscellany," p. 44; *Black Hills Pioneer*, Apr. 21, 1877; *Montana Radiator*, Mar. 31, 1866; *Owyhee Avalanche*, Apr. 7, 1866; Bancroft Scraps, "Idaho Miscellany," p. 18.

9. PROBLEMS OF URBANIZATION

1. The composite picture was drawn from the following sources: *General Ordinances of the City of Aspen; Ordinances of the City of*

Virginia; The Charter and Ordinances of the City of Central; Harry H. Anderson, ed., "Account of Deadwood," *South Dakota Department of History Collections,* 31 (1962), pp. 341-43; *Park Record,* Mar. 11, 18, 1882; *Ouray Times,* Feb. 15, 1879; *Montana Post,* Mar. 11, 1865; *Silver World,* Feb. 19, 26, Apr. 8, 29, 1876; Jim Berry Pearson, *Maxwell Land Grant,* pp. 29-30.

2. Anderson, ed., "Account of Deadwood," pp. 344-45, 349; *General Ordinances of the City of Aspen,* pp. 39-40; *Tombstone Epitaph,* Jan. 23, 1882; *Ordinances of the City of Virginia,* pp. 12-14; Eugene Irey, "Social History of Leadville, Colorado" (diss., Univ. of Minn., 1951), pp. 387-88; *Silver World,* Jan. 15, Apr. 29, 1876.

3. Irey, "Social History," pp. 215-17, 389; *Daily Chronicle,* Oct. 7, 1879. See also *Aspen Times,* Apr. 11, 1885 for another camp with a similar idea.

4. *Silver Reef Miner,* Jan. 17, 1880; *Tombstone Daily Nugget,* Oct. 13, 1880; *Sweetwater Mines,* June 16, 1869; *Herald,* June 2, 1877; *Silver World,* Apr. 29, 1876; *The Charter and Ordinances of the City of Central,* pp. 49-51, 54-55; *Ordinances of the City of Virginia,* pp. 11-12; Lewis A. Kent, *Leadville in Your Pocket,* pp. 156-57.

5. *Solid Muldoon,* Feb. 16, 1883.

6. *Ordinances of the City of Virginia,* pp. 31-32; Anderson, ed., "Account of Deadwood," p. 347; *Southwest Sentinel,* May 19, 1883; *Park Record,* Sept. 15, 1883; *Montana Post,* June 17, 1865, Feb. 23, 1867; *Pinal Drill,* Oct. 30, 1880, Sept. 24, 1881; *Silver World,* June 19, Nov. 13, 1875, Mar. 10, 1877; *Ouray Times,* Nov. 1, 1879; *Silver Reef Miner,* May 11, 1881.

7. Sources for the discussion of city ordinances are found in the following: *General Ordinances of the City of Aspen; Ordinances of the City of Virginia; Charter and Ordinances of the City of Central; Silver World,* Jan. 15, 1876; *Tombstone Daily Nugget,* Nov. 20, Dec. 5, 1880; Irey, "Social History," pp. 248-49.

8. *Sweetwater Mines,* Apr. 7, 1869; *Butte Miner,* Nov. 13, 1877; *Helena Herald,* Oct. 31, Nov. 21, 1867.

9. Matthew Dale, "Letter to Brother," Jan., 1860.

10. H. J. Hawley, "Diary," Colorado State Historical Society, pp. 21-22,31.

11. George W. Parsons, *Journal,* p. 256. Throughout the journal are references to his political activity.

12. A. K. McClure, *Three Thousand Miles,* p. 254.

13. *New Mexico Interpreter,* Aug. 22, 1890; *Tombstone Daily Nug-*

get, Oct. 22, 1880; Solid Muldoon, Apr. 6, 1883; Helena Herald, Nov. 29, 1866; Black Hills Weekly Times, Nov. 4, 1877.

14. Ouray Times, Aug.-Oct., 1878, presents a good example of a local campaign. Charges of corruption were leveled by Francis C. Young, Echoes from Arcadia, pp. 31, 32; Carlyle C. Davis, Olden Times in Colorado, p. 236, and Daily Miners' Register, Apr. 2, 1867. See also Charter and Ordinances of the City of Central, pp. 26-28, and Ordinances of the City of Virginia, pp. 26-30.

15. Daniel Tuttle, Reminiscences of a Missionary Bishop, p. 141.

16. The composite picture was drawn from the following sources: McClure, Three Thousand Miles, p. 292; Parsons, Journal, pp. 156, 158-59, 178; Montana Post, Aug. 31, 1867; Park Record, Aug. 7, 1880, Aug. 5, 1882; Boulder County News, Sept. 7, 1870.

17. W. Turrentine Jackson, Treasure Hill, p. 94. See also Rodman W. Paul, Mining Frontiers, Chapter 8, and Charles M. Hough, "Leadville, Colorado 1878-98, A Study of Unionism" (thesis, Univ. of Colo., 1958), p. 35.

10. THE MATURE CAMP

1. Montana Post, Mar. 2, 1867; Ouray Times, Oct. 27, 1877; Owyhee Avalanche, Jan. 27, 1866.

2. Sources for the preceding section: Bayard Taylor, Colorado, pp. 51-59; Robert G. Athearn, "Life in the Pike's Peak Region," Colorado Magazine, 32 (Apr., 1955), p. 93; Park Record, July 15, 1882, Feb. 24, 1883; Tombstone Epitaph, July 3, 1880, Jan. 16, 1882; Black Hills Weekly Times, May 31, 1879; Butte Miner, Dec. 11, 1877; Owyhee Avalanche, Oct. 29, Nov. 16, Dec. 14, 1867; Pinal Drill, Apr. 16, 1881; Rocky Mountain Sun, Jan. 7, 21, 1882; Weekly New Mexican, Feb. 11, 1873; Montana Post, Jan. 28, Apr. 1, 1865; Herald, Sept. 29, 1877; Silver Reef Miner, Apr. 27, June 28, Oct. 1, 1881.

3. Silver Reef Miner, May 18, 1881; Aspen Times, Dec. 19, 1885; Butte Miner, Oct. 23, 1877; Herald, Jan. 5, 1878; Park Record, Dec. 16, 1882; Ouray Times, July 23, Nov. 24, 1877; Silver World, Jan. 15, 29, 1876.

4. Leadville Weekly Herald, Nov. 15, 1879; Maurice Morris, Rambles in the Rocky Mountains, p. 131; Albert D. Richardson, Beyond the Mississippi, p. 479.

5. Francis C. Young, Echoes from Arcadia, pp. 32-33; Silver Reef

Miner, May 29, 1880, Jan. 21, June 10, 1882; *Idaho World,* June 17, July 1, Sept. 23, 1865; *Montana Post,* Dec. 17, 24, 1864; *Aspen Times,* Jan. 16, 1886; *Black Hills Pioneer,* May 26, 1877; *Sweetwater Mines,* June 19, 1869.

6. For material on Langrishe see: *Helena Herald,* Sept. 26-Nov. 14, 1867; *Black Hills Pioneer,* Aug. 5, 1876; Daniel Tuttle, *Reminiscences of a Missionary Bishop,* p. 170; Ethelbert Talbot, *My People of the Plains,* pp. 96-97; Taylor, *Colorado,* p. 60; Estelline Bennett, *Old Deadwood Days,* pp. 120, 125-26; Melvin Schoberlin, *From Candles to Footlights,* pp. 40-44.

7. Andrew F. Rolle, ed., *Road to Virginia City,* pp. 81-97, has comments on plays he witnessed. Eugene Irey, "Social History of Leadville, Colorado" (diss., Univ. of Minn., 1951), p. 169; Lynn I. Perrigo, "Social History of Central City, Colorado" (diss., Univ. of Colo. 1936), p. 296; Jerry Bryan, *Illinois Gold Hunter,* p. 32; Carlyle C. Davis, *Olden Times,* pp. 246-47; Clair E. Willson, *Mimes and Miners,* p. 133; Schoberlin, *From Candles,* p. 145, 194.

8. A. K. McClure, *Three Thousand Miles,* pp. 332-35, 411, gives a vivid account of an early court. For a picture of the frontier judge, see Bennett, *Old Deadwood Days,* pp. 41-43.

9. *Pinal Drill,* Oct. 22, Nov. 12, 1881; *Ouray Times,* Oct. 27, 1877; *Ordinances of the City of Virginia,* p. 45.

10. Thomas A. Marshall, *Early Records of Gilpin County, Colorado,* p. 185; A. K. McClure, *Three Thousand Miles,* p. 335; Agnes W. Spring, ed., *Pioneer Years in the Black Hills,* p. 121; Harry H. Anderson, ed., "Account of Deadwood," *South Dakota Department of History Collections,* 31 (1962), pp. 310-11; Lewis A. Kent, *Leadville in Your Pocket,* pp. 143-44.

11. Isaac W. Rogers, "Diary January-December, 1865," Montana State Historical Society, Jan. 12, Feb. 8, 13, 14, 1865; Rolle, ed., *Road to Virginia City,* p. 82; *Daily Chronicle,* June 14, 1879; Granville Stuart, *Forty Years on the Frontier,* pp. 257-58; William B. Thom, "In Pioneer Days," *The Trail,* 19 (Oct., 1929), p. 13; *Helena Herald,* Mar. 7, 1867.

12. J. A. Burkhart, "The Frontier Merchant and Social History," *The Montana Magazine of History,* II (Oct., 1952), p. 8; *Boulder County News,* Nov. 27, 1874, Feb. 2, 1877; Samuel Leach, "Excerpts from the Autobiography of Samuel Leach, 1837-1911," Montana Historical Society, Sept. 1, 1868.

13. Bryan, *Illinois Gold Hunter,* p. 28.

14. *Daily Chronicle,* June 6, 1879. See also A M. Holter, "Pioneer Lumbering in Montana," *Contributions to the Historical Society of Montana,* 8 (1917), pp. 251-55.

15. *Silver Reef Miner,* Nov. 19, 1881.

16. *Park Record,* Dec. 10, 1881. See also the same paper Nov. 28, 1881, Mar. 24, May 12, 1883, and *Ouray Times,* June 23, 1877.

17. *Daily Chronicle,* July 7, 1879; Morris, *Rambles,* p. 127; Anderson, ed., "An Account of Deadwood," p. 315; Holter, "Lumbering," p. 261; *Herald,* Aug. 29, 1875; *Park Record,* July 22, 1882; *Sweetwater Mines,* July 3, 1868.

18. George W. Parsons, *Journal,* p. 242; *Yankee Fork Herald,* Dec. 20, 1879; Davis, *Olden Times in Colorado,* pp. 262-66; Irey, "Social History of Leadville, Colorado," p. 134.

19. *Pinal Drill,* Nov. 5, 1881; *Butte Miner,* Mar. 5, Apr. 2, 1878.

20. *Report on the Agencies of Transportation in the United States,* vol. IV, pp. 17-26; *Park Record,* Aug. 20, 1881; Mar. 11, 1882; *Pinal Drill,* July 23, 1881; *Ouray Times,* July 13, 1878; *Butte Miner,* Mar. 19, 1878; *Silver World,* Oct. 20, 1881; Irey, "Social History," p. 278.

21. *Caribou Post,* Oct. 14, 21, 1871; *Daily Central City Register,* Jan. 8, Apr. 30, 1873; *New York Times,* Sept. 28, 1876; *Boulder County News,* Apr. 28, 1876, Apr. 20, Oct. 5, 1877.

22. *Black Hills Weekly Times,* June 28, 1879; *Park Record,* Aug. 7, 1880; *Ouray Times,* May 10, 1879.

23. *Santa Fe Daily Gazette,* Nov. 30, 1867; *Santa Fe Weekly Gazette,* Apr. 18, 1868; *New Mexican,* Mar. 31, June 23, 1868; Bancroft Scraps, "New Mexico Miscellany" (Bancroft Library), p. 36.

11. COMMUNITY LEADERSHIP

1. Agnes W. Spring, ed., *Pioneer Years in the Black Hills,* p. 119.

2. *Montana Post,* Feb. 2, 1867.

3. *Helena Herald,* Nov. 7, 1867.

4. *Union-Freeman,* June 24, 1883; Lynn I. Perrigo, "Social History of Central City, Colorado" (diss., Univ. of Colo., 1936), p. 236.

5. The composite picture was drawn from the following sources: Fred Rogers, "Adam Aulback Interview 1931" (Bancroft Library); *History of Arizona Territory,* pp. 267-68; James H. Mills, "Reminiscences of an Editor," *Contributions to the Historical Society of Montana,* 5 (1904), p. 282; Agnes W. Spring, ed., *Pioneer Years,* pp. 271-73; James

Louder, "Autobiography" (Bancroft Library), pp. 7-10; *Butte Miner,* Dec. 25, 1877.

6. *Solid Muldoon,* Mar. 30, 1883; W. J. Howlett, *Life of the Right Reverend Joseph P. Machebeuf,* pp. 296-97; George W. Parsons, *Journal,* p. 203. See also Daniel Tuttle, *Reminiscences of a Missionary Bishop,* pp. 161, 178-79; *Montana Post,* Nov. 12, 1864; George M. Darley, *Pioneering in the San Juan,* p. 168; Ethelbert Talbot, *My People of the Plains,* pp. 87-91; John L. Dyer, *Snow-Shoe Itinerant,* pp. 334-35; George Edwards, "Presbyterian Church History," *Contributions to the Historical Society of Montana,* pp. 296-99; Darley, *Pioneering in the San Juan,* pp. 108-109.

7. *Tombstone Epitaph,* Oct. 1, 1880; *Idaho World,* July 15, Aug. 19, 1865; *New Mexico Interpreter,* Jan. 31, 1880; *Park Record,* Dec. 24, 31, 1881; *Pinal Drill,* Nov. 19, 1881; *Silver Cliff Miner,* July 18, 1879.

8. *Tombstone Epitaph,* Sept. 27, 1886.

9. Andrew F. Rolle, ed., *Road to Virginia City,* pp. 76-77.

10. *Arizona Silver Belt,* May 16, 1879; *Butte Miner,* Aug. 29-Nov. 7, 1876; *Montana Post,* Dec. 8, 1866; Lynn I. Perrigo, "Life in Central City" (thesis, Univ. of Colo., 1934), pp. 45-46. For further information on Sunday in the camps, see Isaac W. Rogers, "Diary January-December 1865," Montana Historical Society, Jan. 1, 8, 22, Mar. 12; James H. Morley, "Diary," Montana Historical Society, June 19, 1864; Tuttle, *Reminiscences,* pp. 141-42; Dyer, *Snow-Shoe Itinerant,* pp. 145, 148; Talbot, *My People,* p. 89; *Yankee Fork Herald,* Apr. 24, 1880.

11. *Butte Miner,* Dec. 18, 1877; United States Bureau of the Census, *Statistics of the Population of the United States at the Tenth Census,* p. 917.

12. *Black Hills Weekly Times,* June 28, 1879.

13. Matthew Dale, "Letters," Jan. 22, 1860; *Daily Chronicle,* Feb. 18, 1879.

14. *Ouray Times,* Aug. 4, 1877.

15. *Pinal Drill,* Dec. 24, 1881.

16. Dale, "Letters," Aug. 31, 1860; *Arizona Silver Belt,* Nov. 7, 1878, Feb. 7, 1880; *Owyhee Avalanche,* Apr. 13, 1867; *Rocky Mountain Sun,* July 16, 1881; *Yankee Fork Herald,* Dec. 27, 1879, Jan. 17, 1880.

17. Augusta Tabor, "Cabin Life" (Bancroft Library), p. 4. See also Granville Stuart, *Forty Years on the Frontier,* p. 213; Irving W. Stanton, *Sixty Years in Colorado,* p. 58; H. H. [Helen H. Jackson], "To Leadville," *Atlantic Monthly* (May, 1879), p. 576; Parsons, *Journal,* p.

230; *Daily Denver Times,* Feb. 2, 1879; Rodman W. Paul, *Mining Frontiers,* pp. 164-65.

18. H. S. Salt, *The Life of James Thomson,* p. 79. See also Lola M. Homsher, ed., *South Pass, 1868,* pp. 80-81; Maurice Morris, *Rambles,* p. 134; Grace Greenwood [Sara J. Lippincott], *New Life,* p. 63.

19. *Silver Reef Miner,* July 1, 1882. All newspapers have accounts of activities of the fraternal organizations, particularly when a lodge was being established, or was involved in some community project.

20. *Helena Herald,* May 2, 1867; *Silver World,* Feb. 12, 1876; *Herald,* Oct. 13, 1877; *Aspen Times,* Apr. 11, 1885; *Park Record,* June 12, 1880.

21. William S. Greever, *The Bonanza West,* p. 41.

12. LIFE WAS NEVER EASY

1. *Herald,* Jan. 20, 1877; *Park Record,* Nov. 12, 1881; *Daily Chronicle,* Feb. 6, 1879; *Silver Reef Miner,* June 28, 1879, Feb. 14, 1880; *Black Hills Pioneer,* Aug. 12, 1876.

2. *Rocky Mountain Sun,* July 9, 1881. For a particularly painful experience, see George W. Parsons, *Journal,* p. 265. See also the *Arizona Silver Belt,* Oct. 25, 1879; *Park Record,* Sept. 15, 1883; *Helena Herald,* Nov. 21, 1867; William A. Douglas, *A History of Dentistry in Colorado, 1859-1959,* pp. 4-10.

3. Bayard Taylor, *Colorado,* pp. 68-69.

4. H. S. Salt, *The Life of James Thomson,* p. 38.

5. *Owyhee Avalanche,* Sept. 30, 1865; *Arizona Silver Belt,* Dec. 6, 1879; *South Pass News,* Oct. 27, 1869; *Idaho World,* Apr. 15, 1865; *Herald,* Aug. 29, 1875; George T. Ingham, *Digging Gold Among the Rockies,* pp. 184-85.

6. Frank Fossett, *Colorado,* p. 219.

7. Interview with Horace Tabor, *Denver Daily Tribune,* Mar. 12, 1879; Bronson C. Keeler, *Leadville and Its Silver Mines,* p. 31.

8. *Statistics and Technology of the Precious Metals,* pp. 105, 157, 159.

9. *Weekly New Mexican,* Jan. 30, 1877. A letter from Elizabethtown, New Mexico, Feb. 9, 1870, is quoted in Herbert O. Brayer, *William Blackmore,* p. 350. Material for the rest of this paragraph is found in: *Black Hills Weekly Times,* Aug. 9, 1879; *Denver Daily Times,* Mar. 12, 1879; *Daily Chronicle,* June 14, 1879; Andrew F. Rolle, ed., *Road to Virginia City,* pp. 82, 101-102; *Mineral Resources of the States*

and Territories West of the Rocky Mountains, pp. 197, 261, 307, 311.

10. Matthew Dale, "Letters," Aug. 20, 1859. It was publications such as *Sweet's Carbonate Camps, Leadville and Ten-Mile of Colorado,* p. 8, that generated the rumor that the camp was a poor man's paradise.

11. Lola M. Homsher, ed., *South Pass, 1868,* pp. 74-75.

12. Vernon H. Jensen, *Heritage of Conflict,* p. 8-9; Eugene Irey, "Social History of Leadville, Colorado" (diss., Univ. of Minn., 1951), pp. 112-13; Charles M. Hough, "Leadville, Colorado, 1878-1898" (thesis, Univ. of Colo., 1958), pp. 29-33.

13. *Daily Chronicle,* Jan. 29, July 23, 1879; *Leadville Weekly Herald,* June 19, 1880; Jensen, *Heritage of Conflict,* p. 21; Hough, "Leadville, Colorado," pp. 44-60; Irey, "Social History," p. 102.

13. A TIME FOR RELAXATION

1. *Silver World,* July 10, 1875; *Black Hills Pioneer,* July 7, 1877; *Montana Post,* June 24, July 8, 1865; *Rocky Mountain News,* July 9, 1859; *Las Vegas Daily Gazette,* July 16, 1881; *Pinal Drill,* July 9, 1881; *Helena Herald,* July 17, 1867; *Sweetwater Mines,* July 18, 1868; *Yankee Fork Herald,* July 17, 1880.

2. *Arizona Silver Belt,* Jan. 3, 1880; *Ouray Times,* Dec. 29, 1877; *Butte Miner,* Dec. 18, 25, 1877, Jan. 8, 1878; *Herald,* Dec. 8, 29, 1877; *Sweetwater Mines,* Dec. 30, 1868, Jan. 9, 1869; *Helena Herald,* Jan. 2, 1867; *Owyhee Avalanche,* Dec. 30, 1865; *Idaho World,* Dec. 23, 1865; *Silver Reef Miner,* Dec. 17, 24, 31, 1881; George W. Parsons, *Journal,* p. 192.

3. *Black Hills Daily Times,* Dec. 26, 1878.

4. See Ernest Ingersoll, *Knocking Around the Rockies,* pp. 70-71, for a description of a male dominated dance. All mining camp papers have descriptions of dances and suppers. Some reporters become very flowery when describing the affairs and the ladies' dresses. H. S. Salt, *The Life of James Thomson,* p. 90, and Granville Stuart, *Forty Years on the Frontier,* p. 268, give the views of actual participants.

5. Andrew F. Rolle, ed., *Road to Virginia City,* pp. 91, 92-97. See also Parsons, *Journal,* pp. 191-220; Anne Ellis, *Life of an Ordinary Woman,* pp. 126-27.

6. *Constitution and by-laws of the Harrison Hook and Ladder Co.,* pp. 7-27; *Daily Chronicle,* Jan. 29, 1879. For other clubs see *Silver Cliff Miner,* Nov. 20, 1879; *Tombstone Daily Nugget,* Oct. 15, 1880; *Tombstone Epitaph,* Mar. 13, 27, 1882; *Idaho World,* Oct. 14, 1865.

7. *Idaho World,* June 17, July 1, 1865. For the circus in general, see *Montana Post,* July 6, 1867; *Helena Herald,* July 17, 1867; Parsons, *Journal,* p. 165.

8. *Pinal Drill,* Dec. 25, 1880-July 9, 1881, follows its ball team. *New Mexico Interpreter,* June-July, 1887; *Montana Post,* May 26, 1866; *Black Hills Daily Times,* July 7, 22, 1878; *Helena Herald,* Sept. 26, 1867; *Silver World,* Apr. 29, 1876.

9. James H. Morley, "Diary," Montana Historical Society, Sept. 25, 1864. See also *Montana Post,* Oct. 1, 1864.

10. *Black Hills Weekly Times,* Mar. 16, 1878. See also *Montana Post,* Jan. 5, 12, 1867; *Owyhee Avalanche,* Dec. 22, 1866; *Butte Miner,* Jan. 29, 1878.

11. *Park Record,* Feb. 24, 1883.

14. THE TIGER IS FOUND

1. *Herald,* July 18, 1875.

2. Quoted in William Jackson, "Railroad Conflicts in Colorado in the Eighties," *Colorado Magazine,* 23 (June, 1946), p. 17.

3. *Daily Chronicle,* June 7, 1879. See also *Park Record,* Oct. 14, 1882; *Caribou Post,* July 8, 1871; *Aspen Times,* Mar. 6, 1886; Bancroft Scraps, "Idaho Miscellany" (Bancroft Library), p. 154.

4. *Daily Central City Register,* June 12, 1870; *Ouray Times,* Jan. 17, 1880; *Daily Chronicle,* June 4, 1879; *Owyhee Avalanche,* Apr. 28, 1866; *Sweetwater Mines,* June 19, 1869; Charles Liftchild, manuscript (Arizona Pioneer's Historical Society), p. 3. William J. McConnell, *Early History of Idaho,* p. 138.

5. Mark Twain, *Roughing It,* pp. 339-40.

6. Granville Stuart, *Forty Years on the Frontier,* pp. 67-68. See also Jerry Bryan, *Illinois Gold Hunter in the Black Hills,* p. 34.

7. Harry H. Anderson, ed., "Account of Deadwood," *South Dakota Department of History Collections,* 31 (1962), p. 326. See also *Silver Reef Miner,* Mar. 27, 1882; Lynn I. Perrigo, "Life in Central City, Colorado" (diss., Univ. of Colo., 1936), pp. 188-89.

8. *Leadville Daily Herald,* Mar. 2, 1881.

9. Agnes W. Spring, ed., *Pioneer Years in the Black Hills,* p. 291; W. A. Goulder, *Reminiscences of a Pioneer,* pp. 236-37; Glenn C. Quiett, *Pay Dirt,* p. 23.

10. W. P. A. Writer's Program, *Cooper Camp,* p. 175.

11. *Tombstone Epitaph,* Mar. 13, 1882.

12. *Black Hills Weekly Times,* July 12, 1879.

13. *Evening Chronicle,* Apr. 26, 1887. See also Apr. 11, 13. For Red Stockings' account see *Daily Chronicle,* Apr. 16, 1879. For further information on prostitution in the camps, the census returns are helpful but require much searching. Many accounts mention it in passing.

14. Margaret Ronan, "Memoirs" (thesis, State Univ. of Mont., 1932), pp. 41-42.

15. George W. Parsons, *Journal,* p. 139. The two preceding comments were found in Estelline Bennett, *Old Deadwood Days,* p. 30, and Annie D. Tallent, *Black Hills,* p. 355.

16. *Georgetown Daily Miner,* Jan. 27, 1873; *Solid Muldoon,* Feb. 16, 1883.

17. *Denver Daily Tribune,* Sept. 21, 1878.

18. Bernard De Voto, *Mark Twain's America,* p. 124; C. L. Sonnichsen, *Billy King's Tombstone,* p. 94.

19. For a description of the hurdy-gurdies see: Thomas J. Dimsdale, *Vigilantes of Montana,* pp. 12-14; McConnell, *Idaho,* pp. 138-39; Albert D. Richardson, *Beyond the Mississippi,* p. 480; Stuart, *Forty Years,* p. 266; *Montana Post,* Oct. 15, Nov. 12, 1864; *Owyhee Avalanche,* Mar. 30, 1867.

20. A. K. McClure, *Three Thousand Miles,* pp. 412-13. See also Dimsdale, *Vigilantes of Montana,* p. 14, and McConnell, *Idaho,* p. 139.

21. *Montana Post,* Jan. 14, 1865, Mar. 17, Dec. 22, 1866. See also the *Owyhee Avalanche,* Apr. 14, July 28, 1866, and *Daily Miners' Register,* July 1, 1866.

22. *Butte Miner,* May 7, 1878. See issues from Jan. 8 through May 7 concerning the coming and closing of the hurdy-gurdy.

23. Eddie Foy and Alvin Harlow, *Clowning Through Life,* pp. 123-24, 159; Parsons, *Journal,* p. 121; Bennett, *Old Deadwood Days,* pp. 106-10; McConnell, *Idaho,* pp. 60-61; Carlyle C. Davis, *Olden Times in Colorado,* pp. 117-18; Eugene Irey, "Social History of Leadville, Colorado" (diss., Univ. of Minn., 1951), p. 151; Claire E. Willson, *Mimes and Miners,* pp. 10-13, 21, 29-35, 135.

24. *Leadville Democrat,* Sept. 8, 1880. Ernest Ingersoll, "Camp of the Carbonates," *Scribner's Monthly* (Oct., 1879), p. 824, said of the last show, it "beggars description for all that is vile."

25. *Tombstone Epitaph,* Sept. 4, 1880; *Daily Chronicle,* June 16, 1879; *Black Hills Weekly Times,* Aug. 19, 1879; Davis, *Olden Times,* pp. 118-19.

26. Spring, ed., *Pioneer Years,* pp. 199-200; Anderson, ed., "Account

of Deadwood," *South Dakota Department of History Collections,* 31 (1962), p. 322; *Black Hills Pioneer,* June 23, 1877.

15. THE PROMISED LAND

1. Richard C. Wade, *The Urban Frontier,* p. 1.
2. See Billie Barnes Jensen, "The Woman Suffrage Movement in Colorado" (thesis, Univ. of Colo., 1959), for a study of one state.
3. *Yankee Fork Herald,* July 31, 1879.
4. *Solid Muldoon,* Oct. 19, 1883.
5. Jim D. Hill, "Early Mining Camp in American Life," *Pacific Historical Review,* 1 (1932), p. 311.
6. Charles H. Shinn, "California Mining Camps," *The Overland Monthly* (Aug., 1884), p. 173.
7. C. M. Chase, *The Editor's Run in New Mexico and Colorado,* p. 62, quoted in Jim Berry Pearson, *Maxwell Grant,* p. 83.

abortions, 231
Adams, Charles F., on Leadville, 221
agriculture, miners welcome, 124-26; development around camps, 126-28; problems, 127-28; in Colorado, 128-30; in Montana, 130-31; significance of, 131-32, 140-41; changes in settlement pattern, 133-34; *see* ranching
alcoholism, 204
Alta, Utah, dispute over land title, 73
Americans, majority in mining camps, 24-25
animals, domestic problem, 150
Aspen, Colo., 144; unions, 202
architecture, little original, 75-76
Arizona, 14, 36; wages, 200

balloon ascensions, 213
banking, role in camp, 171-72
Bannack, Mont., school, 114
Baptist church, frontier faith, 111
baseball, universal popularity, 213-15
Blackfoot, Mont., 65
Black Hawk, Colo., description, 49
Black Hills, S. D., 14, 164; Indian vs. miner, 52; miners' courts, 87-89
Black Hills Pioneer, 173; on Indians, 38; lack of crime in Deadwood, 81
Black Hills Times, 216
blacksmith, 16; wages, 200
Bonanza City, Idaho, 66
boxing, 215-16
British Columbia, 1858 mining rush, 12
British Isles, immigration from, 26

Bryan, Jerry, on fluctuating prices, 168
Bryan, William J., 248; 1896 election, 160
bullfight, in Montana, 217
Bullock, Seth, on miners' courts, 89; on gambling, 225
business, lodging, 64-65; district, 100-103; East-West trade, 140; profits, 167-68; problems, 168-69; credit buying, 169-70; banking, 170-72; businessmen's contributions, 172; *see* merchant
Butte, Mont., 227; Indian question, 51; unions, 202
Butte Miner, 225; opposes poaching, 215; opposes hurdy-gurdy, 235-36

California, 1849 gold rush, 3; mining camps, 11-12; mining camp tradition, 12; lured the Easterner, 26; municipal government, 142
Caribou, Colo., lack of crime, 81; business profits, 167; struggles to promote itself, 174-75
Catholic church, universally found in camps, 110
celebrations, *see* holidays
census, camps examined, 25n
Centennial Exhibition of 1876, 174
Central City, Colo., 175, 188; Horace Greeley visits, 13-14; age of residents, 28; Negroes in schools, 35; description, 49; growth, 76; railroad to, 136; politics in, 155-56;

Central City—*cont.*
high cost of living, 197-98; tourist center, 250
Cherry Creek, Colo., gold discovery, 13
Chicago, Ill., trade with camps, 140
children, effect of environment on, life in camps, 23; death, 194; *see* education, sports
Chinatowns, 33
Chinese, increase of, 26; discrimination of, 29-34, 39; mob action, 87; ordinances against, 151; blamed for opium, 239
Chisholm, James, on miners' religious beliefs, 105; hardship in camps, 201
Christianity, *see* religion
Christmas, how celebrated, 208-209
churches, *see* religion
circus, 213
Clark & Gruber, banking establishment, 171
Clark, William A., Montana businessman, miner, 172
clubs, private, 212-13; athletic, 220
cockfighting, 217
Collier, David, attacked for newspaper article, 180
Colorado, 36, 164, 216, 234, 242; 1859 mining rush, 3, 12; agricultural developments, 128-30; corrupt politics, 156; wages, 199; women's rights, 248
confidence games, varied in camps, 226-27
cooperation, needed to open camp, 23-24
courts, capstone of law enforcement, 165; *see* miners' courts, police
culture, lecturers, 160-61; music, 161-62; support by fraternal lodges, 190; *see* theater, opera, education

Custer, Ida., population, 26-27
Custer City, S. D., description, 42

Dahlonega, Ga., 18n
Dale, Matthew, on effect of environment, 22; on life in camps, 75; on books, 118
dances, 210n; popularity of, 210-12
Deadwood, S. D., 4, 79, 177; reputation, 81, 239-40; stage robberies, 121; telephone, 173; jealous of Leadville, 175; prostitution in, 231
democracy, in the camps, 47-48
dentists, 195-96
Denver, 13, 76, 129, 185, 248; cost of living, 197-98
Denver & Rio Grande Railroad, effect of camps on, 138
Dick, Everett, *Sodhouse Frontier,* 220
Dimsdale, Thomas, *Vigilantes of Montana,* 83, 85
diphtheria, 194
diseases and epidemics, 194
doctors, 195
Donald, William, career, 25-26
Dyer, John, 108; on miners in church, 19

editor, newspaper, 100; responsibilities and rewards, 177, 180
education, church supports, 111; private and subscription, 111-12; public, 112-15; financial difficulties, 113-14; school problems, 115; significance, 116-17; teachers, 183-84
Elizabethtown, N. M., cooperation in building ditch, 23-24; challenged by rival, 176; food prices, 197-98; ghost town, 252
entertainment, *see* theater, opera, saloons, culture, dancing, celebrations
epidemics, 194

Episcopal church, 111

Fenians, 190
fire, danger of, 93-98
Fort Benton, Mont., 56
Foy, Eddie, on variety theater, 237
Freeman, Legh, office burned, 180
freighting, role in camp, 68-71

gambling, permeated camps, 224-25; hall, 225; the gambler, 226; significance, 227
Garland, Hamlin, *A Son of the Middle Border,* 220
Gayville, S. D., miners' court, 87-88
German States, immigration from, 26
German Turnverein Society, 190
Globe, Ariz., 132; vigilante committee, 84; cost of living, 197-98; unions, 202
Good Templars, temperance, 190
government, municipal, time lag, 46-48; need for, 89-90; organization, 90-92, 142-45; street problems, 92-93; financial problems, 145-48; revenue, 146-47; public services, 148-50; ordinances, 151-53; politics, 154-55
Grand Army of the Republic, 191
Grant, Ulysses S., visits Central City, 175
Greeley, Horace, 21, 44; visits Central City, 13-14

Hale, Horace, on education, 112-13
Harper's Weekly, 79
Harrison Hook & Ladder Company of Leadville, Colo., 212
Helena, Mont., 76, 178-79, 248; Chinese problem, 33; lawlessness, 79; baseball, 214

Helena Herald, 72, 80, 211; newspaper rivalry, 178
Hickok, James (Wild Bill), 239; death and miners' court, 89
holidays, July Fourth, 206-207; Christmas-New Year, 207-209; others, 209
Homer, N. Y., food prices, 197-98
horse racing, 216-17
hospitals, 195
Hughes, Richard, on home guard, 51; on miners' courts, 87-89; on newspaper editor, 177
humor, in camps, 19
hunting and fishing, 215
hurdy-gurdy houses, dance hall, 234-36; decline in public estimation, 235-36

Idaho, 164, 234; 1860s mining rush, 12, 14; wages, 200; tent shows, 213
Indians, effect of camps and frontier on, 29, 37-38; problem, 51
Ingham, George, on Pitkin, Colo., 45

Jackson, W. Turrentine, study of White Pine Mining District, Nevada, 158
jails, 153
Jefferson Territory, 245-46
July Fourth, means of celebrating, 206-208
justice, *see* courts, police, ordinances, lawyers

laborers, 199; pay scale, 200; unions, 201-203
Lake City, Colo., early peacefulness, 81
Langford, Nathaniel, describes boredom of camp life, 75; on vigilantes, 85-86

Langrishe, John S., career, 163-64
law enforcement, by police, 122-23;
of ordinances, 152; *see also* police,
ordinances, lawyers, courts
lawlessness, environment conducive,
80; types, 80-81; public indifference, 82-83; stage robberies, 121;
declines, 123, *see* police and courts
lawyers, 16, 59; camps profitable,
165-66
Lead, S. D., unions, 202
Leadville, Colo., 4, 79, 123; inhabitants, 20-21; Mormon question, 37;
Tabor, 62-64; office rent, 71; criminal record, 81; fire department,
96; bonanza wealth, 101; railroads
fight for, 138; prostitution as
source of revenue, 147; corrupt
politics, 156; restaurant profits,
167; lumber industry, 168; telephone, 173; jealousy, 175; cost of
living, 197-98; wages, 199; union
activities, 202-203; C. F. Adams describes, 221; business census, 223;
reputation, 240
Leadville Daily Chronicle, 237
Leavenworth, Kan., food prices, 197-
98
library, organization, 118; finances,
119
Locke, George, on vigilante justice,
84
lodges, fraternal, role in camps, 189-
90; activities, 190n
Louisville, Ky., 243

Machebeuf, Joseph, 107; locks doors
of church, 181
markets, role of camps, 124-25
McClure, Alexander, describes placer
camp, 65; discusses Montana farming, 130-31; on politics, 155; on

lawyers, 166; experience with
hurdy, 235
McConnell, William, Idaho farming,
127
medical profession, 195; dentists, 195-
96; quacks, 196
Memorial Day, 209
merchant, 16, 59; role in camp, 60;
profits of trade, 71-72; progressive
leadership, 100
Methodist church, frontier faith, 111
Miller, James, business profits, 167;
Sunday, 182; salary, 200; "over the
bay," 212
miner, object of interest, 21, *see* laborers
miners' court, 87-89; strengths and
weaknesses, 88-89
mining camps, stereotyped image, 4;
urbanization, 4-9; not unique in
trans-Mississippi frontier, 10-11; optimistic nature of residents, 18;
humor, 19; nature of inhabitants,
19-23; cosmopolitan appearance,
24-28; youthful population, 27-28;
Indian question, 37-38; society, 39-
40, 185; humble beginnings, 42-44;
growth pattern, 45; democracy, 47-
48; in relation to mines, 57; defined, 57-58; inflation in real estate, 71-72; land title, 72-74; initial
boom, 75; architecture, 75-76, fails
to catch public's fancy, 78-79; fire
danger, 93-98; instability, 99-100;
as market, 124-25; rivalry, 176; improvements, 191; unsanitary, 193-
95; high cost of living, 196-98;
weather, 203-204; mobility, 204-
205; winter activities, 217-18; image shaped by red-light district,
239-40; contradictions, 241, 246-47;
urban center, 243-44; urban dweller,

246; safety valve, 230, 247; significance, 248-52

mining districts, described, 46-48

mining frontier, break with tradition, 9; instability, 10; effect on Indian question, 37-38

mining speculator, 59-60

ministers, *see* religion

Missouri River, in Montana rush, 55-56

Mitchell, Robert, 176

Mollie May, career, 229-30

Montana, 127, 164, 216, 234; 1860s mining rush, 12, 14; agricultural developments, 130-31; tent shows, 213; bullfight, 217

Montana Historical Society, founded, 161

Montana Post, 17, 19, 35, 149; on Indians, 38; criticizes hurdy-gurdies, 235

Morley, James, transformation of camp, 45; on governments, 154

Mormons, discrimination, 29, 36-37; A. Richardson on, 110; farming, 125-26

Morris, Esther, justice of the peace, 188

Morris, Maurice, on Negroes, 34-35

Mountain City, Colo., age of residents, 28

municipal government, *see* government, municipal

music, 161-62, *see* culture, theater, opera.

narcotics, 231, 239; opium dens, 222

Negroes, 34-36; not welcomed, 29, 34, 39; participate in Chinese discrimination, 35

Nevada, 1859 mining rush, 3, 12

New Mexico, 14, 36; early farming, 125; wages, 200

New Mexico Interpreter, 184

Newspapers, on Indian question, 38-39; significance, 65-66; problems, 67-68; on municipal government, 91; editor, 100; responsibilities and rewards, 177, 180; supports agriculture, 127-28; promotes camp, 174

New York, N. Y., 140

Niles Register, 126

Oklahoma!, 124

Omaha, Neb., 140

opera, cultural distinction, 162

Orem, Con, boxer, 215-16

Ouray, Colo., jealous of Leadville, 175; tourist center, 250

Owyhee Avalanche, 32, 112; comments on society, 40n; advertises for opera house, 162; promotes camp, 178

Palmer, William, interest in camps as market for railroads, 137

Park City, Utah, Negro children in schools, 35; Mormon question, 36-37; telephone, 173; jealous of Leadville, 175

Park Record, 133

Parsons, George W., optimistic nature, 18; on youth of camps, 27; on ministers, 108; on politics in Tombstone, 155; on collecting money for church, 181; on prostitution, 231; on Tombstone's reputation, 240

Paul, Rodman, railroads and mining frontier, 139-40

Pinal, Ariz., 177; population, 26-27

Pinal Drill, 182; advocates abolishing courts, 165

Pitkin, Colo., 45

Pittsburgh, Pa., 4, 243

Plummer, Henry, vigilantes and career, 83

pneumonia, susceptibility, 194

police, duties, 122-23; enforcement of ordinances, 152

politics, came early, 154-55; corruption, 156; entertainment value, 157; significance, 158

population, geographical origins, 24-27; age of, 27-28

post office, significance, 186; problems faced, 186-87

Presbyterian church, 111

private clubs, role, 212-13

prostitution, 39, 59; raise city revenue, 147; ordinances against, 151-52; the prostitute, 227-32; flourished, 227-28; census, 229n; hard life, 230-32; movement against, 232-33; why tolerated, 233; significance, 233-34; dance halls, 235; variety theater, 238

railroads, mutual need, 134, 137; blessings promised, 134-35; and Central City, Colo., 136; W. Palmer on, 137; Denver & Rio Grande, 138; significance of camps, 137-38, 140-41; some disadvantages, 139; greatest development, 250

ranching, effect of camps on and significance of camps to, 132-33

Randall, George, miners' religious beliefs, 105-106

real estate, inflation, 71-72

recreation, *see* baseball, dancing, mining camps, track, etc.

Red Stockings, career, 229-30

religion, the minister and his role, 16, 106-107, 180-81; miners' reaction to, 19; effect of miners on, 105-106; problems faced, 105-108;

Baptist, Catholic, Episcopal, Methodist, Presbyterian, 110-11; social status, 160; obstacles for minister, 181; Sundays, 182-83; Christmas, 208; Easter, 209

Richardson, Albert, Christianity and the Mormons, 110

roads, need for, 53-54; significance of, 53; toll, 54-55; public most popular, 55

robberies, stagecoach, 121

Rocky Mountains, description, 12

Rocky Mountain News, 128

Rogers, Isaac, on business profits, 167

safety valve, role of camps, 230, 247

St. Louis, Mo., 4

salesman, 60

saloons, saloonkeepers, 16, 59, 222, 224; ubiquitous nature, 65; ordinances controlling, 152; social status, 160; recreation-gambling, 217-18; apex of masculine society, 222

Sandwich, Ill., growth compared to camps, 76

San Francisco, Cal., 76, 185

sanitation, and municipal government, 144-45, 149-50; water supply, 148-50; animal problem, 150; general problem, 193-95

Scandinavians, 26

scarlet fever, 194

schools, *see* education

scurvy, 194

sheep raising, little impact of camps, 132-33

Sherman, William T., discusses plains, 125

Shinn, Charles, *Mining Camps,* 142; camp's image, 251

Silver City, Ida., growth, 76; cost of living, 197-98

Silver City, N. M., reaction to Indians, 51-52; becomes cattle center, 132

Silver Reef, Utah, Mormon question, 36-37; growth, 77; food prices, 197-98

Silver Reef Miner, 204; warns against draw poker, 226

skating, 219-20

smallpox, 194-95

society, of mining camps, 39-40; 185

South Pass, Wyo., 46, 177; decline, 76-77

Spanish-Americans, frequently not welcomed, 29; small factor in most camps, 36; wage discrimination, 200

speculation, in mining, 59-60

sports, 207; popularity, 213-20

stagecoach, significance, 119-22; robberies, 121

Storms, Charles, career, 226

Story, Nelson, 132

Stuart, Granville, gambling hall, 225

suicide, 204; of prostitutes, 231

Sweetwater Mines, 103; attacks *Helena Herald,* 179

Tabor, Horace, as mining camp merchant, 61-64; investments, 172

Tabor Opera House (Leadville), description, 162

Talbot, Ethelbert, on ministry, 107

Taylor, Bayard, impressed by audiences, 161

teachers, *see* education

telegraph, significance, 172-73

telephone, readily accepted, 173-74

tent shows, in Idaho and Montana, 213

Thanksgiving, 209

theater, 117; opera house, 162; actors, 162-64; impact of urbanity, 164-65;

significance, 164; variety, 237-38, 238n

Thomson, James, discusses women, 188-89

Tice, John, conclusions on agriculture, 131-32

titles, land, 72-74

toll roads, 54-55

Tombstone, Ariz., 123, 227; reputation, 240

Tombstone Nugget, 223

track, professional, 216

transportation, *see* railroads, stagecoach, roads, freighting

Tuttle, Daniel, on Negroes, 34; on lodging, 64; examines ministry, 106-107; on camp politics, 157

Twain, Mark, describes rush for toll roads, 54; stagecoaching, 121-22; saloonkeepers, 224

unemployment, 201-202

Union Pacific Railroad, 134

unions, in camps, 202-203; Leadville strike, 203

urbanization, 4-9, 243-52, *see* mining camps

Utah, 14, 164; impact of camps, 133; women's rights, 248

vigilantes, in Montana, 83-86; controversial legacy, 83-85; California influence, 83, 86

Viola, career, 232

Virginia City, Mont., 64; children in, 23; restricts Chinese, 32; government, 46; opinion of, 49; vigilantes, 83, 86; secures telegraph, 172-73; declining, 178; tourist center, 250

Virginia City, Nev., fire, 96

Virginia City, N. M., challenges Elizabethtown, 176

Wade, Richard, *Urban Frontier,* 243
wages, 199-202; in new camps, 202
Wall, David, early Colorado farmer,
   128-29
water supply, 148-50
weather, effect on people, 203-204
Weekly Register-Call, 232
White Oaks, N. M., 135, 177
White Pine Mining District, Nevada,
   158

women, 16; scarcity of, 21-22; role
   in camps, 187-89; diversions, 212,
   219; affected by environment, 219;
   rights, 248, *see* prostitution
Wyoming, 14, 164; women's rights,
   248

Yankee Fork Herald, 119; praises
   Idaho, 250
"Young America," definition, 17